CHANGING
THE
LAWBREAKER

PRENTICE-HALL INTERNATIONAL, INC., *London*
PRENTICE-HALL OF AUSTRALIA, PTY., LTD., *Sydney*
PRENTICE-HALL OF CANADA, LTD., *Toronto*
PRENTICE-HALL OF INDIA (PRIVATE) LTD., *New Delhi*
PRENTICE-HALL OF JAPAN, INC., *Tokyo*

Don C. Gibbons
San Francisco State College

CHANGING

THE

LAWBREAKER

The Treatment
of Delinquents and Criminals

Prentice-Hall, Inc., Englewood Cliffs, N. J.

PREFACE

This book is intended to be several things simultaneously —an inventory and assessment of recent theories and research findings regarding causal processes in crime and delinquency, an overview of social patterns in correctional organizations, a theoretical venture in "applied sociology," and a contribution to correctional practice theory. These are all involved in the central conceptual problem that is handled in this book, namely, the business of changing lawbreakers into nondeviant citizens. This work is addressed to questions of the order: "What causes people to violate criminal laws?" and "What should be done in order to repress people from breaking laws or to change the conditions that encourage criminality?"

If the "something" which impels individuals to break laws is to be altered, changed, or removed, that something must be clearly identified. Inescapably then, rehabilitation of offenders depends upon basic knowledge of the causal factors in criminality. This book sets forth some central propositions and hypotheses about the causes of crime and delinquency which emerge from the socio-logical literature. But it does this in a particular way. Most of the causal analysis in this volume is set within a typological framework. Briefly put, this book argues that questions of the form "What causes crime or delinquency?" do not make sense, for crime and de-linquency are phenomena that are as varied as social life itself. Criminals and delinquents exhibit nearly the full range of social characteristics. They are from various social circumstances, they exhibit happy and miserable family backgrounds, they show many different personality structures, and they vary in nearly every other way worth noting. Accordingly, the sensible question becomes "What causes criminal behavior of type 1, 2, or 3?" Having said this, it should be pointed out that the task of specifying the forms which criminal and delinquent behavior takes is no easy or obvious one. There are many ways in which offenders could be sorted out into types. It is not the case that one of these leaps out as the "right" one; instead someone must venture a reasoned judgment as to which is the most significant basis of classification. Chapter Two of this book deals with this matter at considerable length.

Behavioral change is conditional upon an understanding of the nature of the behavior to be altered. Rehabilitative ventures are also influenced by the nature of the social environments in which they are attempted. As one illustration, therapy programs in prison must take into account the special nature of the prison milieu, and particularly such things as the informal inmate social system. In the past decade or so, sociologists have learned much about the workings of such social organizations as training schools and prisons. A summary of certain of these findings is presented in Chapter Five, along with some suggestions of how certain organiza-tional impediments to treatment might be circumvented.

This material on the causation of criminalistic deviance and on correctional social organization comprises part of the "ap-plied sociology" in this book. These theories and data have pragmatic consequences for the field of corrections. But the "applied sociology" includes more than this. The discipline of sociology, including the sub-area of social psychology, has much to contribute to the business of tactics of behavioral change directed at lawbreakers. Whatever else that might be said about deviant behavior, it is learned be-havior, acquired in the same basic ways in which conformity is learned. The problem for treatment becomes one of reversing the learning process by contriving methods by which criminalistic behavior and attitudes can be unlearned, or conversely, procedures through which conformity to laws can be inculcated. Parenthetically, the job of therapy may sometimes be directed most profitably at communities and neighborhoods, rather than at specific individuals. Whatever the treatment target, surely anyone who is interested in these activities would be well advised to pay close attention to the sociological commentary on community structure and processes, and to the social-psychological literature on group relations, reference group processes, attitude development and change, socialization influences, and related subjects. In short, this book discusses the major implications of sociological and social-psychological propositions for correctional treatment.

This book is a contribution to correctional practice theory in that one of its aims is to identify some important areas of sociological theory and research which ought to be incorporated into the training of treatment workers in corrections. But it does not provide a complete statement regarding occupational knowledge for correctional employees, for such skills as interviewing, casework techniques, and the like are only tangentially dealt with here.

Hopefully, this volume will make a substantial contribution to criminology and to correctional treatment. A number of individuals have had a hand in its development. In this connection, special mention should be made of Stanton Wheeler, Peter Garabedian, and John Kinch, all of whom encouraged me to write the book. I am also indebted to Donald Garrity, for he and I have collaborated on a number of published and unpublished essays which express some of the themes contained in this work. I am particularly grateful to Herbert Blumer for many important criticisms and suggestions which have influenced the final form of this book. But none of these persons bears any responsibility for errors, omissions, or defects contained herein. These are to be blamed on the author alone.

Don C. Gibbons

San Francisco, California

CONTENTS

one

PRACTICE
THEORY
IN CORRECTIONS

Introduction

This book, a primer for the training of correctional workers, is concerned with the identification of (1) the sorts of rehabilitation problems which different juvenile and adult lawbreakers present to the treatment worker, (2) relevant and effective kinds of therapy which can be applied to these individuals in order to change them into law-abiding citizens, and (3) obstacles of various kinds which are present in correctional work settings and which complicate the task of changing deviants. In a general way, this book can be likened to a brief handbook on medical practice in which various forms of sickness would be identified and described, along with some procedures designed to "cure" these illnesses.

The *raison d'être* of this work arises out of the deficiencies in much of the existing literature on tactics of correctional treatment. For one thing, because discussions regarding strategies of intervention are scattered around in a variety of places and are not collected up in a single text no one book on therapy has been available

1

which could be used in the training of students. Moreover, much of the existing literature is defective in that it has failed to utilize the full amount of available criminological and sociological theory and research. Probably all persons would agree that rehabilitative ventures should be based upon valid causal arguments which identify the character of the problems to be remedied. In short, to "cure" criminals and delinquents implies knowledge of the nature and causes of criminal "sickness." Pursuing this metaphor further, it seems also the case that if offenders vary in terms of the kinds of "criminal illness" they manifest, therapy programs need to take that fact into account. Now, it seems obvious enough that law violators do vary markedly in terms of behavior, attitudes, social backgrounds, and the like. Impressionistic, common-sense observations from a variety of sources quickly demonstrate the heterogeneity of criminalistic deviance. Yet much of what now passes for treatment theory implies that offenders are all quite similar, that they all became involved in deviant behavior as a result of personality problems and deficiencies, and that a single form of therapy (usually some version of individual psychotherapy) will work equally well with all of them.

This volume takes issue with much of the existing treatment theory. It argues that delinquents and criminals are not all alike, that instead, they fall into a number of different behavioral types or patterns. The book also develops the claim that existing treatment theory is usually vague, ambiguous, and often invalid. Tactics of therapy have been suggested which are not suitable for many kinds of offenders. To replace this existing material, different specific treatment forms need to be clearly defined and explicitly linked to particular offender patterns for which they are relevant.

The Nature of Practice Theory

This volume is an expanded explication of diagnostic and treatment problems originally raised in a short essay several years ago.[1] In that article, Greenwood's model of the nature of practice theory in an applied field provided the framework of argu-

---

[1] Don C. Gibbons, "Some Notes on Treatment Theory in Corrections," *Social Service Review*, Vol. 36 (September 1962), 295-305.

ment. Greenwood's commentary is worth examining again because his presentation succinctly defined the basic problems of practice theory. His comments were concerned with the nature of practice fields such as social work, and in turn, with their relationships to basic social science disciplines, such as sociology and psychology.

Greenwood places social work within the general category of the technologies, that is, "disciplines that aim to achieve controlled changes in natural relationships via relatively standardized procedures that are scientifically based." He distinguishes two basic forms of technology, "engineering" which deals with nonhuman materials, and "practices" which involve human subjects.[2] According to Greenwood, the general pattern of activity which the practitioner should follow is noted below:

Ideally, the practitioner should function in the following manner: He is confronted with a problem, which is a state of disequilibrium requiring rectification. He examines the problem situation both internally and externally. On the basis of the facts ascertained, he appraises the problem situation. On the strength of his appraisal, he prescribes a mode of solution. He then undertakes the solution, which re-establishes the equilibrium. This process is customarily referred to as *diagnosis* and *treatment*. . . .

To diagnose a problem implies that, on the basis of certain facts observed in the problem situation, it is correctly placed within an already existing typology. A typology is a classification scheme in which each category or type represents a distinct constellation of factors. . . . A well-developed practice has at its disposal a highly refined diagnostic typology that embraces the entire gamut of problems confronted by that discipline. There has been formulated for each diagnostic type a series of generalizing propositions, both descriptive and prescriptive. The former propositions describe the properties, behavior, etiology, and life cycle of the type; the latter prescribe the steps to be pursued in ascertaining whether a given problem is classifiable within a type. Together, these propositions make up the diagnostic principles of a practice.[3]

Note the similarity of this *modus operandi* for the professional practitioner to the process of diagnosis in medicine. Indeed, the

---

[2] Ernest Greenwood, "Social Science and Social Work: A Theory of Their Relationship," *Social Service Review*, Vol. 29 (March 1955), 20-32. Also, see his "Attributes of a Profession," *Social Work*, Vol. 2 (July 1957), 45-55.

[3] Greenwood, "Social Science and Social Work," 25.

analogy is a close one, for both the doctor and the social worker are concerned with the solution of human problems. Ideally, both should work within the framework of a valid diagnostic system. Parenthetically, Greenwood *does not* suggest that diagnosis in social work is a relatively mechanical process involving only the placement of problem cases within a diagnostic system. As in medicine, extreme skill is needed in diagnosis, for the diagnostician should be concerned *both* with the assignment of a problem to a set of general types *and* with the discovery of the unique features of a specific instance of problem behavior. He must be sensitive both to the similarity of the case to others and to its unique features in order to achieve controlled changes.[4] Diagnosis involves much more than the insertion of a punched IBM card into a sorter which performs the diagnostic task by dropping the card into a particular slot.

Greenwood also indicates that a well-developed practice field would be characterized by a typology of treatment tactics:

A well-developed practice also has at its disposal a typology of treatment procedures, which become elaborated as novel types of treatment are developed. As in the case of the diagnostic typology, a series of generalizing propositions, or *principles of treatment,* has been formulated for each treatment type. These propositions describe operationally the stages in the treatment, indicate when the treatment is appropriate, and specify the criteria, preferably mensurative, whereby success or failure may be ascertained. The diagnostic and treatment typologies are, of course, employed together by the practitioner. Thus each class description of the diagnostic typology contains implications for a certain type or types of treatment. . . .

The descriptions of the diagnostic and treatment typologies, in all their ramifications, implications, and rationalizations, are the *principles of practice* and constitute the unique body of knowledge of the discipline. This body of knowledge may be labeled "practice theory." [5]

A simplified graphic presentation of this structure of practice principles is shown in Figure 1.

The thesis of this book is that correctional treatment activities should be structured around a body of practice theory of the kind

[4] *Ibid.,* 25-26.
[5] *Ibid.,* 26.

DIAGNOSTIC TYPOLOGY

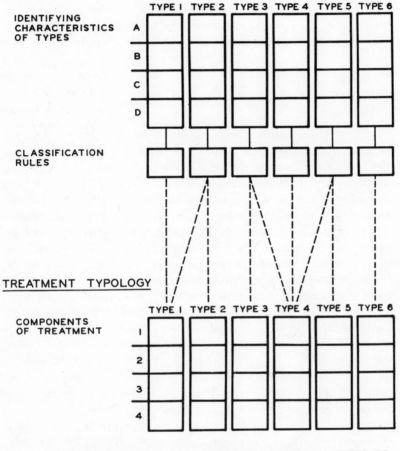

figure 1   **PRINCIPLES OF PRACTICE**

outlined above. Correctional intervention attempts to achieve controlled change in the behavior of law violators. Although there are some special difficulties in the way of achieving such changes within the correctional milieu, nonetheless, the basic aims of correctional treatment are consistent with those of other practice fields. Accordingly, Greenwood's model can be employed as a set of guidelines to the form that correctional practice should take.

Some Defects of Practice Theory

How does the existing material on correctional treatment measure up to these guidelines? Unhappily, the mass of commentary in the form of journal articles, textbooks and other examples of practice theory falls considerably short of the mark.[6] For one thing, many of the discussions of "treatment" are in fact not concerned with rehabilitation at all. Instead, there is a common confusion in the literature between programs which represent humanitarian reforms, or which are simply adjuncts to treatment, and those which are therapy programs, per se. This matter will be discussed in some detail in Chapter Four. It is enough to note at this point that many of the activities which are now called "treatment" have no specific or direct link to rehabilitation. Programs of the kind which try to reduce inmate idleness, to decrease inmate isolation through increased visiting privileges, or to improve the physical appearance of correctional institutions are not treatment activities for they are not directly concerned with attempts to change behavior in any specific way. These are examples of humanitarian reform, of changes in correctional routines and practices which are designed to reduce some of the physical and psychological "pains of imprisonment."[7] They operate to make the matter of "doing time" more tolerable for the individual inmate. Although such

[6] Gibbons, op. cit.; Gibbons and Donald L. Garrity, "Some Suggestions for the Development of Etiological and Treatment Theory in Criminology," Social Forces, Vol. 38 (October 1959), 51-58.

[7] Gresham M. Sykes, The Society of Captives (Princeton, N.J.: Princeton University Press, 1958), pp. 63-83; for some important comments regarding the confusion of treatment with humanitarianism, see Lloyd W. McCorkle and Richard Korn, "Resocialization Within Walls," Annals of the American Academy of Political and Social Science, Vol. 293 (May 1954), 88-98.

changes are to be applauded, they should be recognized for what they are and they should be defended on moral grounds alone.

In a similar fashion, such activities as educational or vocational training are not treatment. Although these programs may be somewhat more directly linked to tasks of rehabilitation, they are not specifically focused upon these ends. They represent adjuncts to therapy which may aid in the resocialization of the offender *when* accompanied by some kind of treatment. For example, vocational training could be a useful adjunct to the treatment of certain kinds of offenders, provided that these persons were also led to modify their earlier attitudes of the form, "only slobs work." But in this case, the term "treatment" should be restricted to those endeavors specifically directed to the goal of controlled change or attitude modification.

A second defect of much contemporary practice theory is that it is based upon crudely articulated behavioral propositions which suggest that most offenders are emotionally maladjusted and in need of intensive individual therapy. Psychogenic theories, holding that lawbreakers are "acting out" emotional problems are, in the first place, incomplete in that they usually fail to account for differential results or outcomes which occur to these assumed problems. That is, some persons with emotional tensions "act out" these problems in noncriminal ways, whereas others are presumed to adopt criminalistic solutions to their difficulties. Psychogenic arguments, however, are usually silent regarding those factors which produce these two different results. In addition, they systematically ignore an abundance of sociological theory and research data which suggest that many forms of unlawful conduct arise out of strains and defects in the social order to which illegal behavior is a "normal" response. Although some sociogenic commentary has begun to creep into discussions of rehabilitation, this material is not prominent in comparison to the mass of psychogenic treatment theory.[8]

Moreover, the problem is not simply that etiological or diagnostic theory shows little sensitivity to sociogenic variables in deviant behavior. Much of this theory also fails to take into account varia-

---

[8] See Stanton Wheeler, "The Social Sources of Criminology," *Sociological Inquiry*, Vol. 32 (Spring 1962), 139-59, for a discussion of some of the reasons why sociological theories have not played an important part in most correctional programs.

tions among types of lawbreakers. There is mounting evidence to indicate that neither a psychogenic nor sociogenic image of causation is sufficient by itself to explain the variety of behavioral forms represented by the total population of offenders. There are many kinds of criminals and delinquents. There are "normal" ones and "abnormal" ones. Some patterns of illegal activity involve personality problems and other characteristics identified in psychogenic models, and others do not. The point of these remarks, in Greenwood's terms, is that correctional diagnostic models are as yet insufficiently developed. They do not identify the range or complexity of the problems that therapy must attack.

The preceding commentary is perhaps an exaggerated description of the present state of affairs in corrections. Doubtless an optimistic observer looking for signs of progress in the direction of empirically sound and effective practices could take heart from recent issues of professional journals. Some analyses of treatment strategies and some examinations of diagnostic typologies for delinquents or criminals have appeared in recent years. In Chapter Two, detailed attention will be given to a number of recent statements regarding offender types and the implications of that work for diagnosis and therapy. Anticipating this later discussion, it should be noted that although these contributions to the correctional literature offer promise for the future much of this work to date has been flawed by a variety of deficiencies.

Also on the optimistic side, some rather good research evidence has been accumulating in recent years regarding the effects of specific programs of treatment upon offenders. In particular, several therapeutic or preventive efforts have been undertaken in the past decade or so which have been directly based upon some sophisticated notions of causal processes in deviant behavior, for example, the Provo Experiment and Mobilization for Youth.[9] In the first case, delinquent probationers in Provo, Utah, have been placed in a program involving several facets but with major emphasis upon group counseling (guided group interaction) as the strategy for inducing behavioral change. This experiment is based upon a complex foundation of behavioral theory regarding the nature of de-

[9] LaMar T. Empey and Jerome Rabow, "The Provo Experiment in Delinquent Rehabilitation," *American Sociological Review*, Vol. 26 (October 1961), 679-95; "A Proposal for the Prevention and Control of Delinquency by Expanding Opportunities" (New York: Mobilization for Youth, Inc.), 1961.

linquency and of effective treatment. The second example, Mobilization for Youth, is a multimillion dollar preventive effort guided by a sophisticated theory of delinquency among lower-class boys which was advanced by Cloward and Ohlin.[10] In brief, this theory holds that delinquency among lower-class youths develops out of perceptions on their part that a significant disjunction or gap exists between their aspirations for material success and their expectations of achieving these goals by conventional means. In turn, the preventive activities are intended to provide a greater supply of legitimate or conventional opportunities for success to these culturally and economically deprived youngsters.

Other examples of this kind will be presented in subsequent chapters. Although these programs are impressive harbingers of the future, several points should be kept in mind regarding them. First, most of these innovations in treatment or prevention are specific to the case of lower-class gang delinquency. This is a reflection of the fact that criminological interest in the past decade has been heavily concentrated upon working-class, subcultural delinquency. Pitifully little theorizing or investigative work has gone on concerning other patterns of juvenile delinquency or forms of adult criminality. In turn, as far as treatment endeavors are concerned, promising innovations outside of gang delinquency programs have been few in number.

A second observation regarding recent innovations in corrections is that most of them have been carried on outside the framework of conventional governmental programs or agencies. A number of these projects have been directed by some university-affiliated group of individuals and have been supported by foundation moneys. There are few programs which represent a significant departure from the *status quo* in county and state correctional systems. One incisive indictment of official correctional organizations and personnel for their failure to develop new lines of rehabilitative thinking has been made by Cressey.[11] His thesis is presented in musicological terms; thus, he finds that most of the commentary in the literature emanating from representatives of official correctional

[10] Richard A. Cloward and Lloyd E. Ohlin, *Delinquency and Opportunity* (New York: The Free Press of Glencoe, Inc., 1960).

[11] Donald R. Cressey, "The 'Square' Theory of Probation"; unpublished paper delivered before the annual meeting of the California Probation, Parole and Correctional Association, June 1960.

systems is "square" in content. Those themes that appear in such places as professional journals don't "swing"—they are repetitious, vague, superficial, and probably, in many cases, erroneous as well. In Cressey's view, those relatively few new and promising ideas which have appeared in the past decade or so—the "cool jazz" of corrections—have been contributed by persons outside of the official structures of probation, institutions, or parole.

My own assessment of the state of correctional thinking and practice is similar to that of Cressey. This evaluation has been built up out of a number of years of experience of several kinds with correctional employees, most of whom were "treatment" agents. Parenthetically, most of these contacts have been with workers in California, the state which is widely regarded as having the most progressive programs and the most "professional" employee group to be found anywhere in the United States. It appears that many workers have been insufficiently trained in etiological theory and research or in treatment tactics that are relevant to the various forms of offender behavior. Instead, many of them are equipped only with some relatively vague, psychogenic notions about criminal or delinquent deviants. In the same way, treatment is at present little more than an activity in which "someone does something to someone else" with indeterminate or unknown results. The use of unshared and intuitive treatment procedures by different workers is the norm. These tactics are frequently vague and ambiguous, even to the worker, and are not based on empirical evidence regarding the nature of offenders or the efficacy of certain tactics. Instead, they are compounded out of gross behavioral theories and treatment notions, along with speculative hunches arrived at by trial and error in the work setting. Discussions and comments by correctional workers frequently take the form of allegations that the job of the agent is to "help the person handle his problems" but without any detailed indication of what this goal implies or how it is to be accomplished. In short, there is little warrant for the use of terms such as "professional correctional work" or "correctional profession" to describe the present situation of correctional practice. It is hard to find much evidence that workers possess a body of uniform, special knowledge and skills which they employ in treatment and which would justify the appellation, "profession."

Much the same kind of analysis could be made of those developments in several states in which research evaluation of programs has become a permanent part of the operation. For example, in California, both the adult and juvenile correctional systems are involved in the study of the impact of programs upon offenders who are classified according to diagnostic devices developed there. No doubt much will be learned in the long run from such research, but it appears that so far the majority of correctional agents in California have been little influenced by the findings of that research operation. Research results have not filtered down to lower-level employees in the system, nor is there any indication that the activities of workers have been much influenced by research discoveries to date.

What should be done about the theoretical deficiencies of corrections? Explicit attention might be given to articulating an improved brand of practice theory. In the chapters to follow, some of the existing knowledge regarding causal factors in crime and delinquency will be organized in the form of diagnostic typologies which have treatment implications. Chapters Two and Three are devoted to this topic. Also, a discussion of therapy which distinguishes treatment goals and forms from various kinds of humanitarian reform or adjunct programs and a typology of therapy tactics is presented in Chapter Four. Chapter Five is concerned with some of the major obstacles to the attainment of treatment goals within different correctional situations such as probation or institutions. For example, one major problem standing in the way of managed behavioral change in prisons is the inmates' social system which lays major emphasis upon antiadministration, antitreatment attitudes as the measure of the conforming prisoner. Although this is not an insurmountable obstacle, it must be recognized and effectively circumvented if therapy is to be successful. The presentation goes on to link up types of treatment with relevant offender types. Attempts are made in Chapters Six and Seven to indicate which of the various forms of therapy are most likely to be effective with types of lawbreakers. Finally, some directions for theory and research regarding the effects of treatment upon offenders are suggested in the concluding chapter.

Much of the argument must necessarily be speculative in tone in view of the gaps in the existing knowledge regarding crime and delinquency causation and the paucity of available evidence concerning the effectiveness of treatment strategies. But speculative and contentious remarks have a place if, in the long haul, they provide the stimulus for attention to problems of diagnostic or treatment typologies. An explicit analysis of diagnostic types and therapy procedures, framed in speculative terms, may help to accelerate the collection of research evidence on offender types and on the efficacy of forms of therapy. Seen in this light, this book represents a series of hypotheses for testing from which an empirically based body of practice theory might accrue.

Some Disclaimers

There are a number of things which this volume is *not* designed to accomplish. For one, no attempt is made to draw together and to synthesize all the existing theory and research on causal questions. Thus this text is not an abbreviated version of conventional criminology or delinquency textbooks in which the accumulation of theory and research results is presented in its entirety. Furthermore, this book is not represented as a full analysis of all the existing literature regarding treatment theory or therapy tactics. Instead, the contents of this volume provide a skeleton upon which specific, detailed reports of pieces of treatment research might be meaningfully placed. This work is not an expedient alternative to a conscientious study of the literature on rehabilitative ventures, nor is it a parallel to several existing penology treatises on treatment.[12] Such matters as variations in administrative structures within which treatment is attempted are discussed in those books; for example, youth authority programs are contrasted to other administrative forms for juvenile correctional agencies. Although organizational patterns represent important administrative facts which the correctional worker should know about, they are not directly germane to the purposes of this text. The chapters to follow contain some tangential observations on the forms of correctional organization, but no effort is made to do full justice to the details of these systems and of their operations because these organizational forms are viewed as *enabling structures* for therapy rather than as treatment. To the extent that a particular form of

---

[12] Paul W. Tappan, ed., *Contemporary Correction* (New York: McGraw-Hill Book Company, Inc., 1951); American Prison Association, *A Manual of Correctional Standards* (New York: American Prison Association, 1954).

correctional structure acts as an impediment, or conversely as an aid to therapy, such functions will be noted.

Existing penology texts are concerned with matters which are not dealt with in detail in this text. In addition, the several penology textbooks do not give much attention to matters of diagnostic typologies, treatment patterns, and the like. Accordingly, this text is directed at problems different from those which are discussed at length in penology books so that it should be viewed as complementary to, rather than competitive with, penological works.

Along the same line, the comments in this book generally exclude any detailed investigation of the forms, procedures, and operations of various specific implementation devices within large correctional operations. These matters are taken up in penology textbooks. Specific implementation devices include such parts of correctional processes as classification, educational programs such as correspondence courses and academic schools, prerelease planning and prerelease units, reception and diagnostic centers, and so forth. These different patterns of operation limit the amount of treatment that can be accomplished. To illustrate, a well-developed program of classification which includes an intensive examination of the offender, along with periodic and systematized reclassification procedures, is obviously required if correctional diagnoses are to be carried out effectively. Reference will be made at various points in the following pages to other structural prerequisites to treatment, but not all the important administrative questions will be covered.

Still in this same vein, no detailed analysis is attempted of the multiple functions and conflicting demands which are imposed upon actual correctional agencies as they go about the business of dealing with offenders. Whereas services such as probation are involved in treatment operations, they also have other functions which are assigned to them or which they have taken upon themselves. Punishment, collection of fines, public relations activities in which probation personnel attempt to assure segments of the general public that probation does not involve "softness" toward lawbreakers, and other activities are all involved in probation work. In turn, a probation service or prison system which is confronted with a hostile, punitively oriented public or one which demands that other nonrehabilitative ventures be carried out in great number is going to find the implementation of treatment to be extremely difficult. Reference will be made to matters of this kind, but no pretense is made that this book represents a detailed socio-logical analysis of the structure of correctional programs or of the impact of the surrounding social environment upon correctional organizations.

In essence, this analysis of practice theory in corrections takes an "other things being equal" stance. The commentary on treatment tactics is designed to be practical and realistic, and it is oriented toward a discussion of those procedures that could be employed within a reasonably tolerant and treatment-oriented community. Thus no proposal is made to "break down the walls" and to handle lawbreakers as though they were mentally ill and not responsible for their actions. Such a proposal would be unrealistic for it is extremely doubtful that the general public would support such a venture. Then, too, there are serious questions about the prac-ticality of such a recommendation, given such facts as the lack of agreement on the part of offenders with the proposition that they are "sick." Some violators must be forcibly restrained before any treatment can be undertaken, or else they will not be available for treatment. Also, if the rehabilitation of law violators is contingent upon the creation of an intensive program of psychiatric therapy carried on by psychiatrists, treatment should be abandoned on the grounds that it is an illusory goal. There are simply not enough psychiatrists available even to begin to implement such programs. In the same way, other types of therapy which might be suggested on logical grounds—such as licensed drug clinics for narcotic ad-dicts who would be dealt with as "sick" persons—seem outside the realm of the practical or achievable in the near future. Accordingly, the discussion of rehabilitative tactics here attempts to suggest pro-grams which have a reasonable likelihood of acceptance and success.

In conclusion, the question posed is this: "What kind of practice theory would be needed, assuming that a reasonable organizational structure exists for the implementation of such theory, and assum-ing that general tolerance exists among the public for treatment-oriented correctional practice?"

Is Treatment Possible?

This book is based upon the assumption that it is pos-sible to apply various measures to juvenile and adult offenders which will result in lower rates of recidivism or reinvolvement in criminality than can be achieved in a system of corrections structured entirely around punitive goals. Prevailing opinions on this issue tend toward polar extremes. One rather common view regarding the treatment of offenders is that once an appropriate structure is provided for rehabilitative efforts, including larger budgets, smaller case loads, wider use of probation, better classification programs, more trained workers in corrections, higher salaries, and the like, dramatic reductions in recidivism will quickly follow. This is a position of unbridled and undue optimism, for there is little empirical basis for such a faith. Improvements in correctional structure could have little effect upon recidivism until improvements are also made in the practice theory of treatment, and even then, dramatic reductions in delinquency and criminality may be unlikely.

On the other hand, there are persons who express an extremely pessimistic view of the prospects for rehabilitation. They argue that the almost inevitable consequence of the segregation of the offender into a special class, "criminals" or "delinquents," is that he is forced to reject society and its rehabilitative devices. According to this line of argument, the law violator has two alternatives to choose from when he is singled out as a deviant: he can take on the societal definition of himself as a "bad" person, or he can reject this conception by contriving rationalizations which exclude him from blame for his deviant conduct. The psychological costs to the offender of the first course of action are frequently too high. If he takes the latter course, which he usually does, he is then quite well immunized against treatment and behavioral change. In a similar vein, these pessimistic observers argue that even in those few instances where an offender is led to a position of attitude change in the direction of prosocial sentiments, his status in the community remains that of a "bad" person, an "ex-convict," and a societal reject. Consequently, any change which is effected in the individual is likely to be short-lived. Some offenders do retire from criminal careers, but only because they decide that they are too old for such a life, not as a result of rehabilitation through therapy.

The correctional pessimist would usually admit that there are some violators who do not fit this kind of characterization, who do regard themselves as persons in need of change and who do represent cases amenable to treatment. But the rejoinder is then made that those individuals are capable of self-correction and need no treatment. Consequently, the pessimist points to the large majority of offenders who are immersed in a supportive social system such as the inmate culture of the correctional institution and concludes that with these persons, who represent the major rehabilitation problems in corrections, little can be accomplished by therapy, however structured.

This view of the prospects of treatment is also one based largely on speculation rather than on evidence. There is little sound empirical evidence regarding the effects of rehabilitation programs upon offenders. At first glance, the data which do exist seem to point to the ineffectiveness of therapy. But, on closer examination, it may well turn out that the failure of previous research to demonstrate the efficacy of treatment stems more from the methodological and logical inadequacies of the research than from the inherent untreatability of offenders.

Succeeding chapters in this monograph will be concerned with some of the existing evidence regarding the treatment potential of criminals and delinquents. As that material is evaluated, it appears to show that at least some modest increase in the effectiveness of therapy is within the range of the achievable. At any rate, the following chapters proceed upon that assumption.

On Correctional Training

This book is concerned with a critique and explication of practice theory in corrections. It is an essay on the *content* of correctional knowledge, rather than on the pedagogical question of where and how correctional training should take place. However, the preceding arguments regarding practice theory have some obvious implications in training for correctional work. If these views are valid, workers should be consistently trained and provided with a common core of knowledge. Ideally, responsibility for training should be lodged within some specific academic field or discipline in order to insure comparability of training. Training should include the detailed study of causal theory and research data, diagnostic models, and principles of treatment. In effect, this educational program would be analogous to that in medical schools and other professional schools, where the basic curriculum content remains constant from one specific training institution to another.

It is certainly not the case that correctional education has this character at present. Instead, the heterogeneous mixture of backgrounds now represented among treatment workers vitiates any claim that there is a profession of correctional work in existence. Persons with backgrounds of social work, sociology, correctional administration, criminology, psychology, and other undergraduate majors all find their way into correctional employment.

In recent years, opinions on the question of where responsibility for training should be lodged have become relatively polarized. One highly vocal group has maintained that social work education prepares persons for correctional work, so that treatment workers should be hired from among social welfare graduates. Persons with social work backgrounds have entered correctional employment in considerable numbers, and there have been concerted efforts made by the social welfare field to "capture" corrections as a social work area of practice.

Those who would define corrections as a subarea of social work claim that the goals of correctional therapy are consistent with those of social welfare and that, as a consequence, correctional activities can be considered social work. According to this line of thinking, training in "generic" social work principles, case work techniques, eclectic behavioral theories, and so forth is adequate to the task of rehabilitating offenders.

The opponents of social work in corrections point out that social workers are products of different programs of generic social welfare training so that they do not get consistent educational content. In addition, aside from the variations that exist among these programs, there is serious doubt that such educational backgrounds prepare workers for the task of rehabilitation of lawbreakers. Whatever the merits of generic education, such training does not provide social welfare workers with clear guidelines concerning how they are supposed to deal effectively with the rather special problems that are presented by correctional "clients," many of whom do not fit the conventional model of the social work agency voluntary client.[13]

[13] Lloyd E. Ohlin, Herman Piven, and Donnell M. Pappenfort, "Major Dilemmas of the Social Worker in Probation and Parole," N.P.P.A. Journal, Vol. 2 (July 1956), 211-25.

In this view of things, social welfare training fails to provide the agent with necessary knowledge regarding the causes of crime and delinquency, variations among offenders, societal restrictions upon correctional agencies, and kindred matters. As a result, the social worker's skills do not equip him for the tasks he is called upon to perform in corrections.

A related comment on this issue has been made by Cressey. He quite accurately notes that many of the functions performed by different employees within correctional agencies are not concerned with behavioral change. Record keeping, dentistry, work supervision, and custodial supervision are cases in point. Consequently, he argues that in a correctional division of labor social workers and a variety of other occupational types should be employed. Although social workers might have general responsibility for implementation of rehabilitation goals, they would not be responsible for other goals. Cressey questions the wisdom of incorporating all the varied components of correctional processes under the authority of some single occupational group such as social workers.[14] Cressey's arguments have merit. Because correctional operations include more than attempts to change behavior, correctional work is not simply a specific milieu and set of behavioral difficulties within which social welfare principles can be applied.

The social work field has responded to some of these criticisms. Several social work schools have drawn sociologists into their programs, presumably in order to develop a greater degree of interaction between behavioral theory and research and social work practice. Also, a number of curricula development projects have been carried out in social welfare in an effort to improve training in this area. A most convincing case for correctional social work has been made by the Project on Social Work in Corrections, an activity of the Council on Social Work Education.[15] The publication from that curriculum development project maintains that correctional social workers need generic social welfare training, along with some specialized knowledge, skills, and attitudes in order to demonstrate competence in correctional work. According to that report, the social worker in corrections requires

---

[14] Donald R. Cressey, "Professional Correctional Work and Professional Work in Correction," *N.P.P.A. Journal*, Vol. 5 (January 1959), 1-15.

[15] Elliot Studt, *Education for Social Workers in the Correctional Field* (New York: Council on Social Work Education, 1959), pp. 6-29.

Knowledge of corrections as one of the fields of public social service, with understanding of its historical development, legal base, agency structure, central professions, functions of various personnel, community and agency interrelationships, and major policy issues.

Knowledge of the offender case load including the social and personal problems leading to crime and delinquency, the social selection process involved in official identification of offenders, the common stress experiences characteristic of this intake process, the personality disorders represented in the case load, and the subcultures characteristic of this group.

Skills in working as a member of the criminal justice team, motivating the involuntary client, using authority for making decisions and for exerting control over behavior as a part of treatment, working with the constellation of persons in the family and in the community who are related to the client in each case, contributing to the process of change in the development of services in his agency.

Attitudes of patience, perspective, flexibility and readiness to act arising from understanding of the field, its tasks, and the people with whom it deals, and requiring resolution of personal problems with authority.[16]

This report outlines a series of core concepts and educational objectives oriented around the concepts required for social welfare practice in corrections. These include *deviance, social selection of case load* (differential law enforcement practices, ethnic and economic biases in correctional handling, and the like), *subcultures,* and *acting out disorders.* Other key concepts include *handicapped status, stress, agency structure as a determinant of service, authority as a dynamic in service relationships, responsibility for value-change,* and *the institution as a tool in treatment.*[17] A brief indication is given of the knowledge, skills, and attitudes centering around these concepts which are needed by workers.

It is difficult to find major points of issue with the general curriculum statement of the Council of Social Work Education. As a programmatic essay setting out a skeletal outline of curriculum content, it is an admirably lucid and succinct presentation. Any educational program structured along those lines, whether within social welfare, sociology, corrections, or criminology departments, would offer reasonable educational preparation for correctional employment.

The fundamental task in correctional education is probably not

[16] *Ibid.,* p. 29.
[17] *Ibid.,* pp. 30-50.

to decide which discipline should have proprietary rights on training programs. Rather, there is room for several patterns of educational preparation for employment. The major job ahead is to "flesh-out" the "bones" of the curriculum content identified above. In the chapters to follow, attention is focused upon various kinds of knowledge and information which are viewed as important elements in the occupational knowledge of correctional workers.

two

CAUSAL ANALYSIS
AND
OFFENDER
TYPOLOGIES

Introduction

Chapter One outlined the problems of practice theory as involving the development of diagnostic and treatment typologies along with a rationale linking up types of offenders to forms of therapy. This chapter takes up the problems of typology development and construction, the immediate concern centering around diagnostic typologies for use in treatment. But at the same time, this chapter and several others to follow involve observations of significance to causal analysis. In particular, the criteria for typologies and the assumptions behind such taxonomies represent excursions into etiological theory. Also, the two typologies put forward in Chapter Three constitute the beginnings of causal theories, albeit rough and tentative ones.

In the plan of this chapter, some general remarks will first be made about typological thinking in the criminological literature, indicating that criminological analysis in the past decade or so has taken a decided turn in the direction of description and explanation of specific patterns of criminal and delinquent deviation. This emphasis upon different types of behavior has replaced, to a considerable extent, a search for unitary and general theories which account for "crime" or "delinquency." In a very general sense, this growing interest in typological studies of causation can be likened to the search for explanations for specific patterns of physical illness rather than for a unitary theory of sickness.

These general comments will be followed by an overview of recent attempts to develop useful taxonomic systems or classifications of offenders. These endeavors have been of several kinds, including speculative statements which suggest a comprehensive set of offender patterns and a number of specific pieces of research that have investigated some single kind of lawbreaking behavior such as "naive check forgery."

Following the résumé of existing typological contributions, attention then turns to some logical and theoretical requirements of an adequate system of criminal or delinquent types. The major point here is simply this—there are an almost infinite number of ways in which law violators might be classified or "typed," but these taxonomies may not all be equally important for explanatory or treatment purposes. For example, one simple scheme for sorting deviants into types would be on the basis of specific legal offenses with which they are charged. However, there are several problems with such a system. For one, processes such as "plea copping," in which the person pleads guilty to a lesser charge than the one with which he was originally charged, means that legal categories do not accurately distinguish various offender patterns. Even more important, legal offense categories often fail to reflect significant dimensions or aspects of the social behavior which has been made the subject of social control agency attention. Thus the legal category of "rape" includes patterns of deviant activity which are quite varied in form, so that some "rape" involves force, violence, and unwilling participation by the victim, whereas in other cases these elements are missing.

Another problem with offense categories as the basis of classification is that offenders do not, in many cases, consistently commit only a single kind of deviant act; thus a person who is labeled a "burglar" today becomes a "larcenist" tomorrow. However, the most serious difficulty with legal classifications is that they do not identify theoretically significant types. There is little reason to suppose that persons who are characterized as "burglars" or who are typed in terms of some other specific legal offense are the product of a uniform causal process. Accordingly, the study of causal patterns in deviant behavior is not likely to be advanced through the use of such taxonomic schemes. It will be aided only through the discovery of classification categories which sort persons into types in which a single causal process does characterize the individuals who are included in a specific type.

Violators can be classified in terms of a multitude of variables: offense, hair color, race, urban-rural residence, age, and so forth, *ad infinitum*. The criminologist who hopes to settle upon a causally significant classification must take a calculated risk. He must choose one system from the many that are available. Hopefully, his choice will be a significant one so that when individuals are sorted out in terms of the selected scheme the result will be homogeneous types in which the etiological process is the same for all members of the class or category. But there is no one obvious or "right" way to classify violators which jumps out at the observer from the facts of criminality. The decision to sort out deviants by means of variable X rather than variable Y can only be made in terms of some logic or rationale, some argument in defense of a particular choice of variables. It is not possible to be certain, in advance of research tests, that a particular classificatory scheme is causally significant. It is this part of taxonomic work that justifies the use of the term, "calculated risk."

The business of developing a diagnostic classification to be used in therapy is plagued with the same difficulties. There are many ways in which offenders could be categorized for treatment purposes, but the different schemes may well not be equally useful. To use an extreme illustration, suppose that violators are sorted out into ethnic categories, with a different form of therapy used with each particular ethnic group. It is doubtful that success in treatment would be increased more than if no taxonomy of offenders was used. But, what would a significant diagnostic scheme be like? Again, some kind of a priori choice of a particular system must be made in advance of empirical evidence in support of the choice.

The latter portion of this chapter will put forward a "role-career" perspective regarding the classification of offenders. According to this view, violators can be meaningfully categorized in terms of certain variables such as "offense patterns," "interactional setting," "attitudes," and "self-images." That is, various deviant types such as the "naive check forger" or "gang delinquent" can be identified on the basis of these dimensions. In turn, this book claims that the types which result from the use of these classificatory dimensions represent significant categories in both causal and treatment terms. The latter part of this chapter attempts to support this claim with an extended justificatory argument.

The Development of Typological Views

Anyone studying recent criminological textbooks or the contents of journals in psychology, psychiatry, or sociology could not avoid noticing the extent to which emphasis has turned toward the study of variations among types of lawbreakers and away from analysis of "crime" and "delinquency." For example, textbooks by Bloch and Geis,[1] Sutherland and Cressey,[2] Clinard,[3] Korn and McCorkle,[4] and Cavan[5] all are structured around the viewpoint that "crime" and "delinquency" represent heterogeneous grab bags of behavior. These authors also promote the proposition that within these behavioral collections of miscellany homogeneous patterns of deviant conduct can be identified. Their conclusion is that attention must be directed toward the investigation of specific offender types.

Much of this commentary is pointed toward the development of causal propositions rather than toward treatment theory. It is widely argued that no single theory of crime or delinquency, however broad or complex, is going to be equal to the task of accounting for the various forms which these phenomena take; thus etiological

---

[1] Herbert A. Bloch and Gilbert Geis, *Man, Crime, and Society* (New York: Random House, 1962), pp. 135-37, 311-43.

[2] Edwin H. Sutherland and Donald R. Cressey, *Principles of Criminology*, 6th ed. (Philadelphia: J. B. Lippincott Co., 1960), pp. 237-50.

[3] Marshall B. Clinard, *Sociology of Deviant Behavior*, rev. ed. (New York: Holt, Rinehart and Winston, Inc., 1963), pp. 204-91.

[4] Richard R. Korn and Lloyd W. McCorkle, *Criminology and Penology* (New York: Holt, Rinehart and Winston, Inc., 1959), pp. 42-156.

[5] Ruth Shonle Cavan, *Juvenile Delinquency* (Philadelphia: J. B. Lippincott Co., 1962), passim; Cavan, *Criminology*, 2nd ed. (New York: Thomas Y. Crowell Co., 1955), pp. 3-31, 125-250.

"theories of the middle range" specific to particular forms of deviant conduct will have to be developed. In the long run, it may be possible to discover some general theory which will subsume specific explanations for particular offender types, but in the short run, it is widely held that the search for specific theories offers the most promising avenue for theory construction and research.

Now, if it turns out that typological theories which make causal sense out of forms of criminality and delinquency can be developed, they would be directly relevant to the matter of practice theory. Indeed, typological schemes are presently sufficiently developed so that they could be applied to problems of diagnostic systems, even though they leave something to be desired in clarity, empirical validity, and so forth.

Certain defects are contained in existing typological statements in the criminological literature.[6] On the one hand, there are a number of general assertions to the effect that criminality is not homogeneous but that particular patterns of similar behavior can be observed. However, in most of this commentary, vague, incomplete, anecdotal, and logically ambiguous classification systems are suggested. Commonly, someone advances the argument that there are types of offenders and then proceeds to list some rubrics such as "egocentric, wayward offender," "professional criminal," or "gang delinquent," within which offenders are said to fall. These categories are not well defined, and they are often illustrated by case histories rather than by explicit statements of the identifying attributes of the types. The underlying logic on which such schemes are based is left largely unspecified. As a result, it is rather difficult to visualize research tests of such claims, for unless a classification scheme is made explicit and detailed, it is unlikely that different researchers would classify particular individuals in the same way or within the same categories.

The criminological literature is made up of more than general statements about offender types. There is a sizeable body of theory and research which has focused upon single patterns of behavior held to represent criminal or delinquent types. Theories have been advanced regarding the nature and causes of "gang delinquency,"

---

[6] For a discussion of the present status of typological assertions and some defects of these arguments, see Don C. Gibbons and Donald L. Garrity, "Some Suggestions for the Development of Etiological and Treatment Theory in Criminology," *Social Forces*, Vol. 38 (October 1959), 51-58.

"automobile theft," and a number of other forms of behavior. Research investigations also have been conducted regarding many kinds of juvenile lawbreaking. Similarly, theorizing relative to specific patterns of adult criminality, as well as a number of pieces of research which have studied "naive check forgers," "embezzlers," and other criminal types, has been developed. By and large, the development of general statements of a typological sort and the exploration of specific offender patterns have been occurring simultaneously, so that each endeavor has fed back into the other. Much of the support for general assertions comes from the results of specific research studies to date, whereas further encouragement for particular pieces of investigation has derived from these general typological frameworks.

However, the studies of narrowly defined types have not been without serious shortcomings. The principal defect of this activity is that it has been unguided by any kind of broad, organizing theory. Most of the types that have been the subject of investigation so far have been defined *ad hoc*. The distinctions made among offenders have frequently been dictated by considerations of convenience—by the kinds of information on violators now available in records and other data sources. Consequently, studies have compared rural versus urban offenders, male and female delinquents, juveniles diagnosed as representing different psychiatric types, criminals classified in terms of information recorded on "rap sheets," and so on. There are nearly as many versions of specific types as there are persons who have conducted research studies. Although the resultant body of empirical data is of great importance, that material does not have the same cumulative impact as would a collection of data structured in terms of a single, over-all theoretical view which has defined the range of offender patterns.[7]

It is truly unfortunate that a detailed, explicit, comprehensive, and empirically verified offender typology does not exist. It is regrettable that the typologies which now are around are somewhat vague, so that it is not entirely clear as to how real-life individuals might be sorted out within such devices. The task of developing

---

[7] *Ibid.* This paper contains a detailed listing of arguments about general types and specific research studies on types. For another inclusive listing of typological works, along with a compendium of other criminological sources, see Dorothy Campbell Tompkins, *The Offender, A Bibliography* (Berkeley: Institute of Government Studies, University of California, 1963).

practice theory would be much easier if a system of valid offender types existed which could be taken over as the basis of a diagnostic typology. However, an incomplete or partially inadequate set of diagnostic categories is better than none at all, which is the only alternative to a tentative statement of treatment principles. Therapy efforts oriented around even a relatively crude classificatory system are probably going to be more effective than activities unguided by any kind of diagnostic system. Moreover, it is not possible to simply stand by and wait until a better diagnostic system can be generated. The articulation of sound taxonomic devices will probably take place in stages, where an initial one is refined and improved as it is applied to problems of rehabilitation.

In the next section, attention turns to a more detailed survey of some of the typological statements in the literature. This section is designed to illuminate the preceding comments and also to indicate the nature of the existing material out of which diagnostic systems might be molded.

Some Typological Precedents

ADULT OFFENDERS

There is no useful purpose to be served by a detailed listing and discussion of all the individual statements that have been made about criminal behavior patterns throughout the history of criminological study. Such comments have been made as far back as the writings of Lombroso. Many of these have been listed in a paper by the author and Donald L. Garrity.[8] A few examples will be sufficient for the purposes here.

In one general statement regarding criminal types, Cavan has classified forms of criminality in terms of the degree of the individual's withdrawal or exclusion from the control of the dominant social organization. She concludes that there are five major types and a number of subtypes of criminal behavior. These include persons who are conformers to a subcultural group (Quaker conscientious objectors, for example), essentially law-abiding violators, segmental criminals, professional criminals, and maladjusted offend-

---

[8] Gibbons and Garrity, op. cit. See also Gibbons and Garrity, "Definition and Analysis of Certain Criminal Types," Journal of Criminal Law, Criminology and Police Science, Vol. 53 (March 1962), 27-35.

ers. These categories are illustrated in anecdotal fashion by case histories; but in the several chapters of the textbook where these patterns are singled out for attention, the reader can get some sense of the nature of the categories even though the discussions are generally discursive in tone.[9]

This system of classification is no doubt quite useful in a textbook analysis of criminality. Then, too, it would be generally conceded that Cavan's distinctions among offenders are a reflection of some real differences among criminals. But the classification is relatively crude and is not well suited as a basic structure on which to hang etiological theory. These distinctions are not clear enough in the first place, and additionally, they are probably not sufficiently detailed so that each pattern is causally homogeneous. For example, there may be a number of specific patterns of professionalized criminality, each of which is produced by a different causal process.

Another general statement on criminal types which is open to the same sort of criticism is represented by Bloch and Geis. These authors handle, as separate types of crime, professional criminality, organized crime, homicides, assaults, sex offenses, property crimes, petty offenses, and white-collar crime. These distinctions are useful as a first approximation to a detailed set of types, particularly within a textbook format.[10] However, this example is also one in which a discursive examination is given to offender patterns and where, consequently, the classification is not sufficiently developed to serve as the basis for causal theory or treatment principles.

As indicated earlier, a number of specific statements and research reports have appeared in recent years. For example, a series of studies by Roebuck and his associates are all based on one sample of 1,155 prison inmates in the District of Columbia reformatory and concern the characteristics of such types as "Negro armed robbers," "Negro drug addicts," "Negro drinkers and assaulters," and "Negro jack-of-all-trades offenders."[11] Roebuck developed a ty-

[9] Cavan, Criminology, pp. 20-29.

[10] Bloch and Geis, op. cit., pp. 135-404.

[11] Julian B. Roebuck and Mervyn L. Cadwallader, "The Negro Armed Robber as a Criminal Type: The Construction and Application of a Typology," Pacific Sociological Review, Vol. 4 (Spring 1961), 21-26; Roebuck, "The Negro Drug Addict as an Offender Type," Journal of Criminal Law, Criminology and Police Science, Vol. 53 (March 1962), 36-43; Roebuck and Ronald Johnson, "The Negro Drinker and Assaulter as a Criminal Type," Crime and Delinquency, Vol. 8 (January 1962), 21-33; Roebuck and Johnson, "The Jack-of-all-Trades Offender," Crime and Delinquency, Vol. 8 (April 1962), 172-81.

pology based on legal categories of offense behavior, studied within the framework of *criminal careers,* so that prison inmates were sorted into types based on their over-all crime career as shown in their cumulative arrest records. One type consisted of persons involved in a single pattern of robbery, another of offenders involved in a single pattern of narcotics violations, another of individuals whose careers consisted primarily of burglaries, and so forth. In all, thirteen criminal career patterns were identified.

After inductively constructing the typology from the data on prisoners, Roebuck then compared single types with the balance of the offender group. In the case of Negro armed robbers, those persons were examined against the rest of the inmates in order to uncover significant differences between the robbers and the other offenders. He found that the robbers differed significantly from the residual class of inmates in twenty-two of thirty social and personal characteristics. In general, robbers were from more disorganized home backgrounds and from more deteriorated and criminalistic areas of urban communities than were the other prisoners. They were also characterized by a kind of short-run hedonism in that they had no long-term plans and were relatively spontaneous and uncommitted in attitudes.

Similar results were obtained in the other comparisons reported. Addicts were seen to differ from other inmates in that they were generally younger, from family backgrounds that were more favorable, and from homes in which maternal dominance was common. Roebuck concluded that addicts are frequently dependent personalities who take refuge in drugs as an escape from intolerable social situations. Differently, Negro drinker-assaulter inmates were from less criminogenic backgrounds than other prisoners and were from family situations which distinguished them from other offenders. Finally, Negro jack-of-all-trades offenders turned out to be introverted, "marginal" persons who had failed to experience learning opportunities in which they could acquire skill and sophistication in criminal activities.

These studies have much to recommend them. For one thing, Roebuck suggests some techniques for overcoming the limitations imposed on research when investigations are restricted to only the most recent offense. His attention to career aspects of crime is an important contribution. In addition, these reports comprise part of the intellectual capital out of which a typological theory of crime might be constructed. Nonetheless, there are some problems with this material, one of the most serious of which is concerned with the ethnic orientation of the classificatory system. In all likelihood, ethnicity is not an important definitional variable for separating homogeneous types of offenders. There is little reason to suppose that *Negro* armed robbers are significantly different from *Caucasian* armed robbers in terms of causal background, and the same point holds for most of these other types as well; thus, the ethnic aspect of this typology seems to be an incidental and largely irrelevant distinction.

A second difficulty with the methodology employed by Roebuck is that such inductively derived typologies could easily mount up to a total number of specific types which would be unmanageable as a basis for treatment diagnosis or for causal analysis. Inductive discovery of types could develop into a never-ending process, in which as many patterns could be defined as there are ways of classifying persons. If this line of activity were followed indefinitely, etiological study would be faced with a problem of separate explanations for hundreds of specific types of criminalistic behavior. In contrast, perhaps a system of types could be stated a priori, involving a limited number of types which would subsume most of the specific patterns arrived at inductively. If so, at least some energy should be expended in such speculation about offender types which would provide a theoretical base for research.

Other recent typological studies of adult offenders include the investigation of assaultive and nonassaultive criminals by Peterson, Pittman, and O'Neal[12] and Lemert's several studies of different kinds of forgers.[13] All of these represent important sources of information regarding variations among criminals. However, each of these lines of inquiry has proceeded independently of the others rather than out of a single typological frame of reference. Consequently, since the degree of overlap that is represented by the different studies is not entirely clear, direct parallels cannot be seen between certain of Roebuck's types and those of Lemert or Peter-

[12] Richard A. Peterson, David J. Pittman, and Patricia O'Neal, "Stabilities in Deviance: A Study of Assaultive and Non-Assaultive Offenders," *Journal of Criminal Law, Criminology and Police Science,* Vol. 53 (March 1962), 44-48.

[13] Edwin M. Lemert, "The Behavior of the Systematic Check Forger," *Social Problems,* Vol. 6 (Fall 1958), 141-49; Lemert, "An Isolation and Closure Theory of Naive Check Forgery," *Journal of Criminal Law, Criminology and Police Science,* Vol. 44 (September-October 1953), 296-307.

son and associates. In turn, the data which emerge from these investigations do not have the same impact as would a body of findings about a common set of types that have been studied by different researchers.

The typological works reviewed so far have been concerned with types "at large," that is, with patterns of criminal behavior that are not specific to a particular correctional setting. But there have been several recent reports regarding role behavior among prison inmates which represent still another kind of typological material. The work of Schrag is a particularly impressive instance of this kind. He has shown that a pattern of four sets of inmate roles oriented around certain focal issues exist in the prison community. These role patterns are identified in the argot of inmates by the labels of "square John," "right guy," "outlaw," and "politician," but Schrag has retitled these with a more neutral terminology.[14]

According to Schrag, prosocial inmates (square Johns) consistently define role requirements in terms of the legitimate norms of the civilian community of law-abiding citizens, whereas antisocial inmates (right guys) perceive role requirements in terms of the norms of the prisoner society. The latter are loyal to other convicts and engage in minimal contact with prison officials. Pseudosocial prisoners (politicians) shift their allegiance between legitimate norms and prisoner standards and are engaged in interaction with both inmates and administrators. Finally, asocial inmates (outlaws) are rebels against both legitimate norms or prescriptions and the standards of inmate society.

Schrag has summarized a series of studies which demonstrate that these role patterns are of primary importance in understanding inmate behavior within prisons. Among other observations, he notes that each of these role types is the product of a relatively distinct constellation of background experiences. Prosocial offenders usually are involved in crimes of violence or naive property offenses. They exhibit few prior arrests and little in the way of delinquency records. They appear to be the products of situational stress of various kinds, rather than of long-term conditions of family instability or other kinds of disorganization. On the other hand, anti-

[14] Clarence C. Schrag, "Some Foundations for a Theory of Correction," in Donald R. Cressey, ed., *The Prison* (New York: Holt, Rinehart and Winston, Inc., 1961), pp. 309-57; Schrag, "A Preliminary Criminal Typology," *Pacific Sociological Review*, Vol. 49 (Spring 1961), 11-16.

social inmates are highly recidivistic, they are frequently involved in crime careers which started at an early age, and they are usually from urban, slum area backgrounds. In a word, they are gang delinquents "grown up." Pseudosocial inmates have engaged in sophisticated and subtle property crimes involving the manipulation of other persons rather than in those involving coercion and violence. They tend to be the products of relatively stable and comfortable economic backgrounds. Finally, asocial prisoners have been involved in violent, bizarre forms of crime, and they closely resemble descriptions of "psychopaths." In most cases, such individuals seem to be the product of backgrounds of early and severe parental rejection.

In addition to differences in social backgrounds, Schrag notes other correlates of these role patterns. Social participation within the institution varies between these different types, as do the inmates' responses to various prison experiences such as treatment programs or punishment. To take one example, prosocial inmates associate differentially with other prosocial inmates and also engage in frequent contacts with staff members. Prosocial prisoners also make considerable use of the various treatment programs in the prison, in contrast to other types who shun such activities.

Similar facts regarding inmate types in prison have been presented by Sykes, who indicated that at least eleven role patterns exist and are recognized in the inmate argot of a New Jersey institution. The prisoner language designates these role patterns by such colorful labels as "rats," "gorillas," "center men," "ball busters," "merchants," and "hipsters." [15] It appears that most of the inmate roles specified by Sykes are paralleled by the role patterns listed by Schrag. For example, "gorillas," "ball busters," and "toughs" are apparently quite similar to prisoners who are called "outlaws" in other institutions.

These reports regarding inmate types represent extremely important contributions to criminological knowledge, especially since they are the product of a series of empirical investigations of inmate groups, guided by a central theory of role patterns, and carried on by means of rather careful research techniques. Thus it can be declared with some confidence that clear-cut differences

---

[15] Gresham M. Sykes, *The Society of Captives* (Princeton, N. J.: Princeton University Press, 1958), pp. 84-108.

among prison inmates do exist. Inmates fall into relatively homogeneous types, not only with respect to criminal backgrounds and preprison social experiences, but also in terms of variations in social-psychological characteristics. Prisoner incumbents of different roles perceive the world in different ways. These observations about inmate types are involved in the typological systems discussed in Chapter Three, in that the typological perspective advanced is a parallel of that employed in Schrag's work. That is, the view of the author is that criminal and delinquent behavior should be examined from a role approach in which variations among criminals and delinquents are identified in terms of (1) offense patterns and (2) self-image, normative orientations and other social-psychological characteristics. Attempts should be made to isolate among offenders role patterns similar to those defined by Schrag, but which are not restricted to a specific correctional setting. In this regard, it does appear that such types as "square Johns" are not indigenous only to correctional institutions but exist in probation case loads, jail populations, and other situations.

JUVENILE DELINQUENTS

Two things can be said at the outset about typological activities in delinquency study. First, there have been more of them than those concerning adult criminality, so that the existing supply of typological statements is quite large. Second, classificatory activities, particularly of a "subculture" form, are very much alive right now. In the past decade or so, a rejuvenation of the field of delinquency study has occurred, and a number of efforts have been made to identify specific forms of group-related, organized "subcultural" delinquency and to develop sociological theories to account for the development and persistence of these different patterns. A brief summary of this material follows.

In one overview of typological statements, Kinch reports on fifteen instances of typologies that have been advanced in the delinquency literature.[16] Most of these are ambiguous to some degree and generally discursive in tone. The logic of classification on

[16] John W. Kinch, "Continuities in the Study of Delinquent Types," *Journal of Criminal Law, Criminology and Police Science*, Vol. 53 (September 1962), 323-28.

which most of them are based is not clear. Nonetheless, Kinch suggests that most of the authors of taxonomies have been identifying rather consistently three major types: prosocial, antisocial, and asocial delinquents. He shows that most of these arguments distinguish among juvenile offenders, either explicitly or implicitly, in terms of the reference group orientation of different delinquents. Prosocial juvenile law violators are the adolescent parallels of Schrag's prosocial inmates, and antisocial and asocial delinquents appear to be similar to antisocial and asocial prisoners in adult institutions.

Kinch has also reported data regarding variations in self-images among training school delinquents who were previously classified as prosocial, antisocial, or asocial offenders on the basis of social background data.[17] In the same way, Fisher's study of institutionalized offenders suggests the existence of three types of delinquents, distinguished from each other in terms of their major reference group orientations. He maintains that training school residents include "delinquents of conventional perspective" (prosocial), "delinquents of the delinquent subculture perspective" (antisocial), and "delinquents of ambivalent perspective." Because these three types are differentiated on the basis of social attitudes and definitions of the situation, they are not analogs of psychiatric or psychological types.[18]

Any survey of typological approaches to delinquency would be incomplete without mention of the work of Richard L. Jenkins. He has identified three basic offender patterns through research in several different studies of delinquents. He has shown that there is a group of unsocialized aggressive offenders (asocial), a group of socialized or pseudosocial offenders who are members of delinquent subcultures, and an emotionally disturbed group in the population of serious delinquents. Further, he suggests that these are fundamental patterns of delinquency which are generated by causal processes that vary among the offender types. A background of severe parental rejection emerges as the most important causal experience in the genesis of unsocialized aggressive behavior, whereas parental neglect and exposure to criminalistic influences character-

[17] John W. Kinch, "Self-Conceptions of Types of Delinquents," *Sociological Inquiry*, Vol. 32 (Spring 1962), 228-34.

[18] Sethard Fisher, "Varieties of Juvenile Delinquency," *British Journal of Criminology*, Vol. 2 (January 1962), 251-61.

izes socialized delinquents.[19] Closely parallel to the investigations of Jenkins, a study of Cook County, Illinois, juvenile court probationers by Reiss provides additional confirmation of the existence of these types.[20]

Clinard and Wade have presented evidence regarding juvenile vandalism as a subtype of delinquency.[21] Similarly, several theorists have attempted to explain middle-class delinquency, implying that this is a relatively discrete form of delinquent behavior.[22] Several recent reports have also appeared concerning automobile theft by juveniles, and the impression emerges that still another pattern of juvenile misbehavior has been identified.[23]

The recent attention to sociological explanations of juvenile illegality, triggered by Albert K. Cohen's *Delinquent Boys,* has been one extremely impressive development in the field of delinquency study. That slim volume, published in 1955, redirected attention toward the sociological perspective and away from traditional, multiple-factor orientations. In his essay, Cohen argued that working-class gang delinquency represents a *delinquent subculture,* a social movement among juvenile deviants. This subculture arose as a solution to *shared* problems of low status among working-class boys. These problems are a consequence of the boys' placement in the social order: working-class boys experience status-threats when

[19] Richard L. Jenkins and Sylvia Glickman, "Patterns of Personality Organization Among Delinquents," *Nervous Child,* Vol. 6 (July 1947), 329-39; Lester E. Hewitt and Jenkins, *Fundamental Patterns of Maladjustment: The Dynamics of Their Origin* (Springfield: Illinois State Printer, 1947); Jenkins and Hewitt, "Types of Personality Structure Encountered in Child Guidance Clinics," *American Journal of Orthopsychiatry,* Vol. 14 (January 1944), 84-94.

[20] Albert J. Reiss, Jr., "Social Correlates of Psychological Types of Delinquency," *American Sociological Review,* Vol. 17 (December 1952), 710-18.

[21] Marshall B. Clinard and Andrew L. Wade, "Toward the Delineation of Vandalism as a Sub-Type of Juvenile Delinquency," *Journal of Criminal Law, Criminology and Police Science,* Vol. 48 (January-February 1958), 493-99.

[22] Ralph W. England, Jr., "A Theory of Middle-Class Juvenile Delinquency," *Journal of Criminal Law, Criminology and Police Science,* Vol. 50 (March-April 1960), 535-40; Joseph W. Scott and Edmund W. Vaz, "A Perspective on Middle-Class Delinquency," *The Canadian Journal of Economics and Political Science,* Vol. 29 (August 1963), 324-35.

[23] William Wattenberg and James Balistrieri, "Automobile Theft: A 'Favored Group' Delinquency," *American Journal of Sociology,* Vol. 57 (May 1952), 575-79; Leonard D. Savitz, "Automobile Theft," *Journal of Criminal Law, Criminology and Police Science,* Vol. 50 (July-August 1959), 132-43; Erwin Schepses, "The Young Car Thief," *Journal of Criminal Law, Criminology and Police Science,* Vol. 50 (March-April 1960), 569.

they are evaluated in terms of a middle-class measuring rod. The subculture of the gang provides them with a social setting in which they can become insulated from these assaults upon their self-esteem.[24]

Cohen's initial formulation has been widely hailed as eminently sociological and as an important theoretical exposition which makes sense out of many disparate facts about lower-class delinquency. However, the theory has not been without critics. Among those who have taken issue with parts of the formulation are Kitsuse and Dietrick,[25] Sykes and Matza,[26] and Wilensky and Lebeaux.[27] These criticisms have been salutary rather than destructive in their impact upon the study of delinquency for they have directed attention to issues not previously considered and they have provided new insights.

Cohen's original essay has also stimulated a number of theoretical works which represent alternative arguments rather than criticisms of selected parts of the Cohen thesis. For one, Bloch and Niederhoffer have attempted to show cross-cultural parallels in the forms taken by adolescent gang behavior.[28] They argue, not entirely convincingly, that gang delinquency is more of a generic form of adjustment to problems of adolescence than a class-linked response to status-frustration. Yablonsky takes issue with the Cohen notion of subcultures by arguing that delinquent gangs are "near groups" rather than collectivities characterized by social solidarity.[29] Miller has provided still another alternative view regarding gangs.[30]

---

[24] Albert K. Cohen, *Delinquent Boys* (New York: The Free Press of Glencoe, Inc., 1955).

[25] John I. Kitsuse and David C. Dietrick, "Delinquent Boys: A Critique," *American Sociological Review*, Vol. 24 (April 1959), 208-15.

[26] Gresham M. Sykes and David Matza, "Techniques of Neutralization: A Theory of Delinquency," *American Sociological Review*, Vol. 22 (December 1957), 666-70.

[27] Harold L. Wilensky and Charles N. Lebeaux, *Industrial Society and Social Welfare* (New York: Russell Sage Foundation, 1958), pp. 187-207.

[28] Herbert A. Bloch and Arthur Niederhoffer, *The Gang* (New York: Philosophical Library, 1958).

[29] Lewis Yablonsky, "The Delinquent Gang as a Near-Group," *Social Problems*, Vol. 7 (Fall 1959), 108-17; Yablonsky, *The Violent Gang* (New York: The Macmillan Company, 1962).

[30] Walter B. Miller, "Lower Class Culture as a Generating Milieu of Gang Delinquency," *Journal of Social Issues*, Vol. 14, No. 3 (1958), 5-19; Miller, "Implications of Urban Lower Class Culture for Social Work," *Social Service Review*, Vol. 33 (September 1959), 219-36.

He asserts that they must be examined from the perspective of lower-class culture, rather than in terms of middle-class behavioral norms. He sees gang behavior as a consequence or by-product of certain values or "focal concerns" of lower-class culture.

Cohen has not been inattentive to criticisms of his original statement. In a 1958 essay, he and Short presented a classification of types of delinquent subcultures.[31] This taxonomy developed in part as a response to critics who maintained that lower-class gang delinquency is not all of the same kind. Cohen and Short aver that the gang subculture described in *Delinquent Boys* represents the "parent subculture," that is, the basic form of gang behavior from which a number of variant patterns of delinquent activity have developed. They also provide some answers to a number of other criticisms regarding the initial Cohen formulation.

Another major analysis of gang delinquency which was originally stimulated by the work of Cohen is the "opportunity structure" theory of Cloward and Ohlin.[32] The essentials of this theory are as follows: Lower-class boys share a common American value commitment to "success," measured largely in material terms. But unlike middle-class youths, they do not have access to legitimate means or avenues to attain these "success" goals. Or, if they have access to legitimate means, they perceive their chances of success as limited. Thus for many lower-class boys, a severe gap exists between their aspiration levels and their expectations. Pressures to engage in deviant behavior are generated by this "means-ends disjunction." In turn, the particular deviant adaptation which develops is a function of "opportunity structures" for deviant behavior, at least in part. Some lower-class areas are characterized by integration of criminalistic and conformist patterns of social organization, whereas others are lacking in stable criminalistic patterns. In the organized, criminalistic area, "criminalistic" gang subcultures develop in which boys are involved in instrumental acts of theft and the like and in careers which eventually lead to adult criminal behavior. On the other hand, in areas lacking criminalistic patterns, gang delinquency tends to take the form of "conflict" subcultural behavior, in which "bopping" (gang fighting) predominates. Finally, there are

[31] Albert K. Cohen and James F. Short, Jr., "Research on Delinquent Subcultures," *Journal of Social Issues*, Vol. 14, No. 3 (1958), 20-36.
[32] Richard A. Cloward and Lloyd E. Ohlin, *Delinquency and Opportunity* (New York: The Free Press of Glencoe, Inc., 1960).

some boys who are failures in both the legitimate and illegitimate opportunity structures who engage in "retreatist" behavior and become narcotic users.

Several attempts have been made to subject this argument to test, directly or indirectly, by Spergel,[33] Elliott,[34] and Reiss and Rhodes.[35] The theory has also received some criticism from Schrag[36] and Bordua,[37] among others.

It is impossible to detail the entire variety of hypotheses and counterarguments about gang delinquency which have appeared in recent years. At present, complete consensus regarding the nature of gang behavior or the causal processes involved does not exist. In addition, some new hypotheses are brought forward from time to time to further muddy the subject.[38]

There is, however, one point on which most subcultural statements do agree. There is substantial consensus that gang delinquency does take several forms, so that in some cases "bopping" is the usual activity of gangs, whereas in others predatory theft constitutes the most frequent kind of deviant behavior.

Most of the theorizing about subcultures has been centered on groups and delinquent organizations rather than on the specific characteristics of individual deviants. For example, Cloward and Ohlin define a subculture as an organization of juveniles in which performance of delinquent acts is a requirement for membership. Willingness and ability to carry out deviant acts is at the heart of role-performance.[39] If subcultures exist, it should be possible to

---

[33] Irving Spergel, "An Exploratory Research in Delinquent Subcultures," *Social Service Review*, Vol. 35 (March 1961), 33-47; Spergel, *Racketville, Slumtown, Haulburg* (Chicago: University of Chicago Press, 1964).

[34] Delbert S. Elliott, "Delinquency and Perceived Opportunity," *Sociological Inquiry*, Vol. 32 (Spring 1962), 216-27.

[35] Albert J. Reiss, Jr., and Albert L. Rhodes, "The Distribution of Juvenile Delinquency in the Social Class Structure," *American Sociological Review*, Vol. 26 (October 1961), 720-32.

[36] Clarence C. Schrag, "Delinquency and Opportunity: Analysis of a Theory," *Sociology and Social Research*, Vol. 46 (January 1962), 167-75.

[37] David J. Bordua, "Delinquent Subcultures: Sociological Interpretations of Gang Delinquency," *Annals of the American Academy of Political and Social Science*, Vol. 338 (November 1961), 119-36; Bordua, "Some Comments on Theories of Group Delinquency," *Sociological Inquiry*, Vol. 32 (Spring 1962), 245-60.

[38] David Matza and Gresham M. Sykes, "Juvenile Delinquency and Subterranean Values," *American Sociological Review*, Vol. 26 (October 1961), 712-19; Matza, *Delinquency and Drift* (New York: John Wiley and Sons, 1964).

[39] Cloward and Ohlin, *op. cit.*, p. 7.

specify characteristics of individual actors which identify them as members of such groups. In other words, it should be possible to provide descriptions of the characteristics of members of delinquent subcultures. Accordingly, in the typology of delinquents in Chapter Three, some individuals will be seen who are held to be members of delinquent subcultures.

Some Criteria for Typologies in Causation and Treatment

The major thread of criticism throughout the preceding commentary has been that existing typologies of criminals and delinquents are ambiguous and lacking in specificity. It is now time to take up in detail the requirements which taxonomies must satisfy if they are to be useful, either in causal analysis or in providing diagnostic systems for treatment purposes. Some of the major criteria are as follows: First, an explicit statement must be made regarding the functions any classificatory system is supposed to serve and the form it should take. The point is that several kinds of typologies could be developed, depending upon the use to which a scheme is to be put. Next, the assumptions upon which a classificatory device is based should be made public. Any typology involves assumptions about behavior and these should not be left implicit or unstated; one or more of them may be faulty, which would vitiate the usefulness of the scheme, and defective presuppositions are not likely to be easily recognized unless they are set out for examination. In addition to these two requirements, the identifying or definitional variables in a typology must be specified. The rationale for the choice of definitional variables derives out of the behavioral assumptions. Finally, an adequate typology should provide detailed and specific indicators of the descriptive ingredients of the categories in the system in order that the claims can be checked against empirical evidence. There may be other criteria as well, but these are some of the more important ones.

The Functions and Structure of Typologies

The functions of typologies are twofold. They are needed as the first step in the construction of explanatory theory; until a sharp break is made with the traditional approach which looks upon offenders as a relatively homogeneous class, little progress is likely to be made toward explanation and prediction of crime and delinquency. Instead, investigators will continue to find that no single variable or combination of factors exists in the backgrounds of all violators such that when these are present deviant behavior can be expected to occur. The goal of prediction will continue to elude the criminologist. Hopefully, causal processes will eventually be identified when types are made the focus of theory and research, and predictions—such as "If A, B, C, and D occur, X will occur"—will be possible.

Typologies can also provide the basis for diagnostic systems to be used in treatment. It seems but a small jump from the view that the causes of illegal behavior vary among types of delinquent or criminal careers to the conclusion that efficacious therapy procedures similarly vary with the kind of behavior to be treated or changed.

Regarding these two functions, perhaps a single typology of delinquents or of adult offenders could serve both ends. It may not be necessary to employ one classification in etiological theory and a different one as the basis for diagnosis, in that the two purposes of taxonomies are closely related. The task of treatment is to modify those role characteristics of offenders which are responsible for their involvement in deviant activities. In turn, an adequate etiological typology would be one that identifies those characteristics of deviant individuals which distinguish them from nonoffenders. In many cases, the salient differences are concerned with deviant self-images and antisocial attitudes, or in other words, with the social-psychological concomitants of deviant role behavior. In these cases, causal analysis would seek to discover the factors which produced such role-conceptions, and treatment would be aimed at the modification of these characteristics.

Role-career notions are taken up in detail later in this chapter. For the moment, assume that the kind of typologies needed for etiological and treatment purposes are ones which identify role patterns among offenders. Now, in the case of causal theory and research, it would be wise to restrict a typological classification to a set of descriptions of the deviant behavior and role-conceptions exhibited by different lawbreakers. Such a scheme would consist of a set of assertions about the forms that criminal or delinquent behavior takes, and statements about the background or situational correlates of these types would be kept separate. For example, assertions about the social class background, family pattern, and other social characteristics of a particular type would be made independently of the definition of that type so that research could examine the accuracy of the former. Ultimately, assertions about background patterns would be made in the form of causal propositions, stating that "offender type A is the product of factors 1, 2, 3, and 4." Over time, the allegations regarding the forms of illegal behavior and the claims about etiological experiences producing these types would represent a relatively formal propositional system about criminality or delinquency, or in short, a theory. Figure 2 indicates the basic structure of such a pattern of argument.

The major justification for a clear separation between descriptions of types and statements about backgrounds is that not enough evidence is now at hand to lend complete credence to either of these sets of claims. Consequently, it makes sense to divide up the labor of empirical investigation. For example, research may show that certain defined types of offender roles do exist but that some of the hypothesized causal backgrounds are in error. If so, those types which have real-life counterparts would be retained, and the incorrect statements about backgrounds would be modified. In other words, only that part of the argument which is defective would be discarded. This might not be so easily accomplished if definitional statements about role patterns were mixed in with allegations about background characteristics, for in that case, the investigator might not know precisely how much or which part of the argument should be discarded.

There is now the question of what form typological systems should take in diagnostic practice. Although definitional claims should be distinguished from comments about backgrounds, *both* should be incorporated into a diagnostic device or instrument; the more relevant information the diagnostician employs, the greater the confidence he can feel in the accuracy of the diagnosis finally established. Moreover, although the background correlates of criminalistic roles are not entirely clear, enough information does exist to indicate that certain backgrounds do usually accompany certain role patterns. For example, it is possible to define as an offender type the pattern of predatory gang delinquency on the basis of certain forms of offense behavior and accompanying self-images

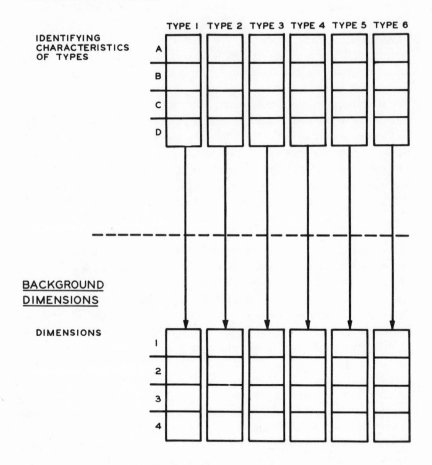

OFFENDER TYPOLOGY

figure 2   **THE STRUCTURE OF TYPOLOGICAL ARGUMENTS**

and attitudes. The available data suggest that delinquents who fall into this category are usually from lower-class, urban backgrounds and from large families in which other members of the family are frequently involved in criminality. The diagnostician who finds a juvenile with this kind of offense career and background can be quite certain that the person would be correctly identified as a predatory gang delinquent.

Some Basic Assumptions of Typology

The typologies in this book rest upon some basic premises which need to be identified. These are in the nature of basic sociology textbook propositions which may strike the reader as pedestrian in the extreme. Nonetheless, there are different perspectives from which deviant behavior could be examined, and assumptions must be dragged out into the open for public scrutiny. If a different set seems more valuable, then quite probably the scheme based on these postulates should be viewed rather skeptically.

In the presentation that follows, a list of seventeen brief and for the most part simple propositions will first be set forth. Most of these premises are presented as self-evident, so that no extra discussion will be given to them. Some additional discussion will be presented regarding certain notions about deviant roles and the like which are contained in these assumptions. However, the following set of statements is not put forward as a theory of criminality; rather, this section should be viewed as a brief prolegomenon to some of the elements that would be included in a detailed theoretical discussion of etiology.[40]

---

[40] The frame of reference utilized in this book and discussed in this section is a relatively straightforward one. For the most part, it is in the mainstream of sociological thinking regarding deviant behavior. In turn, this general perspective is a compound of observations and insights taken from some of the author's teachers. The view here also derives, in part, from discussions with colleagues, particularly with Stanton Wheeler, Peter G. Garabedian, Donald L. Garrity and John W. Kinch. Finally, the point of view has been influenced in considerable measure by certain published statements on deviant behavior. These include Lemert, *Social Pathology* (New York: McGraw-Hill Book Co., Inc., 1951), especially pp. 3-98; Clinard, *op. cit.*, pp. 3-59; Howard S. Becker, *Outsiders* (New York: The Free Press of Glencoe, Inc., 1963), passim. The customary note should be added that those persons bear no responsibility for the mixture the author has brewed up using their ingredients.

Some of the seventeen claims are extremely simple ones. Look at statement two, which declares that social roles are a social product. That proposition is in no way controversial. The point of the remark is simply to record a denial that biological factors play any direct part in social behavior, whether criminal or noncriminal in form. In other words, this is an "antibiogenic" postulate. Take assumption six as another case in point. That proposition declares that "badness" tends to be specific rather than general in character. There is no reason to suppose that individuals who are "bad guys" as far as criminality is concerned are "bad guys" in all other ways as well. There is no necessary reason to expect that offenders also beat their wives and children, that they belong to the Communist Party, or that they express atheistic beliefs. However, the opposite assumption about generic "badness" is often involved in commonsense beliefs about deviants. One dramatic illustration of this point is the "drug fiend" mythology, which attaches all kinds of beliefs about personal vices and reprehensible motives to drug addicts. There is no factual basis for most of these imputations.

Some of the statements in the list below are extremely terse. For example, the fourteenth proposition will be recognized by many readers as a capsule version of Mertonian arguments about deviant behavior, including criminality.[41] As such, it cannot serve as a substitute for a detailed examination of the "ends-means disjunction" schema of Merton. Although this book cannot take lengthy etiological detours into such areas, the reader is strongly enjoined to explore these byways on his own.

The seventeen assumptions follow:

1. The members of a society are the carriers of an organization of social roles, that is, behavior patterns reflecting different social statuses or positions. (In other words, it is meaningful to approach the description of the behavior of individual persons by paying attention to the related but independent component activities or roles making up their behavior.)

2. Social roles are the product of social organization and socialization, that is, of the ongoing structure of society and of learning processes in primary groups. (In other words, the developmental process in human behavior centers around the acquisition, by the person, of a col-

---

[41] Robert K. Merton, *Social Theory and Social Structure*, rev. and enlarged ed. (New York: The Free Press of Glencoe, Inc., 1957), pp. 131-94.

lection of social roles made available to him by the society in which he is found.)

3. Various patterns of social organization and socialization exist in complex societies so that, in turn, a variety of statuses and roles exist in them. There is a variety of nondeviant roles as well as a great many deviant ones (radical, homosexual, criminal, and so forth).

4. All people play criminal or delinquent roles at one time or another, if only symbolically. (In other words, petty violations of law are engaged in by nearly every person in the course of his lifetime. Also, many individuals entertain deviant and criminalistic motives but do not act upon them; thus they play deviant roles symbolically.)

5. Sociologically, "criminals" or "delinquents" are persons who play criminalistic roles heavily and/or who are identified by "society" as criminals or delinquents. (Persons who come to be tagged as offenders by the legal processes are frequently ones who are involved in repetitive and serious acts of law violation; but individuals who engage in petty and isolated acts of illegality are also sometimes reacted to as violators. Both of these groups are "criminals" or "delinquents" because they have been so labeled by the official machinery of social control.)

6. Criminal or delinquent behavior is one social role, but not the only one, that persons play. Criminal or delinquent individuals also play roles as "citizen," "father," "employee," and so forth.

7. Among persons identified as criminals or delinquents, there are variations in the character and intensity of the deviant role. These include variations in both (a) actual deviant role behavior and (b) role-related social-psychological characteristics. The illegal acts carried on by offenders vary from one individual to another. Also, some persons have no self-image as a deviant, whereas others exhibit such self-definitions. In turn, among individuals with deviant or nondeviant self-conceptions, variations are exhibited in the particular kind of image held ("tough guy," "right guy," "smart hustler," and so on).

8. Stable patterns of criminal or delinquent roles, involving recurrent forms of deviant activity accompanied by uniform social-psychological role characteristics, can be observed in the population of offenders. In these terms, it can be said that types of criminalistic deviance exist.

9. Although behavioral and social-psychological changes occur in specific criminal or delinquent roles during the development of the role, these changes are limited, orderly, and identifiable. As a result, it is possible to define specific, stable criminal and delinquent role-careers. Of-

fenders do not engage in random and unpredictable patterns of role-behavior; they do not "play the field" of offenses.

10. The specific etiological process that leads to one particular kind of criminalistic role behavior involves a number of causal variables and differs from that which produces another criminal role. In this sense, criminal and delinquent behavior is the product of multiple-causation. At the same time, it is possible to identify the different etiological processes which are implicated in the various forms of criminalistic deviance.

11. The learning of criminal and/or delinquent roles is maximized in a criminalistic society, and the United States is such a society.

12. Much, but not all, criminal and delinquent behavior in the competitive, materialistic American society is societally generated and takes the form of assaults upon property. Property crime is not usually the expression of hidden motives but, rather, of surface ones. (Offenders steal to "make a living" rather than to commit symbolic incest and so on.)

13. Crime and delinquency in complex societies are encouraged in a variety of ways by that complexity. For example, police ineffectiveness is a correlate of a democratic, complex, urban social organization. In turn, ineffectual police work aids in the commission of crime and is an encouragement to criminality. (In a society which demands that law enforcement agents behave according to strict rules of arrest, search and seizure, interrogation, and the like, many offenders are inevitably going to avoid apprehension or conviction for crimes. Additionally, in a society in which relatively few policemen are employed to maintain surveillance over a large population living in metropolitan communities, the law enforcement persons are not going to be able to observe most illegal acts that occur. As a result, the risk of being apprehended for deviant acts will appear to be slight to many individuals.)

14. Some criminalistic roles are mainly the consequence of social-class variations in socialization and life experiences, along with other social-structural variables. In particular, situations in which legitimate avenues to the attainment of common American goals or values are blocked are importantly involved in certain forms of crime and delinquency.

15. Some criminalistic roles are produced by family and other socialization experiences which are not class-linked or class-specific. Among these are "parental rejection," "deviant sexual socialization," and others. These kinds of experiences occur at all social class levels.

16. The "defining agencies" (police, probation services, courts, and so forth) play a part both in the definition of deviants and in the continuation of deviant roles. The result of apprehension and "treatment" may be quite contrary to the expected result. In other words, although one official function of correctional agencies and processes is the reformation of the offender, the actual outcome is often the isolation of the person, reinforcement of the deviant role, and rejection of society by the offender, the final result being nonreformation.

17. Variations can be seen in societal reactions to criminality of different kinds. Personal offenses and crude, visible attacks upon property are likely to be severely dealt with and punitively handled. Accordingly, embezzlers and similar persons are reacted to differently than gas station stick-up artists or strong-arm robbers. In addition, societal reactions to criminal deviants are based upon other characteristics of the individual than criminal role behavior. Middle-class delinquents, for example, are accorded a societal reaction different from that directed toward working-class individuals involved in similar delinquent behavior. In turn, these reactions have implications for involvement in, and continuation in, criminality.

These propositions commit the user of them to a certain view of crime and delinquency causation. Among other things, this frame of reference eschews the pursuit of the causes of "crime" or "delinquency." Instead, the search is directed toward discovery of the causes of particular criminalistic role patterns. These premises also suggest the major dimensions according to which law violators can be studied as incumbents of social roles. The causal framework contained in them emphasizes "multiple-causation," while at the same time implying that scientific explanations of criminality are attainable. In other words, these claims aver that the etiological factors in criminality are numerous and that they enter into different patterns of conduct in varied ways and with different degrees of importance. But these variables are also finite or limited, so that, ultimately, propositions such as "If A, B, C, and D occur, criminality of type X will result" can be stated. Finally, the preceding statements announce that much American criminality is carried on by "normal" persons who are pursuing conventional goals by illicit means. On a more specific level, the causes of particular forms of illegal deviation are located in the general areas of social class relationships, family and peer interactions, and contacts with agencies of social control.

Types as Role-Careers

One major assumption contained above is that the total behavior of individuals can be meaningfully examined *as a pattern of social roles*. Social roles represent the particular ways in which persons interact with other actors in terms of their various statuses or positions within social systems. Statuses are "jobs" in a social division of labor (social system) involving a pattern of normative expectations or rules that the status occupant is expected to follow in the pursuit of some interactional end or objective. The task of case worker in a correctional institution is an example of a status, for this position involves a set of expectations that any particular case worker will behave in specified ways toward inmates, other staff members, and the general public. The actual performance activity of a specific case worker represents role behavior within this particular status. The important point is that the sociological perspective on behavior is not a disguised version of the study of personality systems. Statuses are not identified solely or mainly by characteristics internal to the actor, but rather, in terms of the expectations of other persons in the external situation in which the status incumbent is placed. Also, a status and role-related activities of any individual person are not descriptive of that person as a totality but of only a part of the entire behavior of the individual.

The fact that criminal and delinquent statuses are often pariah ones, involving expectations that persons occupying these positions will behave in ways which are evaluated negatively, does not alter the fact that criminalistic behavior can be approached from a status-role direction. There are many statuses and roles in addition to criminalistic ones that are negatively defined by some group or groups. Also, invidious evaluation of criminal or delinquent statuses is relative to particular group definitions. Within associations of offenders, deviant statuses are frequently evaluated positively, so that the thief who can steal most cleverly is regarded as an exemplary person by his peers.

Criminal statuses and roles represent only one of many statuses and roles in which real-life persons are involved. It may well be that in some cases criminality has primacy over other roles, so that the various positions occupied by the offender become heavily colored by his involvement in illegal role behavior. As a case in point, the occupational role of the ex-convict is often altered rather markedly as a result of the "parolee" label attached to the person. The difficulties of gaining and holding jobs are exacerbated when the individual's "parolee" identity becomes known. In turn, the employment instability that sometimes develops is more a function of his "ex-convict" reputation than of his lack of skills.

Even though deviant statuses may exercise differential impact upon behavior, there is no reason to suppose that delinquent or criminal individuals differ in all important ways from nonoffenders. For example, there is little reason to assume that they are less patriotic or less committed to family values than are nonoffenders. Similarly, there is little justification for an unquestioned assumption that criminals differ in total personality structure from nondeviants. This may seem obvious enough, but much research has proceeded on a different implicit presupposition that the deviant is a generally different person than the nondeviant. Quite probably, the failure of investigators to discover traits which distinguish criminals from noncriminals is due, in many cases, to the invalidity of this built-in assumption.

Let it be understood that the description of offender roles includes analysis of the social context within which role behavior occurs. Indeed, the notions of status and role are virtually meaningless when divorced from the role-expectations of others. Thus it is not enough to indicate that an offender engages in role activity taking the form of burglary. Additional questions must be asked. Did that role behavior take place within the structure of a group of participating role players, that is, other burglars? Is the behavior of the person part of a pattern of activities within some kind of deviant subculture in which illegal acts are encouraged by other individuals? Or are the burglaries of the offender usually carried on in isolation? Although those behavioral acts which identify a person as a law violator and which run counter to legal statutes are necessary components of any description of offender types, attention must also be paid to other aspects of role behavior. Some deviant roles such as embezzlement are enacted surreptitiously because nonembezzlement is defined as the appropriate behavior within the system of action in which defalcations occur. Other kinds of criminality represent role activities which are positively evaluated by the associates of the offender, even though they may be negatively regarded by the larger social organization.

Two basic components of social roles are employed in this analysis: actual behavioral acts or role behavior, and role-conceptions, which refer to self-image patterns and role-related attitudes. The importance of this distinction between acts and social-psychological states of being is illustrated in everyday life where predictions are made about the future behavior of an individual. The knowledge that he has committed an assault is not sufficient information on which to predict that additional episodes of violence will occur in the future. However, confidence in such a judgment is enhanced when it becomes known that the assaultive individual defines himself as a "tough guy" and views other persons as "mean" and not to be trusted. Quite a different prognostication would be in order following observations that the assaulter acted in this fashion under conditions of severe personal stress and that he is now contrite and repentant in attitude.

This illustration is paralleled in real life by numerous cases wherein behavior that is ostensibly similar for separate persons has quite different meanings to the actors. One cannot assume that every case of criminal role behavior of a certain kind is accompanied by similar role-conceptions among all the persons in question. This distinction between behavior and role-conceptions is closely related to the notions of *primary* and *secondary* deviation.[42] Lemert, the originator of these concepts, points out that deviant behavior is often primary in character, in the sense that the person does not regard his criminal behavior as meaning that he is actually a criminal. Such an individual lacks a self-image as a deviant. On the other hand, some patterns of deviant behavior develop into secondary deviation in which the actor ultimately comes to integrate his deviant activity within his total personality structure. In this process of *sociopathic individuation,* he eventually undergoes a degree of personality reorganization in which deviant behavior becomes a role recognized by the person himself and symbolized in self-reference statements of the form "I am 'gay,' " "I am a 'hype,' " "I am a thief and proud of it," or "I am a 'lush.' " However, while primary deviation precedes the development of secondary deviation, the latter does not always follow from involvement in initial deviancy. One clear illustration of this point, in degree at least, is

[42] Lemert, *Social Pathology,* pp. 73-98.

the "square John" in prison who persistently asserts that he is not a "real criminal."

Roles can also be analyzed longitudinally in terms of *role-careers*. Many nondeviant roles, such as occupational ones, continue over extremely long periods of time and involve a series of changes of behavior as particular social situations change. A medical career illustrates this point nicely. This pattern could be said to originate at the point where initial decisions are made by persons to become doctors and where activity is undertaken to implement such plans. Medical school is a further stage in the career, and still a further segment is involvement in professional employment as a physician. Medical role-incumbents exhibit behavior patterns that are somewhat different in each of these stages. They also show role-conceptions that are not identical in each of these periods.[43] Nonetheless, these varied behavior patterns and role-conceptions can be treated as parts of a long-term career, for they "hang together" in ways which are obvious.

Some more specific comments about deviant role-careers are as follows. First, role-careers vary in duration. There are some criminal patterns in which role-performance is begun and terminated in a single illegal act, and there are others in which involvement in the deviant role continues over several decades or more, as in the instance of professional criminals. Some delinquent roles lead to adult criminality, whereas other delinquent roles are terminal ones, for they do not normally precede or lead to involvement in adult deviation. In turn, some criminal roles have their genesis in juvenile delinquent behavior, whereas certain other forms of adult criminality develop in adulthood and are not presaged by delinquent careers. Then, too, some role-careers involve more changes in the component episodes of the pattern than do others. Semiprofessional property offenders are one illustration. This pattern begins at the onset of minor delinquent acts in early adolescence. Such a career line frequently leads to more serious forms of delinquency with advancing age: repeated police contacts, commitment to juvenile institutions, "graduation" into adult forms of illegal activity, and more contacts with law enforcement and correctional agencies.

[43] Howard S. Becker, Blanche Geer, Everett C. Hughes, and Anselm L. Strauss, *Boys in White: Student Culture in Medical School* (Chicago: University of Chicago Press, 1961).

Over this lengthy developmental sequence, the social-psychological characteristics of offenders also change. For example, the degree of hostility toward policemen and correctional agents exhibited by the adult semiprofessional criminal is likely to be considerably greater than the antagonism demonstrated by the same person at an early age. The same comment could be made regarding changes in self-image, attitudes, and other matters.

To summarize the preceding line of exposition, no assumption is made that criminal or delinquent roles involve only a single specific kind of illegal act, on the one hand, or that criminalistic behavior is made up of all sorts of random behavioral activities of individuals, on the other hand. Instead, it is assumed that identifiable changes occur in role-career patterns of different offender types. There is some supporting evidence regarding behavioral stabilities among deviants, at least with respect to illegal activities. The papers by Peterson *et al.*[44] and by Roebuck[45] are cases in point, as is a report by Frum.[46]

In the typologies in Chapter Three, offenders are grouped according to a fourfold system of variables. They are categorized in terms of the patterns of illegal role-behavior which they exhibit and also in terms of the social context within which their actions occur. Thus two dimensions are used to distinguish different forms of role-behavior. Violators are then differentiated on dimensions concerned with role-conceptions, namely, self-image patterns and role-related attitudes. A time dimension is included also, as a summary role-career description of offenders in terms of the four dimensions also appears in the typologies. For example, one type is specified as the "predatory gang delinquent," and the identifying characteristics of this type involve

1. a repetitive pattern of serious thefts and burglaries;

2. delinquent behavior which takes place within the context of delinquent peer group associations;

3. a self-image as a "delinquent" and as "cool" and sophisticated;

[44] Peterson, Pittman, and O'Neal, *op. cit.*
[45] Roebuck, *op. cit.*
[46] Harold S. Frum, "Adult Criminal Offense Trends Following Juvenile Delinquency," *Journal of Criminal Law, Criminology and Police Science,* Vol. 49 (May-June 1958), 29-49.

4. antisocial attitudes taking the form of allegations that the police are discriminatory in their operations, that correctional workers are "phonies," that "only slobs work," and so forth.

Such is the pattern of argument for the entire system of types. Types are defined in such a way that no two of them have the same characteristics on all four dimensions. Two or more patterns may share some attributes in common, but they differ in at least one dimension.

Typologies and Causal Arguments

It was indicated previously that the definitional statements about types should be kept distinct from comments about social backgrounds of types, although diagnostic typologies probably should indicate some of the major background characteristics of offender types. Accordingly, in the schemes presented in Chapter Three, statements are made about situational correlates of types. These are placed within four relatively gross categories or dimensions: social class variations, family background variations, peer group associations, and contact with defining agencies.

These categories, singled out as causally important, arise out of the same rationale that underlies the focus upon role-careers. The literature of social psychology indicates that the development of role-behavior is a direct result of the process of socialization. Socialization refers to the complex processes of social interaction through which the habits, beliefs, skills, and standards of judgment are learned. However, not all interaction is equally important to the individual. The person's conception of self, his attitudes, and the motives which he employs in perceiving the world of experience and in formulating his behavior accordingly are most likely to be the product of a special kind of interaction, primary group interaction. Family and peer group associations represent two kinds of primary groups, so that the great attention given to interactional processes within these two groups by social psychologists is not accidental.

However, primary groups do not exist in a social vacuum but are units within societal and cultural systems. Because primary groups function within larger patterns of social organization, the social institution of the family does not refer solely to specific family units. The family institution also involves a body of norms and expectations regarding relationships between nearly all parents and nearly all children which are shared by members of American society. More important, there are some norms and expectations which are indigenous to spatially contiguous groups of a similar social class. Because these norms and expectations influence the particular character of primary group interactions, the structure of primary groups, their norms and values, are affected by their inclusion within larger social systems.

Thus family and peer groups are sources of etiologically significant experiences in the development of criminal and delinquent behavior. Social class is included as an important determinant of the structure and types of actions which occur within these primary groups. Finally, contacts with defining agencies are included because they are social processes which weigh heavily in the kinds of interpretations attached to the behavior manifested as a result of socializing experiences. In an important sense, it is the police and the courts who dramatize "evil" to the community and who determine whether behavior is to be evaluated as "good" or "bad," as "delinquency" or as a "harmless prank," as "morally reprehensible" or as "understandable." Illegal acts which are not identified as "bad" through intervention of the police and courts may have quite different personal consequences than do those which are attended to and acted upon by these agencies of social control. The social experience of involvement with the police and courts may act as a career contingency that influences the experiences and behavior of the individual in the future.

SOCIAL CLASS VARIATIONS

Different offender types are not distributed proportionately in all social class levels. Instead, one of the characteristics of different patterns is that they are most common in certain social strata; that is, they are "class-linked." For example, gang offenders of specific kinds are usually working-class boys, whereas "joyriders" are often from comfortable economic areas.

Class in the sense used above refers to groupings of persons within a community into relatively homogeneous economic categories. However, variations in economic position per se are not responsible for different deviant behavior patterns. Economic position is an indicator of different "life styles" among individuals, and it is these life style patterns which propel behavior. Thus the analysis of class linkages in illegal behavior comes down to a search for life-style variations which play a part in the kinds of deviation that emerge in different strata. For example, it appears that most semi-professional property offenders are working-class persons who come from low-income areas of cities. The suspicion arises that this is not a chance matter. There may be something about the social life of working-class groups that brings forth this particular kind of misbehavior. Some of the observations on pages 35-39 regarding subcultural theories of delinquency suggested the nature of the "something" about life styles. Theories have argued that working-class "focal concerns" and life experiences are in one way or another entangled in delinquency causation. The general view in this book is that such factors are implicated in a variety of criminal and delinquent behavior patterns.

FAMILY BACKGROUND VARIATIONS

Family backgrounds and interactional processes represent another basic dimension in the analysis of offenders. Family structure and activity are critically important in various types of offender behavior. For one thing, the family is one of the vehicles through which social class phenomena are expressed. That is, class values are imparted to persons through interaction in particular family situations, at least in part. To illustrate, Miller has suggested that the values or "focal concerns" of lower-class society are such as to encourage illegal behavior. He alleges that lower-class emphases on "toughness," "having a good time," and "trouble," along with other values, call out deviant activities on the part of many working-class males in particular.[47] Ignoring the question of whether or not this specific hypothesis is correct, focal concerns exert an influence over specific persons only to the extent that they have been acquired by the individual in a process of social interaction. The family is one of the major interactional settings in which such learning and communication takes place.

Although there is evidence that class-linked behavior patterns

---

[47] Miller, "Lower Class Culture as a Generating Milieu of Gang Delinquency."

do exist, it is obvious that much behavioral variation occurs within class groups. Part of this variation is caused by differences in the interactional processes of particular family groups. The values or focal concerns of a social class may be given different emphases in particular families, so that in this sense the family situation conditions the impact of class phenomena on individuals.

In addition to differences of this kind from family to family, families with a shared life style of a particular social stratum vary in other important ways. For example, within working-class families in which the common values of the class are found some parents reject their children, others neglect them, spouses interact in varying ways with each other, and other families behave in accordance with other personal "styles." A number of patterns of criminality seem to be related to these varied interactional patterns and difficulties among family members, particularly between spouses. Incest behavior, assaults, and homicides are all pertinent cases.

PEER GROUP ASSOCIATIONS

The comments about the mediating influence of family structure also apply to peer group associations. Like the preceding two dimensions, this is a general category within which a host of specific comments about the effects of peer group interactions fall. Some of these have to do with the impact of a "youth culture" on adolescents, a youth culture which is transmitted within peer groups. Other specific observations regarding peer groups involve more intimate associations with particular kinds of peer groups, including both delinquent and criminal gangs. Here again, broad class-linked influences have their effects upon specific persons through the particular kinds of social relations within which those individuals are participants. The peer group is one of these organizational networks and an extremely important one as well.

Peer group relationships enter into this analysis in two places. In the statements about defining dimensions of offender role-careers, the interactional context of deviant acts is included as a part of the offense description. Thus the gang offender represents a juvenile who commits certain illegal acts as a member of a delinquent peer group. In turn, peer group processes are included among the body of causally related dimensions. Although there is the possibility of tautological analysis as a consequence, peer associations and their effects can be handled in independent ways so as to avoid circular arguments. It is possible to observe, on the one hand, that certain offenders commit illegal acts with delinquent peers, and on the other hand, to relate this observation to additional and independent observations about peer interactions. As one illustration, it appears that in many conflict-oriented "bopping" gangs, specific acts of gang fighting by juveniles are a response to the fear of status-loss which would be generated by "punking-out" (failure to fight). In the same way, much of the other deviant and nondeviant behavior of gang offenders is generated by membership in the delinquent peer group.

CONTACT WITH "DEFINING AGENCIES"

What about the etiological influences of contacts with "defining agencies"? Defining agencies refer to those official and semiofficial agencies that are given the responsibility for the detection, apprehension, punishment, and treatment of offenders. As stated previously, contact with the police, courts, and other agencies may be an important causal experience. For example, one of the major factors that may impel many juveniles toward delinquency as a systematic role centers around the extent to which the individual has been defined as a "delinquent" and as a "bad boy" by community agencies. In other cases, such contacts may have salutary effects, as seems to be the case with amateur female shoplifters. Cameron found in a study in Chicago that these persons rarely repeated the act of shoplifting after they had been forced by the personnel of a victimized store to admit that they were "thieves" and "criminals." [48] Apparently, the painful social-psychological processes involved in coming to grips with the deviant nature of shoplifting served to deter women from further behavior of this kind.

These possibilities have been given little attention in research. Customarily, the search for causal factors has paid little or no attention to career aspects, that is, to changes in the behavior of offenders over time. However, some years ago, Tannenbaum argued that the effects of official dealings with deviants, ostensibly therapeutic in nature, represent instead a process of "dramatization of evil." He

[48] Mary Bess Cameron, *Department Store Shoplifting*, doctoral dissertation, Indiana University, 1953.

claimed that the outcome of official handling in the courts and elsewhere was frequently quite different from the announced purposes of such actions. Instead of diverting the person from a deviant career, such experiences alert members of the community to the presence of an "evil" or "bad" person in their midst. In turn, once an individual becomes singled out as an "evil" person, he is likely to be regarded as such in the future, quite apart from how he actually behaves. If his deportment does not change, this confirms the original diagnosis in the eyes of the community. If for one reason or another he does alter his behavior, such change is seen as an attempt on his part to hide his true nature. The effect of all this is to narrow the possibilities of action for the individual so designated. In many instances, the deviant develops feelings of being unjustly dealt with which operate as rationalizations for his conduct. Thus, according to Tannenbaum, the end result of treatment is reinforcement of the very behavior which the treatment agents are attempting to eradicate.[49] This thesis is polemic in tone, so that there is room for argument concerning the extent to which the dismal implications of Tannenbaum's view are warranted. Nonetheless, this extremely provocative hypothesis deserves more attention than it has received. Lemert has dealt with similar processes in discussing the factors which create a secondary deviant out of a primary one. He notes that some persons may deviate without defining themselves as "different"; or they may view themselves as deviants, having a body of rationalizations by which they extenuate themselves from self-condemnation. According to Lemert, the latter stage frequently develops when the individual is forced to come to grips with the fact that some group or agency dealing with deviants has singled him out for attention. At this point he can hardly deny that he is a deviant—the mentally disordered person cannot very easily assert that he is normal when he finds himself committed to a mental hospital.[50] In the same way, the delinquent may find it

---

[49] Frank Tannenbaum, *Crime and the Community* (New York: Ginn and Co., 1938), pp. 19-21; a more general statement on some of these processes is contained in Harold Garfinkel, "Conditions of Successful Degradation Ceremonies," *American Journal of Sociology*, Vol. 61 (March 1956), 420-24.

[50] Lemert, *Social Pathology*, pp. 54-72. For some other valuable commentary on societal reactions, see John I. Kitsuse, "Societal Reaction to Deviant Behavior: Problems of Theory and Method," *Social Problems*, Vol. 9 (Winter 1962), 247-56; Becker, *op. cit.*, passim.

extremely difficult to retain his self-image as a "good boy" when confronted with the fact of being in the hands of the police or in the juvenile court. Two alternatives are available to the person at this point. He can adjust his self-conception downward, taking the view of himself held by others. But this can be done only at great psychological cost. The other course of action is to redefine the situation so as to blame others for his predicament. The juvenile offender can argue that although he is a delinquent, he is smart, honest, and a martyr in a system that is unjust. Although the social pains that result from such action may in the long run be very serious, such a redefinition of the situation does save him from great psychological pain.

There is much merit to this line of analysis for it serves to point up the possible causal significance of experiences with defining agencies, even though the available evidence that can be brought to bear upon the argument is sketchy. Contacts with defining agencies could have three different effects: They could be positive in impact, so as to deter the deviant from further deviation, or they could be adverse in effect, driving the person into further violations in response to his changed social identity. A third possibility is that such experiences could be of neutral significance, so that the individual would be neither deterred nor harmfully influenced by them.

Bits and scraps of empirical evidence can be assembled which seem to demonstrate that each of these three possibilities does occur. Cameron's study seems to show that contacts with defining agencies can lead to deterrence of further deviation. On the other side of the coin, some findings from the Highfields project seem to point to negative consequences of contacts with treatment agencies. The Highfields institution, to be discussed in more detail in Chapter Four, is a small, intensive treatment facility in New Jersey. As a part of the research program associated with that place, a projective test, the *Holsopple Sentence Completion Test,* was given to Highfields boys and to inmates of a conventional reformatory in New Jersey at the time of admission and at a later point in their institutional careers. The test results indicated that the reformatory boys moved toward bleaker, darker outlooks on life during their stay in the facility, so that they may have become reconciled to further deviation as a life career. The Highfields boys showed movement in the opposite direction.[51] Thus a double conclusion seems to follow. Traditional penal facilities may operate in harmful ways as far as contributions to criminality are concerned, but at the same time, it may be possible to achieve different results with intensive, specialized programs within institutions.

It seems apparent from these variations in the effect of contacts with defining agencies that there are intervening variables which are interposed in the situation. Thus the outcome of agency intervention is conditional upon a number of other factors. One can speculate about at least four such variables, one of which would be *personality variations* among the subjects who are the focus of agency concern. There are probably some persons who by virtue of certain personality patterns would be responsive to even quite innocuous contacts with agencies and their personnel, whereas others might find such experiences of no important personal consequence.

A second factor which may condition the effects of these experiences has to do with variations in *societal definitions* of behavior. Consider violations of traffic laws as an illustration. Little public condemnation is attached to this kind of deviant behavior, so that the person who is involved with agencies for this reason runs little risk of societal hostility being directed at him. There are other kinds of criminality which are defined as serious by agencies but which are regarded in a more tolerant light by the general public. Persons engaged in these forms of behavior are in a sense shielded from exceedingly negative repercussions from contacts with agencies because of public tolerance.

Not only do societal reactions vary for different forms of deviation, different segments of the community react to the same behavior in discrepant ways. Thus a third factor which probably influences the effects of agency experiences centers around *exposure to antisocial environments*. In other words, the person who has grown up in an antisocial subculture in which antipolice attitudes and other hostile sentiments are indigenous to the situation is not likely to be traumatized by any specific instance of contact with defining agencies. That same individual is immunized against agency pressures by a supportive peer system which assists him in

---

[51] Lloyd W. McCorkle, Albert Elias, and F. Lovell Bixby, *The Highfields Story* (New York: Holt, Rinehart and Winston, Inc., 1958), pp. 122-26.

warding off the negative definitions of himself that flow from these agency contacts. Alternatively, the person who is a product of middle-class, prosocial social circumstances is much more likely to experience any contact with the police or courts as a profoundly important one.

Finally, *agency climate* can be suggested as a fourth consideration which influences the results of agency contacts. Some organizations take a punitive and hostile attitude toward persons who come into their hands, whereas others adopt a more positive and less hostile stance. Thus it might be expected that the effect of being dealt with by an abusive police officer would be somewhat different than the effect of interaction with a polite and pleasant officer. In the same way, correctional institutions vary in the kind of social atmosphere which dominates them, so that they may not all act upon offenders who get into them in precisely similar ways. This is suggested in the Highfields-conventional reformatory data presented above.

One thing seems certain from this discussion: The impact of agency contacts is not simple or uniform on all who come under these contacts. Not all training schools are "crime schools," and those which are do not have the same effect upon all boys who go through them. In the same way, treatment programs sometimes fail to change persons, but sometimes they do manage modifications in behavior. Beyond such general observations, little is known about the influence of these experiences in particular cases. Fragments of tangential evidence can be uncovered which suggest some of the ways in which these processes operate, but definitive findings gathered through careful research are lacking and sorely needed. The discussions of roles in criminality will speculate about the part played by these events in types of offender behavior, which is about all that can be done in the face of a paucity of hard evidence.

Personality Dynamics

One major issue remains to be taken up: the question of personality dynamics in illegal behavior. In part, this aspect is concerned with the extent to which criminality can be said to be the product of personality problems and personality variations. One of the most popular and widespread notions regarding criminality is that this behavior is the result of individual personality dynamics which impel certain persons toward deviant conduct. In this view, offenders are thought of as "acting-out" neurotics, as persons with defective superegos, or as individuals suffering from various anxieties and other personality deficiencies. Looking ahead a bit to remarks to come, this book asserts that *certain* personality patterns are etiologically involved in *certain* forms of criminality. At the same time, there are many forms of delinquency and criminality in which deviant personality patterns are not at all implicated. In many types of illegal deviation, the actors involved are essentially "normal" in terms of personality structure. Also, in those cases where atypical personality patterns are found, the personality pathology in question is relatively specific rather than diffuse in form. In other words, although certain violators such as "naive check forgers" exhibit "dependency" as a personality characteristic, there is little reason to suppose that the same individuals would turn out to be clinically abnormal when measured by other dimensions of personality structure. Accordingly, persons exhibiting "paranoid" characteristics may be randomly distributed in the offender population and may be no more common in that group than in the population of nonoffenders.

A second, and closely related, part of the personality dynamics issue concerns the place of personality variables in diagnostic typologies. The view to be developed in this book is that those personality correlates of deviant behavior common to the members of an offender type should be included in the description of the type. Thus "dependency" ought to be specified as a common social-psychological attribute of "naive check forgers." Conversely, personality patterns or characteristics which are incidental to particular offender types should not be included in a diagnostic typology. Stated another way, if personality variations such as paranoid tendencies are not rather commonly linked to illegal behavior, they should not be put into a diagnostic system. This does not mean, however, that idiosyncratic characteristics of deviants should be ignored in the specific diagnostic process or in treatment, for these may condition or effect the specific therapy plan that is developed for the individual.

Turning to a more detailed examination of these matters, the criminological literature abounds with a wealth of claims regarding the part played by personality characteristics in deviant behavior. Many of these, strictly Freudian in orientation, regard offenders as either neurotic or lacking in superego development. Something has gone awry in the normal processes of the criminal deviant's personality growth, the argument goes, so that he is responding to various instinctual impulses in unconscious or disguised ways. The writings of Aichhorn,[52] Friedlander,[53] and Abrahamsen[54] represent analyses of this sort.

One variation on this theme is represented by neo-Freudian or non-Freudian views which downplay or ignore instinctual processes, but which maintain that offenders suffer from various deficiencies of personality. A recent paper by Grossbard [55] provides one example of this sort of view. He claims that most delinquents exhibit inefficient or underdeveloped ego mechanisms, so that they tend to act out conflicts rather than to handle them by rational means or by symptom formation as do nondelinquents. This view owes something to the psychoanalytic position, but it is not a strictly orthodox version of basic Freudian theory.

Some of the personality dynamics that are discussed in the sources referred to are included within the typologies in Chapter Three. For example, "feelings of hostility," particularly those directed at law enforcement agents and correctional personnel, are noted within self-image and attitude descriptions of lawbreakers. Indeed, it would hardly be surprising if law violators involved in repetitive and serious offenses and who have had extensive contacts with police and correctional representatives did not exhibit hostility, suspicion, and feelings that "nobody cares." These sentiments, however, may be more the *result* of dealings with "defining agencies" and other experiences that have occurred to them after the onset of a deviant career than of anything else. If incarcerated offenders are shown to be suspicious and antagonistic, it does not necessarily follow that such personality characteristics are causal ones, for they may not have preceded involvement in deviance.

Many personality dynamics associated with criminality or delinquency probably are not generic to all offenders or wholly lacking in nonoffenders. Instead, feelings of hostility and the like may

[52] August Aichhorn, *Wayward Youth* (New York: Meridian Books, 1955).

[53] Kate Friedlander, *The Psycho-Analytical Approach to Juvenile Delinquency* (London: Routledge and Kegan Paul, Ltd., 1947).

[54] David Abrahamsen, *Who Are the Guilty?* (New York: Holt, Rinehart and Winston, Inc., 1952); Abrahamsen, *Crime and the Human Mind* (New York: Columbia University Press, 1945).

[55] Hyman Grossbard, "Ego Deficiency in Delinquents," *Social Casework*, Vol. 43 (April 1962), 171-78.

be quite common among lawbreakers of a particular type, say gang delinquents, and uncommon among others. For example, in instances of casual delinquency there is little reason to expect to observe personality peculiarities which distinguish those juveniles from nondelinquents. In the same way, it may be that certain criminals such as "naive check forgers" show "dependent" personality traits, even though these are not exhibited by all offenders. Also, it is not likely that all or most "dependent" personalities become check forgers. Check fraud may represent only one of several problem-solving techniques for such persons.

The additional point should be made that there are doubtless many personality traits which do not differentiate between violators and nonoffenders to any degree. There are probably many personality characteristics which would be exhibited to the same degree by both groups. For example, there is no particular reason to suppose that a scale of "authoritarianism" would differentiate the two groups. Also, there is no apparent basis for supposing that authoritarianism is a common personality characteristic of any specific offender type. It may be that the same point holds with respect to variations in "interpersonal maturity" between criminals and nonoffenders. The notion of interpersonal maturity is presently under investigation in the correctional system of California on the assumption that delinquents and criminals are interpersonally immature.[56] No evidence is yet at hand regarding the relative distribution of maturity types between the deviant and nondeviant groups, but the arguments for the hypothesis that interpersonal immaturity is more common among offenders are not so convincing as to rule out the possibility that the two groups do not differ significantly on this personality dimension. Certainly not all violators are at low levels of interpersonal adequacy, nor are all noncriminals at advanced states of interpersonal maturity.

SOME EVIDENCE

Although this discussion is not a detailed résumé or critique of the literature on personality problems and deviance, some of the salient evidence is examined below.

[56] Clyde E. Sullivan, Marguerite Q. Grant, and J. Douglas Grant, "The Development of Interpersonal Maturity: Applications to Delinquency," *Psychiatry*, Vol. 20 (November 1957), 373-85.

One early and influential report on personality problems and delinquency is represented by the study of Healy and Bronner. These investigators concluded from a comparative investigation of delinquents and their nondelinquent siblings that "It finally appears that no less than *91 per cent of the delinquents* gave clear evidence of being or having been very unhappy and discontented in their life circumstances or extremely emotionally disturbed because of emotion-provoking situations or experiences. In great contradistinction, we found similar evidence of inner stress at most in *only 13 per cent of the controls*" (italics in the original).[57]

This seems to be impressive confirmation indeed of the view that juvenile misbehavior is a response to emotional pressures and personality problems. However, the research suffered from a number of methodological defects, so that these findings are much less convincing than they first seem. In general, subsequent studies have failed to substantiate the Healy and Bronner results.

One review and critique involving some 113 studies of personality characteristics of delinquents and criminals has been reported by Schuessler and Cressey. They concluded that "of 113 such comparisons, 42 per cent showed differences in favor of the noncriminal, while the remainder were indeterminate. The doubtful validity of many of the obtained differences, as well as the lack of consistency in the combined results, makes it impossible to conclude from these data that criminality and personality elements are associated." [58]

Another critique and review, involving data from three surveys of emotional disturbance among cases from an adolescents' court, a psychiatric clinic attached to a juvenile court, and a juvenile correctional institution, has been reported by Hakeem.[59] Among other things, these reports show a diversity of diagnostic categories used by the psychiatrists in the separate studies. One set of labels identifies a number of offenders as suffering from psychoneurosis or neurotic character disturbances, whereas in the other two studies this category does not appear. Similarly, immaturity and mental conflict appear as diagnostic categories in one survey but not in the

---

[57] William Healy and Augusta F. Bronner, *New Light on Delinquency and its Treatment* (New Haven, Conn.: Yale University Press, 1936), p. 122.

[58] Karl F. Schuessler and Cressey, "Personality Characteristics of Criminals," *American Journal of Sociology*, Vol. 55 (March 1950), 476-84.

[59] Michael Hakeem, "A Critique of the Psychiatric Approach," in Joseph S. Roucek, ed., *Juvenile Delinquency* (New York: Philosophical Library, 1958), pp. 79-112.

others. In those cases of comparable diagnostic categories in the three studies, diverse proportions of offenders are found in the separate tabulations. All of this leads Hakeem to conclude that these reports tell more about the biases of the psychiatrists than they do about the offenders! It should also be noted that several categories which appear in these three studies are of dubious validity. Because in one series the diagnosis "conduct disorders" is used to classify about one-third of the cases, the following question must be asked: Were there any identifiable characteristics of offenders used to recognize conduct disorders, apart from the facts of involvement in delinquency? It is quite likely that a tautological procedure is involved here, in which the illegal activity of the juvenile is used to indicate the presence of a conduct disorder. If so, one should not suppose that the diagnosis of conduct disorder explains anything.

One of the studies of offenders and their emotional characteristics cited by Hakeem is the investigation of the Gluecks.[60] The delinquents and controls in this research were subjected to a psychiatric interview lasting about two hours and were also administered *Rorschach* tests, a projective instrument designed to measure basic personality traits. In summarizing the Rorschach findings, the Gluecks report that "Considering first those traits in which the delinquents as a group significantly exceed the nondelinquents, we observed that they are to a much greater degree socially assertive, defiant, and ambivalent to authority; they are also more resentful of others, and far more hostile, suspicious, and destructive; the goals of their drives are to a much greater extent receptive (oral) and destructive-sadistic; they are more impulsive and vivacious, and decidedly more extroversive in their behavior trends." [61] A number of the characteristics identified as more common among offenders through the Rorschach test are not clearly signs of maladjustment. Assertiveness, impulsiveness, and vivacity could be thought of as indications that the delinquents are the better adjusted of the two groups.

The Gluecks also presented psychiatric diagnoses of the offenders and nondelinquent controls in which several points stand out.[62]

---

[60] Sheldon and Eleanor Glueck, *Unraveling Juvenile Delinquency* (Cambridge, Mass.: Harvard University Press, 1951).
[61] *Ibid.*, p. 240.
[62] *Ibid.*, pp. 239-43.

First, the differences between deviants and controls were not pronounced. About half of both groups showed no conspicuous mental pathology. Second, the delinquents classified as showing mental pathology exhibited a variety of disorders, whereas the disturbed nondelinquents were classed as predominately neurotic or as showing neurotic trends! This finding runs counter to many psychogenic arguments in the criminological literature which maintain that delinquency is a form of neurotic, acting-out behavior.

Another body of research data on the psychogenic thesis comes from studies using the *Minnesota Multiphasic Personality Inventory*, an objective personality test designed to measure a variety of personality characteristics.[63] The M.M.P.I., as it is usually called, includes eight scales in which certain responses to questions in each scale are indicative of particular personality patterns. For example, persons scoring high on the Pa (paranoia scale) are ones who give responses similar to those of individuals clinically diagnosed as sufferers of paranoia.

This inventory has been applied to many samples of offenders by Hathaway, Monachesi, and others. One piece of research involving the application of the inventory to over 4,000 Minneapolis ninth-grade pupils was carried on in 1948. In 1950, the same children were traced through the Hennepin County Juvenile Court and the Minneapolis Police Department to determine which ones had acquired records of delinquency. Of the boys, 22.2 per cent had become delinquent, and 7.6 per cent of the girls had become known to the court or police. In analyzing the responses of delinquents and nonoffenders, the researchers found that 27.7 per cent of the boys with high Pd (psychopathic deviate) scale points were delinquent, as were 25.4 per cent of those with high Pa (paranoia) scale points.

[63] Starke Hathaway and Elio D. Monachesi, *Analyzing and Predicting Delinquency with the Minnesota Multiphasic Personality Inventory* (Minneapolis: University of Minnesota Press, 1953); Hathaway and Monachesi, "The Minnesota Multiphasic Personality Inventory in the Study of Juvenile Delinquents," *American Sociological Review*, Vol. 17 (December 1952), 704-10; Dora F. Capwell, "Personality Patterns of Adolescent Girls: II. Delinquents and Non-Delinquents," *Journal of Applied Psychology*, Vol. 29 (August 1945), pp. 289-97; Monachesi, "Some Personality Characteristics of Delinquents and Nondelinquents," *Journal of Criminal Law and Criminology*, Vol. 38 (January-February 1948), 487-500; Monachesi, "Personality Characteristics and Socio-Economic Status of Delinquents and Nondelinquents," *Journal of Criminal Law and Criminology*, Vol. 40 (January-February 1950), 570-83; Monachesi, "Personality Characteristics of Institutionalized and Non-Institutionalized Male Delinquents," *Journal of Criminal Law and Criminology*, Vol. 41 (July-August 1950), 167-79.

Of the boys with "Invalid" responses, indicating uncooperativeness, lying, and so forth, 37.5 per cent were delinquent. Thus there is some tendency for delinquent boys to show disproportionate numbers in some of the scale areas of the M.M.P.I. Substantially similar results were obtained in the case of the girls.

Hathaway and Monachesi carried out a number of detailed analyses of these data which indicated, among other things, that differences in scale responses of offenders are found among those tested before as opposed to after court or police contact; that differences in responses exist among delinquents categorized by seriousness of behavior; and that scale responses varied by age, sex, and other variables. Such variations in the test results make the interpretation of them somewhat difficult and tentative. Hathaway and Monachesi are modest in the claims they make on the basis of these data. In the main, they argue only that the M.M.P.I. possesses some discriminatory power. However, critics have noted the problems of interpretation involved in the variability of results, and they have also pointed out that a number of social factors appear to correlate more highly with delinquency than do M.M.P.I. scores.[64]

Gough's work is still another line of activity in the area of personality patterns and criminality. In a 1948 essay, he identified the major attitudes and traits of psychopathic personality.[65] He also articulated a social-psychological theory to account for the emergence of this pattern. Briefly stated, this is a role-taking theory in which psychopaths are viewed as persons critically deficient in the ability to look upon one's self as an object or to identify with another's point of view (role-taking ability). Thus the psychopath does not experience the social emotions such as embarrassment, contrition, identification, or loyalty. When other persons look at him, they see him as asocial because he doesn't play the social game by rules others share. He is a "lone wolf," not a "team player." [66]

In subsequent elaborations of his views, Gough has explicitly framed the conceptualization of psychopathy as a matter of degree

[64] Clarence C. Schrag, review of Hathaway and Monachesi, *Analyzing and Predicting Delinquency with the Minnesota Multiphasic Personality Inventory,* *American Sociological Review,* Vol. 19 (August 1954), 490-91.

[65] Harrison G. Gough, "A Sociological Theory of Psychopathy," *American Journal of Sociology,* Vol. 53 (March 1948), 359-66.

[66] *Ibid.*

rather than as dichotomous in nature. Instead of viewing psychopathy as a kind of clinical entity clearly marked off from the "normal," he argues for a socialization continuum. Accordingly, a representative sample of the population at large would be expected to show personality patterns ranging from the exemplary citizen at one extreme to persons with negative and positive traits to the markedly asocial individual at the other pole. These differences, in turn, are seen as the product of variations in the depth and validity of the role-taking experiences of persons. Finally, Gough maintains that correlations should be found when variations in socialization among persons are matched up with the social behavior categories in which these persons are located. Individuals who are relatively asocial should be disproportionately criminals and other deviants, whereas well-socialized persons should occupy social positions of trust and repute. However, he notes that "discrepancies are of course to be expected in individual instances between the sociological baseline and the psychological measurement, if for no other reason than that the culture will occasionally make mistakes in putting some men in prisons and others in positions of trust and responsibility." [67]

Gough has also developed measuring techniques and has conducted research to test his theory. His *California Personality Inventory* is a test which includes a number of scales designed to measure particular personality dimensions. One of these, the Socialization (So) Scale, was evolved from the psychopathy theory. The kinds of items in this scale are indicated by the following samples:

1. Before I do something I try to consider how my friends will react to it.

2. I often think about how I look and what impression I am making upon others.

3. I would rather go without something than ask for a favor.

4. I find it easy to drop or "break with" a friend.

Taken together, the 54 items in the scale are intended to provide indices of role-taking deficiencies, insensitivity to the effects of one's behavior on others, resentment against family, feelings of despond-

[67] Harrison G. Gough, "Theory and Measurement of Socialization," *Journal of Consulting Psychology*, Vol. 24 (February 1960), 23-30.

ency and alienation, and poor scholastic achievement and rebelliousness.[68] These are characteristics by which relatively asocial persons are differentiated from relatively well-socialized individuals.

Gough has used this scale to test a number of research samples covering a wide range of the socialization spectrum, from "best citizens" through various occupational and professional groups to known delinquents and prison inmates. The results from these various samples all tend to prove the hypothesis. Persons who occupy social positions of a desirable sort tend to score highly on measures of socialization, whereas those who occupy social categories of an undesirable kind show up as less socialized in terms of this test.[69] But it is also true that between groups of offenders and "good citizens," some overlap exists in role-taking deficiency or ability and other characteristics. Even though the proportion of persons with role-taking deficiencies is greater among offenders, some deviants show positive scores and some nonoffenders show low scores. Thus predictions that persons who score poorly on the So scale are delinquent would be correct in many instances but not in every case. Similarly, predictions that high scorers are nonoffenders would sometimes be in error.

These variations between delinquents and nonoffenders have been substantiated in other studies as well. One case is the research of Reckless and associates, devoted to examining the factors which "insulate" some boys who live in high delinquency areas from delinquent involvement. The potential offenders and nondelinquents in these studies differed in terms of So scale responses in the expected direction.[70]

The last piece of work on personality characteristics of offenders to be mentioned in this brief review is that of Jesness on the *Jesness Inventory*, a personality inventory somewhat similar to that of Gough.[71] This is an instrument developed in the California cor-

[68] Harrison G. Gough and Donald R. Peterson, "The Identification and Measurement of Predispositional Factors in Crime and Delinquency," *Journal of Consulting Psychology*, Vol. 16 (June 1952), 209.

[69] Gough and Peterson, *op. cit.;* Gough, "Theory and Measurement of Socialization."

[70] Walter C. Reckless, Simon Dinitz, and Barbara Kay, "The Self Component in Potential Delinquency and Potential Nondelinquency," *American Sociological Review*, Vol. 22 (October 1957), 566-70; Reckless, Dinitz, and Ellen Murray, "The 'Good Boy' in a High Delinquency Area," *Journal of Criminal Law, Criminology and Police Science*, Vol. 48 (May-June 1957), 18-25.

[71] Carl F. Jesness, *The Jesness Inventory: Development and Validation*, Re-

rectional system which involves eight scales and a delinquency prediction score. The eight scales measure defensiveness, value-orientation, neuroticism, authority attitude, family orientation, psychoticism, delinquency orientation, and emotional immaturity. The first six of these scales involve a priori items, and the last two were constructed from the items in the first six which differentiated among institutionalized delinquents and samples of nonoffenders.

The data from the development and validation studies of this inventory indicate the following: Delinquents and nondelinquents do not differ significantly or markedly in scores on defensiveness, value-orientation, neuroticism, or family orientation. The two groups do vary on authority attitude, with delinquents showing greater hostility toward authority figures. They differ also on psychoticism as the offenders are more suspicious and distrustful of other persons. Additionally, the delinquents can be differentiated from nondelinquents on the two empirical scales, delinquency orientation and emotional maturity. When compared to nondeviants, institutionalized delinquents are more concerned about being normal, exhibit more marked feelings of isolation, are less mature, lack "insight," and tend to deny that they have problems. Finally, the delinquency proneness prediction scale separates the two groups, with some degree of overlap. Some nonoffenders have scores predictive of delinquency proneness, whereas some deviants have scores that are indicative of nondelinquency.

One or two comments are in order on this material. Many of the differences that show up on the *Jesness Inventory* are similar to the self-image and attitudinal characteristics that are involved in the role-conception dimension of the typologies to be presented here, so that the results of the *Jesness Inventory* are not inconsistent with the views of this book. Role-conceptions of institutionalized offenders are expected frequently to involve the sorts of characteristics identified by Jesness. On the other hand, it may well be that not all types of offenders would show these personality configurations. Quite probably, the role-conceptions of certain delinquent

---

search Report No. 29, mimeographed (Sacramento: California Youth Authority, 1962); see also Jesness, *Redevelopment and Revalidation of the Jesness Inventory*, Research Report No. 35 (Sacramento: California Youth Authority, 1963). The 1963 report presents somewhat different findings from applications of the *Jesness Inventory* to additional samples. However, the outlines of the *Jesness Inventory* results from this latter study of delinquents and nondelinquents were not materially altered from those of the 1962 report, discussed in this chapter.

types, particularly casual patterns of offender behavior, are marked by an absence of feelings of hostility, suspicion, and so forth. Further, many of these self-views and attitudes held by serious and incarcerated offenders are probably the consequence of differential involvement with "defining agencies," at least in part. They did not necessarily precede the deviant career, but may have developed correlatively with the growth of the pattern of illegality.

To summarize this line of commentary, certain kinds of personality dynamics common to particular offender roles are noted in the statements made about role-conceptions within the typologies in Chapter Three. There is evidence for the existence of certain common social-psychological correlates of offender behavior. On the other hand, the data suggest that deviants and nonoffenders do not vary over-all in terms of many personality dimensions and that many personality patterns are not common to a single offender type. Typological comments about offender role-conceptions are generally restricted to the first class of variations.

Of course, in actual diagnosis and treatment, incidental personality traits that are not common to most offenders or to most incumbents in a particular type may still be important. Suppose that a certain lawbreaker turns out to be extremely withdrawn and timid, even though other individuals of the same general type do not show such characteristics. Clearly, timidity and withdrawal in the instance at hand would be important information to consider, for it might imply some modification of the usual treatment strategy for offenders of the general type. Idiosyncratic factors should not be ignored. To resort to an overworked analogy, the situation is somewhat comparable to medical practice. The diagnostic types and treatment tactics of medicine are based upon conceptions of general medical problems such as cirrhosis of the liver, arteriosclerosis, and leg fractures. However, in the actual treatment of any particular sick person, consideration must be given to the incidental characteristics of that individual. Some strategies may be ruled out because the heart patient exhibits certain physical peculiarities that are relatively atypical among heart cases. Correctional treatment is essentially similar. Idiosyncratic personal characteristics are not unimportant in treatment, but a statement of general diagnostic types and treatment procedures cannot and should not be sufficiently detailed so as to include mention of all these incidental but important personality characteristics.

Summary

This chapter examined the development and present status of typological thinking in criminology and corrections. Certain defects of existing classificatory schemes were noted. Lengthy consideration was then given to the logical, structural, and theoretical requirements which adequate typologies must meet. The particular frame of reference employed in the typologies in this book was clarified. Finally, attention was given to the issue of personality dynamics in causal or treatment typologies. Chapter Three examines the taxonomic schemes which this chapter has been leading up to.

three

TWO
CANDIDATE
TYPOLOGIES

Introduction

A typology of juvenile delinquents and one of adult criminals is presented in this chapter, and a classification of forms of treatment is presented in Chapter Four. Subsequent sections in this volume are devoted to linking up offender types and forms of therapy strategy.

The discussions to follow are organized in this way: Both the juvenile and adult typologies set forth descriptions of lawbreakers in terms of the role-dimensions introduced in Chapter Two. Offender patterns are described as role-careers within the definitional dimensions of (1) offense behavior, (2) interactional setting, (3) self-image, and (4) attitudes. Then, in addition, comments about background or situational correlates of offender types are made, indicating the social class origins, family background, and other character-istics commonly associated with the defined types.

No systematic attempt is made to amalgamate all the research findings and theoretical arguments about law violators within the types in the typologies. Such an endeavor would resemble an intellectual "con game" in view of the deficiencies, which were discussed in the previous chapter, in much of the existing data. Much of the existing research is not directly related to the framework used here: thus to cite investigations in great number would be misleading, in that this would imply a greater degree of empirical support for the types than is warranted. To illustrate, the several studies of juvenile automobile thieves now in existence do not provide any data supporting certain hypotheses about adjustment problems of the boys who engage in car theft and which are contained in the typological description. The same is true of other investigations of specific types. This is not to say that these offender types are entirely unsupported by evidence, but the descriptions should be taken as tentative characterizations. They are portraits rather than caricatures of real-life persons, but they may be slightly distorted due to the paucity of research findings about them.

A Typology of Delinquents

A typology involving fourteen patterns of juvenile delinquent roles has been presented in an earlier essay by the author.[1] The reader is referred to that discussion for detailed commentary on the procedures involved in the genesis of a type scheme. But in brief, the typological classification was developed through a process of explication, in which existing descriptions of offender patterns in the criminological literature were examined. An effort was made to uncover, by logical analysis, the underlying dimensions or variables that are implicit in these characterizations. In turn, an attempt was made to identify the basic patterns of delinquent conduct that have been discussed by different investigators.

In this book, several of the patterns in the earlier scheme are combined on the grounds that fine distinctions among offenders are not necessary for the purposes at hand, namely, the articulation of treatment theory based on diagnostic categories. The nine role-types examined here can be listed in summary form as follows:

[1] Don C. Gibbons, "Problems and Prospects of Delinquent Typology," *Sociological Inquiry*, Vol. 32 (Spring 1962), 235-44.

    I. Predatory gang delinquent
    II. Conflict gang delinquent
  III. Casual gang delinquent
  IV. Casual delinquent, nongang member
    V. Automobile thief—"joyrider"
  VI. Drug user—heroin
 VII. Overly aggressive delinquent
VIII. Female delinquent
  IX. "Behavior problem" delinquent

Four of these patterns, I, II, III, and VI, represent variants of working-class, gang delinquency, and thus in a sense they "go together." As noted in Chapter Two, a number of persons have suggested that lower-class gang delinquents come in several varieties. In particular, the view is frequently expressed that conflict behavior ("bopping") appears in some working-class, urban areas, whereas it is relatively absent in other low-income neighborhoods. Predatory or criminalistic delinquency is also differentially distributed, for it tends to be most common in working-class areas other than those where conflict activity is found. In turn, a widely held contemporary view is that the causal process in fighting-gang behavior is probably different from that in predatory deviation. One particularly prominent etiological theory of this kind is that of Cloward and Ohlin, which centers upon variations in "illegitimate opportunity structures" as the critical factor in the determination of which pattern emerges in slum areas.[2] According to these writers, the neighborhoods in which predatory activity develops are ones which show integration between criminalistic and conventional social organizational patterns, where stability of social organization is found, and where learning opportunities for careers in crime exist for juveniles. These conditions are relatively absent in conflict areas, which tend more toward "sociological jungles." Whatever the merits of this argument—and it is probably not an entirely satisfactory one—it does appear that these two variant patterns of delinquency do exist.

"Heavy" drug users are differentiated in the typology from other gang delinquents because a considerable literature on juvenile

---

[2] Richard A. Cloward and Lloyd E. Ohlin, *Delinquency and Opportunity* (New York: The Free Press of Glencoe, Inc., 1960).

drug addicts suggests that these youths are not entirely comparable to nondrug users. Addicted heroin users should be distinguished from juveniles who casually experiment with marijuana, or who "joy pop," that is, who try out opiates but who discontinue using them before they become addicted. The former are the ones described in the typology. There is some substantial body of opinion that these juveniles are an atypical group of youngsters who are probably more burdened with personality problems than their contemporaries who do not use narcotics. Finally, casual gang delinquents are separated from other working-class gang types. The literature on gang behavior suggests that the degree of involvement in delinquency varies from one juvenile to another and that there are some who are peripheral members of this subculture. These are the boys here identified as casual gang delinquents.

Patterns IV and V in the typology represent two forms of predominately "middle-class delinquency," in that middle-class juveniles tend to be commonly found in these two types and relatively few middle-class juveniles would be found among gang delinquents. On the other hand, there are lower-class youngsters who steal cars or who are involved in relatively petty, nongang forms of misconduct, but the largest concentration of working-class youths would be found in Types I, II, III, and VI. Although Types IV and V appear to be middle-class forms of deviation, it should also be noted that there are significant differences between the two. "Joyriding" is a serious form of lawbreaking, at least in the eyes of the police and the courts. Boys who are apprehended for car thefts normally receive a marked and formal societal reaction from these sources, and some of them end up in training schools or other institutions. In contrast, casual nongang misbehavior is the kind of activity that most frequently emerges from studies of "hidden delinquency." [3] Investigations involving self-reported instances of deviant conduct by predominately middle-class youths reveal that they engage in a lot of very petty activity, so that delinquency in a very broad sense seems to be widespread. But it is clearly not true that these "hid-

---

[3] James F. Short, Jr., and F. Ivan Nye, "Extent of Unrecorded Juvenile Delinquency, Tentative Conclusions," *Journal of Criminal Law, Criminology and Police Science,* Vol. 49 (November-December 1958), 296-302; Short and Nye, "Scaling Delinquent Behavior," *American Sociological Review,* Vol. 22 (June 1957), 326-31.

den" delinquents are the same as, only "luckier" than, officially recognized offenders. Comparative data on training school residents and "hidden" delinquent, high-school students show quite vividly that the incarcerated subjects differ from the other group. The former indicate that, not only have they committed all the illegal acts reported by the high-school students, but they have also engaged in those acts more frequently. In addition, the training school offenders "cop out" to a large number of serious law violations which are not admitted by the school students.

Three other delinquent role patterns which are not noticeably class-linked in character are specified in the typology. Overly aggressive behavior is the product of parental rejection which can and does characterize families at all class levels. Female delinquency is also a kind of deviance which develops in various social class groups, although this activity is in other ways quite dissimilar to overly aggressive behavior. Finally, "behavior problem" delinquency is a form of misconduct which develops in a variety of socioeconomic settings.

I. Predatory Gang Delinquent

DEFINITIONAL DIMENSIONS

Offense Behavior. This offender is involved in a variety of property offenses, including repetitive and serious thefts and burglaries. These juveniles also frequently become involved in acts of vandalism, automobile theft, and sexual delinquency. "Playing the queers" (submitting to homosexual acts for pay) and "gang shags" are two forms of sexual delinquency sometimes involved. Although this type exhibits versatility in offense behavior, the offender tends to engage most frequently in acts which involve monetary rewards. Conversely, this type is not often active in "rumbles," that is, gang fighting.

Interactional Setting. This juvenile is usually labeled a "gang delinquent," for he frequently associates with delinquent peers. However, gang behavior in these cases varies from involvement in large, highly structured gangs to delinquent acts carried on with two or three delinquent peers. Further, some juveniles of this kind are engaged in deviant acts with different collections of delinquent peers over time. Finally, some are involved in delinquencies with deviant peers who are at the same time siblings. However, in each case, the individual engages in most of his law violations with some supportive group of peers sharing antisocial norms.

Self-Concept. This offender exhibits a delinquent self-image. He views himself as "cool" and as a self-reliant individual. He takes pride in his reputation as a "tough kid" and as a delinquent. He is likely to verbalize sentiments alleging that he has no problems, that "My stealing may be a problem to someone else but not to me."

Attitudes. This type exhibits antisocial attitudes. That is, he shows considerable hostility toward the police, toward probation officers, and other correctional agents, and also toward law-abiding citizens generally. His view of the world tends toward the argument that everyone has a "racket." He shows negative attitudes toward work, arguing that "only slobs work." In general, the attitudes of this offender that are related to involvement in delinquency are ones in which he sees himself as a victim of a society which does not provide opportunities for persons of his kind. Consequently, he maintains that prosocial standards have no validity.

Role-Career. These juveniles usually exhibit a pattern of early entry into delinquent activities, starting around the age of eight or nine. Frequently the offender shows a pattern of increasing entanglement in more serious and repetitive property crimes. He also exhibits rapid progression from an initial stage of a non-delinquent self-image and mildly antisocial attitudes to a delinquent self-image and a structure of hostile, suspicious, antisocial attitudes. By about the age of sixteen, he demonstrates a developed pattern of property offenses, delinquent self-image, and antisocial attitudes. The career development of these views appears to be the joint product of the type of social background from which he emerges and of contacts with defining agencies. That is, to some extent the emergence of a "delinquent personality" is a function of differential association with carriers of criminalistic norms with whom the offender interacts. To some extent, it is also attributable to unpleasant and difficult experiences with law enforcement and correctional agents. Such experiences force the offender to come to grips with the negative definitions of him held by others. The frequent outcome of such contacts is that the person develops rationalizations for his behavior which allow him to "reject his rejectors."

BACKGROUND DIMENSIONS

Social Class.   Delinquents in this type come from work-ing-class (lower-class) backgrounds and from urban areas. They live in deteriorated neighborhoods in which patterns of adult crimi-nality are often readily observable.

Family Background.   The family background of these offenders is one of parental neglect and exposure to delinquency patterns. The family structure is usually not characterized by in-tense interfamily tension. Instead, the family members are on rela-tively good terms with each other. But the offender commonly is not subjected to close parental supervision. On occasion, this type exhibits a family background in which siblings are also delinquent or involved in criminality. In addition, the parents are on occasion involved in forms of criminality, so that differential association with deviant family members plays a significant part in the de-velopment of this career.

Peer Group Associations.   This type of offender is in-volved in interaction within the structure of delinquent gangs or is characterized by a background of differential association with de-linquent peers. In some cases these delinquent peers form a rec-ognizable gang, whereas in others they represent a loose confeder-ation of offenders. However, in either case, the predatory delin-quent shows differential avoidance of nondelinquent juveniles in his community. Commonly this type associates with a group of youths known in the area as troublemakers and delinquents, all of whom share such characteristics as expulsion from school, un-employment, and so on. This peer structure provides him with group support for his hostile and cynical attitudes. The peer struc-ture also provides social rewards for prowess in delinquent acts, in that peers often accord high status to the most delinquent boys.

Contact with Defining Agencies.   This type usually ex-hibits early involvement with the police. In many instances, his police contacts are considerably more common than is indicated by his official record. This type is also well known to the juvenile court. His record is likely to show several probation experiences, culminating finally in placement in a correctional institution. The usual view of persons who have dealt with the offender is that he is a "tough kid," lacking in insight and concern over his delinquent conduct. In turn, the offender's usual view of law enforcement and correctional agents is that such persons are "phonies."

II. Conflict Gang Delinquent

DEFINITIONAL DIMENSIONS

Offense Behavior. This type consists of juvenile males who are members of so-called "hanging gangs" in urban areas (street corner groups) and who engage in "rumbles" and "bopping," that is, gang fights. Much of the activity of such offenders is nondelinquent in form, in which groups of juveniles spend their time in "hanging" or loitering around some favorite haunt. Some of them experiment with narcotics, and others engage in heterosexual acts with girls from the area, either by themselves or in "gang shags." On occasion, members of this type engage in predatory acts. However, these are not carried on as frequently or systematically as in the case of Type I juveniles. The behavior of these offenders which is most repetitive and which causes the most concern among police and youth workers is "bopping." These acts involve groups of boys in mass fighting with members of a rival gang.

Interactional Setting. Unlike members of Type I, conflict gang delinquents are members of rather clear-cut delinquent peer groups. These gangs are frequently identified by articles of apparel adorned with such gang names as the "Cougars," "Viceroys," and so forth and by other paraphernalia of formal organizations. The sense of belonging to a gang is heightened in the case of conflict gang members. Members of such groups are likely to associate almost entirely with other group members. In the nature of gang fighting, delinquent acts are carried on within a peer group structure.

Self-Concept. The self-images of conflict gang members tend to be less criminalistic than those of Type I delinquents. These offenders do not see themselves as delinquents so much as they define themselves as members of a "tough gang." Most members of conflict gangs do not conceive of themselves as neophyte criminals.

Attitudes. The attitudes of conflict gang members center around the view of the world as offering little promise for them.

These delinquents are not so hostile toward conventional work careers as they are doubtful of their chances of obtaining a conventional job. Antisocial attitudes of conflict delinquents center around hostile views of the police, who are held to be unsympathetic to the feelings of gang members.

Role-Career. The role-career of this type is one which begins in the adolescent years. Membership in a conflict gang results in repetitive instances of fighting behavior and other delinquent acts. It appears that many "hanging gang" boys ultimately develop noncriminal, adult adjustments—they get married, obtain jobs, and so forth. One reason for this is that adult criminal models are not readily available for them to emulate.

BACKGROUND DIMENSIONS

Social Class. Offenders of this type are from urban backgrounds and are residents of deteriorated slum areas or of housing project areas. In either case, the areas from which they come tend to be more "disorganized" than the neighborhoods producing delinquents of Type I. They are areas lacking in stable community organizations and in stable patterns of deviant behavior, and they are characterized by high rates of residential mobility. They represent a kind of "sociological jungle" in that they are lacking in social integration. It appears that the most extreme form of conflict gang behavior is to be found in the largest American cities, where conditions of this kind are most pronounced.

Family Background. The family background of conflict gang delinquents tends to be one in which the parents are recent arrivals to the urban area. They are frequently Puerto Ricans or southern migrants. Many of them experience unemployment and considerable general confusion regarding life in a large city. In many cases, they view their children's delinquent activities negatively, but they are unable to control their children. Unlike the parents of Type I offenders, these parents are likely to be carriers of prosocial norms.

Peer Group Associations. As indicated above, most of the delinquent acts of this offender take place within a peer structure of an identifiable gang. These offenders view the gang as representing the limits of their significant social world. Meaningful personal experiences are largely restricted to this peer gang. Personal status or feelings of self-esteem tend to be a function of the general status of the gang as a "tough gang." Involvement in such a gang usually means that the individual juvenile then becomes subject to control by group norms which encourage "heart" (bravery) and which severely condemn those who "punk out" or refuse to fight.

Contact with Defining Agencies. Conflict gang members tend to experience a variety of contacts with community agencies in which they are labeled as "bad." Contacts with community centers sometimes result in the juvenile being expelled from the program for rowdy behavior and boisterous conduct. Similarly, the offender is likely either to have been expelled from school or to have voluntarily withdrawn from it because he views school as unpleasant. He also experiences a number of contacts with the police, but many of these involve no official action by the police. Gangs are "rousted" by the police in order to curtail potential "rumbles," but arrests are not made. On occasion, offenders of this type get "busted" and sent to correctional institutions. Such contacts are productive of hostile feelings toward law enforcement, correctional, and social agencies, but they do not appear to lead to commitment to adult crime as a way of life.

III. Casual Gang Delinquent

A prefatory comment is in order regarding this type. Lower-class, high-delinquency areas are characterized by a variety of juvenile behavior patterns. Some juvenile males are heavily involved in delinquency and fall into Types I and II. Others are essentially nondelinquent in behavior. But, in addition to these patterns, some boys engage in relatively minor and infrequent acts of delinquency, often as peripheral members of delinquent gangs. Such juveniles would not be included in Types I or II but are not nondelinquents either. These offenders have been labeled "Casual Gang Delinquents." The typological description below indicates the ways in which they differ from Types I and II.

DEFINITIONAL DIMENSIONS

Offense Behavior. In some cases, casual gang delinquents participate in conflict activities; and in others, in acts of theft and vandalism. At an early age, their delinquent acts are not distinguishable from those of Types I and II, but as the career develops, these offenders engage in fewer and less serious activities than Type I or II delinquents.

Interactional Setting. This type engages in delinquencies with peers who are members of a gang which may be loosely or firmly structured. However, the offender tends to view this activity as "fun." Furthermore, he is usually regarded by delinquent peers as a fringe member of the group and tends to regard himself in the same way. In any sociometric analysis of gang structure, the offender would be assigned a marginal position in the deviant peer group. That is, he would be considered by most members as a hanger-on and would not be accorded high status within the group.

Self-Concept. Casual gang offenders view themselves as nondelinquents. Although they indicate awareness of the deviant nature of their delinquent activities, at the same time they differentiate themselves from those gang members regarded as "real delinquents." Similarly, the casual delinquent exhibits a relatively ambiguous version of his position within the gang. His commitment to gang norms and gang identification tends to be minimal. He views gang boys simply as "good guys to be around."

Attitudes. Casual gang delinquents exhibit some degree of hostility toward policemen and similar persons. However, such attitudes tend to be relatively generic to working-class persons, so that the casual offender's "antisocial" attitudes are not particularly pronounced within the groups in which he associates. Members of this type exhibit positive attitudes toward conventional work roles. They expect to assume such occupational roles upon adulthood.

Role-Career. Casual gang delinquents frequently begin their delinquent activities at a relatively early age. In some cases, these persist over a number of years; in other instances they terminate relatively quickly. In either case, the usual outcome of casual gang delinquency is adult adjustment as a law-abiding citizen.

BACKGROUND DIMENSIONS

Social Class. Casual gang delinquents derive from working-class neighborhoods in urban areas. In this respect, they are from similar backgrounds as Types I and II.

Family Background. In some ways the family backgrounds of casual gang offenders are similar to those of Type I and

II gang boys: All three types come from working-class families. However, casual offenders are products of families in which greater control and supervision is exercised over the boys. In addition, the parents of the casual offender are infrequently criminalistic. Most important, the parents of the casual delinquent have been relatively successful in socializing him to prosocial norms stressing conventional occupational aspirations, upward mobility, and the like. They have provided a degree of insulation against delinquent norms.

Peer Group Associations. The casual gang member associates with delinquent peers who are viewed by him as friends and as congenial companions. However, he does not interact with delinquent peers to the exclusion of involvement with nondelinquents. Instead, the casual gang boy tends to associate with nondeviants, both at school and in the general community. His time tends to be spent between the two kinds of peer settings. Because of this peripheral involvement in gang activities, the subject fails to clearly identify himself as a gang member, and in turn, is not so identified by the gang itself. In the same way, due to divided peer loyalties, the casual delinquent is less influenced by delinquent norms of gangs.

Contact with Defining Agencies. Because of the lesser degree of participation in delinquent actions than in the case of Types I and II, members of Type III are likely to have fewer police contacts. Those contacts which occur are frequently informal ones in which the police issue warnings but take no further action. It may be that contacts with the police and other agencies sometimes push the offender into greater involvement in, and commitment to, delinquent activities. However, it is probable that the more frequent outcome of such contacts is to deter the delinquent from further interaction with serious delinquents.

IV. Casual Delinquent, Nongang Member

In the multitude of forms of delinquency, there are some patterns which involve juveniles who engage in delinquent acts but who are not members of any clear-cut gang pattern. The casual delinquent, nongang member is one of these. This type designates juveniles who may on occasion commit delinquencies with peers, whereas on other occasions their deviant acts may be carried on as individualistic forms of behavior. In delinquencies committed with peers, the participants are likely to be adolescents who define themselves as "friends." None of the participants regard themselves as delinquents. Delinquent acts are *permitted* activities within the peer group structure, but they are not *required* for membership in the group. Moreover, most of the peer group interaction among these persons is nondelinquent in form. Consequently, it is not appropriate to refer to such behavior as "gang" delinquency, even though it may be peer group activity. It is this meaning which the term "non-gang" has in the following type. At a later point in the typology, forms of delinquency which are truly individualistic in character and in which no peer group interaction is involved will be identified.

DEFINITIONAL DIMENSIONS

Offense Behavior. This type refers to so-called "hidden delinquents"—juveniles who engage in relatively few minor acts of misbehavior. The acts of delinquency include petty thefts, operating a motor vehicle without a license, smoking and drinking, acts of vandalism, and similar offenses. On occasion, such acts may become quite destructive and serious, but this is the exception rather than the rule.

Interactional Setting. This offender interacts with other juveniles who are regarded by adults as nondelinquents and who view themselves in the same way. These peers engage in conventional adolescent behavior for the most part, but on occasion some of them carry on minor delinquencies. Within the group, involvement in delinquency does not result in status-loss, but neither does it produce status-gains for the offender. Such activities are within the range of permissible conduct but are not accorded any special recognition as desirable or laudatory activities.

Self-Concept. Juveniles of this type view themselves as nondelinquents. When apprehended for delinquent acts, they acknowledge the deviant character of their behavior, but they tend to exhibit chagrin and a degree of shame. Delinquent acts are seen by the offenders as "fun" but not as indicators that the person is a "real delinquent."

Attitudes. Prosocial attitudes characterize members of this type. They do not exhibit particularly marked attitudes of hostility toward policemen, occupational roles, and so on.

Role-Career. Offenders of this type begin their delinquent activities at various ages, but most frequently during the teenage period. Their delinquent actions are few in number and generally not serious in character. Such activities terminate when the offender graduates from high school. The delinquent frequently goes to college, where he sometimes becomes a research subject in investigations of "hidden delinquency."

BACKGROUND DIMENSIONS

Social Class. Casual, nongang delinquents are usually from middle-class, comfortable economic backgrounds. They are found both in large urban communities and in smaller urban centers.

Family Background. These offenders are from family backgrounds in which middle-class behavior patterns are exhibited. Parent-child interaction patterns vary somewhat from one offender to another, but in general they are within the range of normal, satisfactory relationships. The parents of the casual, nongang delinquent have been relatively successful in attempts to socialize the juvenile to prosocial norms and to "success" values.

Peer Group Associations. The casual, nongang boy is an accepted member of juvenile peer groups. He belongs to a peer subculture which permits acts of delinquency but which does not require such acts as membership criteria. Instead, the peer subculture is oriented around hedonistic, "fun" values. The emphasis upon short-run hedonistic activities sometimes results in overly exuberant acts of a delinquent sort.

Contact with Defining Agencies. This offender has minimal contacts with the police and other official agencies, due to both the petty nature of his deviant acts and the fact that he is from a relatively stable, comfortable background. The police take no official action against juveniles of this type, because of biases which lead the policemen to regard such juveniles as essentially nondelinquent "pranksters." *Inaction* on the part of the police is more customary than is differential handling which results from interference in police decisions by powerful citizens. The casual offender who is not officially acted against tends to continue to define himself as a nondelinquent. It is likely that official action against some of these offenders acts as a deterrent and restrains them from further deviant acts.

V. Automobile Thief—"Joyrider"

DEFINITIONAL DIMENSIONS

Offense Behavior. Joyriders steal cars for recreational or joyriding purposes, not to "strip" them or for other profit motives. The customary activity is to steal automobiles by the technique of "hot wiring," ride around in them for a short time, and then abandon the car undamaged. Car thieves are sometimes known in the community as "wild" boys who drink and associate with "wild" girls. However, their delinquent activities tend to center around auto theft and they are not usually involved in other kinds of property offenses.

Interactional Setting. Joyriders steal cars within a loosely structured group of fellow joyriders. On any particular occasion, an individual car thief engages in these acts with several other delinquents. Over a series of joyriding incidents, the participants in such acts vary somewhat; thus on one occasion, cars are stolen by boys *A*, *B*, and *C*, whereas another time they are stolen by boys *A*, *D*, *E*, and *F*. Consequently, these boys, *A*, *B*, *C*, *D*, *E*, and *F*, do not constitute a well-structured gang, but they do represent individuals who associate differentially with each other, that is, "birds of a feather." As a group they are likely to be juveniles with adjustment problems in school and elsewhere.

Self-Concept. These offenders define themselves as nondelinquents and distinguish themselves from "real delinquents." On the other hand, they are boys who frequently exhibit a considerable psychological investment in self-notions as "tough" and masculine persons. In general, they regard their delinquent activities as evidence that they are "tough" and "cool."

Attitudes. Joyriders exhibit essentially prosocial attitudes, in that they show conventional attitudes toward work and reveal other conventional norms. Their views of the police are not so much hostile as they are notions that the police are stupid and inefficient.

Role-Career. The role-career of the joyrider begins in adolescence with automobile theft. It may persist over several years and may involve a number of instances of joyriding. Repetitive acts of car theft are likely to result in the arrest of the offender, adjudication as a delinquent, and placement on probation. Some of these boys eventually end up in training schools where they make a reasonably stable adjustment. It appears that most car thieves terminate these actions in the late teenage years and become law-abiding citizens.

BACKGROUND DIMENSIONS

Social Class.   Joyriders are juveniles who specialize in this kind of activity, as distinct from those juveniles who occasionally steal cars but whose acts are normally in the direction of predatory theft. Car thieves of the first sort are usually from middle-class, comfortable economic backgrounds. They live in single-family dwellings in middle-income areas. Their parents are usually white-collar or other types of middle-class workers.

Family Background.   The family situation out of which joyriders emerge is one of relatively close supervision and consistent discipline by the parents. However, joyriders frequently indicate a lack of intense interaction with their fathers. It may be that to some degree the fathers of car thieves fail to provide completely adequate models of adult, masculine behavior to their sons. Another not uncommon characteristic of the families of joyriders is a relatively high degree of occupational and residential mobility. This pattern may sometimes contribute to the marginal status of the boy in the community in terms of peer group membership.

Peer Group Associations.   Joyriders exhibit relatively adequate peer group adjustments. However, although they interact with nondelinquent peers, they exhibit differential association with other car thieves, most of whom have reputations as "wild" and somewhat deviant boys. To some extent, the joyrider appears to be a marginal member of conventional juvenile peer groups.

Contact with Defining Agencies.   Contact with defining agencies in the case of joyriders seems to confirm the person's status as a "tough" individual in his own eyes. Repeated contacts with the police and courts tend to produce negative attitudes toward these groups. However, these contacts do not usually lead the offender to a commitment to adult patterns of criminality. Instead, the joyrider is sufficiently socialized to conventional norms that he ultimately gets a job, gets married, and assumes the behavior of a conventional law-abiding citizen.

VI. Drug User—Heroin

Experimentation with narcotics, particularly marijuana, occurs on occasion among members of Types I, II, and III. Some of these individuals also engage in casual "joypopping" of opiates. However, "mainlining" or systematic use of so-called "heavy" drugs, usually heroin, is uncommon among juvenile offenders. Those adolescents who are addicted to "heavy" drugs form a special class of delinquents. It is these offenders who are defined below.

DEFINITIONAL DIMENSIONS

Offense Behavior. Most juvenile heroin users are boys who specialize in the use of narcotics as deviant behavior. Some of them engage in other delinquent acts, particularly in forms of "hustle" (pimping, and so forth), but only to obtain funds to purchase drugs.

Interactional Setting. Juvenile heroin users are normally members of a drug-user subculture, which sometimes takes the form of a "cat" culture. Differential association with other drug users occurs for several reasons. Association with narcotic addicts involves a system of mutual aid, in which users inform each other about sources of drugs, means of obtaining narcotics by illicit methods, and so forth. In addition, involvement in patterns of "heavy" drug use normally results in expulsion of the user from more conventional delinquent peer groups or in the voluntary withdrawal of the addict from such groups. Narcotic users are often viewed by other delinquents as undependable and bizarre personalities.

Self-Concept. The juvenile narcotic user usually exhibits a self-image as a drug addict rather than as a "delinquent" or "criminal." He maintains that the use of drugs is no more deviant than the various other "kicks" resorted to by noncriminals, for example, drinking or smoking. The narcotic addict views himself as a person who has plenty of justification in his life circumstances for drug use. Further, he argues that he should be allowed to use narcotics and that if he were, there would be few problems either for himself or for society. Some narcotic addicts view themselves as "cats," that is, as individuals who are "cool" and who are able to make a living through various forms of "hustle." In turn, "cats" evidence considerable disdain for "squares" or noncriminal persons.

Attitudes. The attitudes of the heroin user take the form of allegations that he is being harassed by a society which provides few satisfying experiences for persons of his kind. The narcotic user has negative attitudes toward work, but his principal antagonism is directed toward the police. This is, of course, understandable in view of the fact that the addict experiences considerable contact with the police, which he defines as harassment, and is continually under surveillance by narcotic agents.

Role-Career. Narcotic addicts are sometimes juveniles who begin their delinquent careers as members of conventional gangs but who ultimately branch off from such groups as they come to be caught up in narcotic use. On other occasions, the drug user drifted into narcotic use outside the framework of conventional gangs. The juvenile drug user often continues in drug use into adulthood and becomes an adult, criminal drug user.

BACKGROUND DIMENSIONS

Social Class. Drug users are usually from urban, slum area, lower-class backgrounds. They appear to be recruited from those persons in lower-class areas who have the most pronounced feelings of low status, lack of opportunity, and inability to extricate themselves from situations of extreme stress and unpleasantness.

Family Background. For the most part, the family origins of drug users are relatively conventional lower-class ones. However, the drug user tends to be from families in which close parent-child ties are missing. Family life tends to be relatively meaningless and unimportant for the drug user.

Peer Group Associations. Drug users normally associate differentially with other addicts. They normally learn the use of drugs and norms defining narcotics as pleasant from interaction with other addicts. When the "budding addict" becomes seriously involved in drug use, he usually withdraws into almost exclusive isolation from nonaddicts and into interaction with other users.

This interaction has important consequences for his continuation in drug use, for these persons share a set of norms which define narcotic use as acceptable and which suggest that cures for addiction are nonexistent.

Contact with Defining Agencies. Drug users experience numerous contacts with defining agencies during the course of their deviant career. On the one hand, it does not appear that involvement in programs of conventional treatment in which the user is incarcerated, withdrawn from dependence upon narcotics, and then given psychiatric treatment has any pronounced rehabilitative effect. Instead, drug users tend to quickly resume drug habits upon release from treatment. But, on the other hand, it does not appear that contact with defining agencies plays any direct role in drug relapse. Instead, such contacts have only a neutral impact upon drug users.

VII. Overly Aggressive Delinquent

The delinquency literature indicates the existence of varying degrees of individualistic, aggressive, relatively unsocialized behavior by delinquents in addition to patterns of conflict gang behavior. On the one extreme are unsocialized, aggressive delinquents who engage in serious and vicious acts of aggression against human and animal targets. On the other extreme are mildly aggressive delinquents who engage in frequent fist fights and in similar activity. The causal backgrounds of such offenders seem to vary in a similar fashion, so that severely aggressive youngsters are from backgrounds of extreme parental rejection, whereas mildly aggressive children are from parental situations of relatively mild rejection. The typological description to follow refers to delinquents on the severe end of the scale of individualistic aggression.

DEFINITIONAL DIMENSIONS

Offense Behavior. Overly aggressive delinquents are juveniles who engage in seemingly meaningless assaults upon peers and, on occasion, upon adults and animals. Acts of extreme cruelty directed toward either humans or animals are characteristic of such offenders. Most of these persons restrict their activities to hostile acts against various targets, and they do not engage in property offenses and the like.

Interactional Setting.   Overly aggressive delinquents are "lone-wolf" offenders. In view of the nature of their diffuse aggressive activities, interaction with peers is minimal, for these children are avoided by other youngsters.

Self-Concept.   The overly aggressive child does not normally define himself as a delinquent. Instead, he views himself as "picked upon" and as a victim of a hostile environment. The overly aggressive offender exhibits defiance, a kind of chip-on-the-shoulder attitude, and the view that people are not to be trusted. Because of his suspicion of other persons, he lashes out at people with the intent of hitting first before he is punished or harmed by others he suspects of having bad motives.

Attitudes.   The attitudes of the overly aggressive delinquent are not generally antisocial, aside from his notions that other persons are a source of aggression and harm directed toward him.

Role-Career.   Overly aggressive offenders often begin these assaultive and violent acts well before adolescence. Many of them turn up rather early in child guidance clinics and residential treatment centers. The prognosis for adult adjustment in these cases is poor. Many of these juveniles continue aggressive activities into adulthood and become inmates of penal institutions, where their adjustment continues to be poor.

BACKGROUND DIMENSIONS

Social Class.   Overly aggressive delinquents do not come from any single social class background. Instead, such persons are found in several social class groups.

Family Background.   Although the specific family experiences of aggressive delinquents vary somewhat, in nearly every case some kind of early and severe parental rejection appears to be the prelude to aggressive behavior. Aggressive youngsters were usually illegitimate or unwanted pregnancies, rejected and abandoned by the parents at an early age, or underwent severe parental rejection within the home if the offender was not physically separated from his parents. Many of them have lived for extended periods of time in foster homes, orphanages, and the like, rather than with their natural parents.

Peer Group Associations.   Intensive interaction with

peers is an uncommon experience among overly aggressive delinquents because of two factors. First, most aggressive offenders refrain from initiating relationships with peers because they are socially inept and because of their hostile views of people. Second, most eligible peers refrain from contacts with aggressive children because of the potentially violent consequences.

Contact with Defining Agencies. Overly aggressive offenders exhibit considerable contact with police, courts, and child guidance clinics, and they show hostile attitudes toward such agencies and persons. These attitudes are not the product of such experiences, however; they are the result of the diffuse feelings of hostility directed toward people generally by the aggressive person.

VIII. Female Delinquent

DEFINITIONAL DIMENSIONS

Offense Behavior. Delinquent girls are sent to juvenile courts for offenses labeled variously as "ungovernability," "waywardness," "immorality," and "sexual misconduct." However, in most instances, the girl comes to the attention of the authorities for sexual reasons. Either she has been discovered engaging in promiscuous sex acts or else the presumption is that she is about to become so involved. In addition, the sexual misconduct of girls who are dealt with as delinquents has a somewhat special character. That is, there are numerous teenage girls who engage in sexual intercourse, but most of them are not defined as delinquents. It is those who associate with a number of "wild" boys and who engage in relatively visible and promiscuous sex acts with a number of male partners who are likely to be defined as delinquents.

Interactional Setting. Delinquent girls commit delinquencies of a sexual kind with boys, but they do not engage in gang activities with other delinquent girls. Although delinquent females associate differentially with other deviants, they do not form any kind of delinquent gang or subculture. These girls associate with each other because they tend to be shunned by other teenage girls as "wild."

Self-Concept. Female delinquents do not define themselves as delinquents, but they do view themselves as laboring under special problems and difficulties. Many of them see themselves as "tough" and as capable of resisting harsh treatment by other persons. Many of these girls use markedly profane language, particularly in communication with males.

Attitudes. The principal attitudinal characteristics of female delinquents center around hostility toward their parents and toward correctional agents. These girls regard their parents as lacking in affection, sympathy, and understanding toward them.

Role-Career. Sexual delinquency by girls usually begins in postpuberty. It frequently continues for some time, and girl delinquents usually experience probation placement and institutional commitments. However, this is not a career which normally continues into adulthood. Most female delinquents get married during their late teens and make a reasonably law-abiding adjustment.

BACKGROUND DIMENSIONS

Social Class. This type of delinquency is not markedly class-linked, but emerges in different social class settings.

Family Background. The family background of girl delinquents tends to be atypical when compared to that of nondelinquent girls. In some cases the female delinquent has developed in a broken home, whereas in others she has grown up in a physically intact home. However, in either case, the usual background is one of family tension in which the girl is on poor terms with one or both parents. Sexual delinquency by these females is, at least in part, an attempt to find a substitute affectional relationship outside of the home.

Peer Group Associations. Female delinquents are often relatively well adjusted in terms of peer interaction, but they associate differentially with other delinquent girls and with "wild" boys. Group relationships in this case play only an attenuated role in female delinquency, for these offenders do not exhibit the characteristics of a subculture.

Contact with Defining Agencies. Girl delinquents often get involved in police contacts, probation case loads, and institutional commitment. In these settings they are likely to be hostile and defiant toward correctional personnel. However, it does not appear that these experiences have negative consequences which drive the offenders to continue their deviant behavior in adulthood.

IX. *"Behavior Problem" Delinquent*

DEFINITIONAL DIMENSIONS

Offense Behavior. This category represents something of a residual pigeonhole for offenders who commit individualistic, "bizarre" offenses which are often quite serious in nature. Arson, homosexual acts, isolated acts of aggression, and various deviant sexual acts are the kinds of offenses included here. Offenders of this type are frequently diagnosed as "neurotic" or "prepsychotic" by guidance clinics.

Interactional Setting. This offender normally commits delinquencies in "lone-wolf" fashion. Moreover, the juvenile tends to be shy and withdrawn and cut off from frequent interaction with peers. The delinquent acts do not occur within the framework of a supportive peer structure.

Self-Concept. Offenders of this type exhibit nondelinquent self-views. The individual sees himself as "different" from both delinquents and nondelinquents. He is likely to be quite ignorant of behavior patterns of systematic delinquents. The offender is quite introverted, exhibiting a number of private concerns about himself.

Attitudes. Juveniles of this type exhibit conventional attitudes toward the police, schools, and so forth. To the extent that they show deviant attitudes, these are likely to center around sexual themes.

Role-Career. These offenders commit only a few delinquent offenses but ones which are quite serious in character. Consequently, they are likely to get into the hands of the police and the juvenile court. In turn, they frequently are referred to child guidance clinics, to psychiatric facilities, or in some cases, to custodial institutions. They tend to get into further behavioral difficulties in adult life, but frequently these predicaments are not criminal in form. Some of these individuals end up as inmates in mental hospitals.

BACKGROUND DIMENSIONS

Social Class. Because this type of delinquency is not class-linked, it appears at various class levels. The causal variables in this case are largely independent of social class "life styles."

Family Background. The family situation from which these individuals derive tends to be atypical in a variety of ways. In the case of offenders who engage in deviant sex acts, the family atmosphere usually is one in which seductive interaction occurs between parents and children or in which repressive parental attitudes regarding sexual matters are found. In other cases, a more general condition of parental repression exists. Case investigations of these offenders usually turn up abundant evidence of peculiar patterns of parent-child interaction.

Peer Group Associations. These offenders are "lone wolves," both in terms of delinquent activities and in terms of more general behavior. They have few friends and are regarded by their peers as "strange" and "peculiar."

Contact with Defining Agencies. The contacts this offender has with courts, guidance clinics, and the like tend to be of neutral significance as far as continuation in delinquency is concerned. The problems which have led to involvement in delinquency outweigh any negative effects that contacts with defining agencies produce. On the other hand, treatment agencies tend not to have any positive effect upon the offender either.

A Typology of Criminals

The discussion to follow presents a criminal typology based upon earlier work by the author and Donald L. Garrity.[4]

[4] Don C. Gibbons and Donald L. Garrity, "Definition and Analysis of Certain Criminal Types," *Journal of Criminal Law, Criminology and Police Science,* Vol. 53 (March 1962), 27-35. This initial statement of criminal types has recently been subjected to criticism by Roebuck. See Julian B. Roebuck, "A Criticism of Gibbons' and Garrity's Criminal Typology," *Journal of Criminal Law, Criminology and Police Science,* Vol. 54 (December 1963), 476-78. His remarks suggest that the typology is defective because it is not based upon legal offense categories, but rather, upon nonlegalistic criteria. This comment is based on a misconception regarding the definitional variables in the typology.

The following fifteen patterns of adult criminal behavior are identified in the typology:

    I. Professional thief
    II. Professional "heavy" criminal
    III. Semiprofessional property criminal
    IV. Property offender—"one-time loser"
    V. Automobile thief—"joyrider"
    VI. Naive check forger
    VII. White-collar criminal
    VIII. Professional "fringe" violator
    IX. Embezzler
    X. Personal offender—"one-time loser"
    XI. "Psychopathic" assaultist
    XII. Violent sex offender
    XIII. Nonviolent sex offender—"rapo"
    XIV. Nonviolent sex offender—statutory rape
    XV. Narcotic addict—heroin

Nine of these types have careers of property crime, and the remaining six are personal offenders. Types I through VI all show patterns of conventional criminality, that is, forms of criminal behavior which the general public has in mind when it thinks of "crime." Of these, the two professional criminal careers are infrequently encountered in treatment case loads because of the considerable crime skill exhibited by incumbents of these categories. The third type, the semiprofessional property offender, is a major therapy problem in many correctional settings. These are individuals who engage in crime as an occupation, but without much skill, and as a result, frequently end up in the hands of various correctional agencies. "One-time loser," property offenders are also

---

Legal categories are employed, but the typology also pays attention to such matters as variations in crime skills, interactional partners in criminality, and so forth. In this regard, the approach utilized closely follows the recommendations of Cressey, [Donald R. Cressey, "Criminological Research and the Definition of Crimes," *American Journal of Sociology*, Vol. 56 (May 1951), 546-51]. Cressey advises that the criminologist must deal with homogeneous units within the broad and heterogeneous rubric of crime. He also suggests that although the criminologist must work within the limits of legal definitions, he may find it necessary to identify criminalistic behavior systems which cut across or transcend specific legal categories. Roebuck also declares that the Gibbons and Garrity scheme is too inclusive. However, this is a matter to be examined by research designed to investigate a hypothesized set of offender types. It is not an issue to be settled by fiat.

found in agency case loads, but in contrast to semiprofessionals, they do not exhibit well-developed criminalistic attitudes or self-definitions. Members of the fifth type, "joyriders," are adult counterparts of automobile-stealing juveniles. The naive check forger represents another type of deviant who is lacking in criminalistic attitudes and self-image; but unlike the "one-time loser," the check forger engages in repetitive acts of law violation.

Types VII, VIII, and IX all show criminal patterns that are sometimes lumped together under the rubric of "white-collar crime." However, there are good reasons for differentiating the kinds of criminal behavior specified in Type VII from the other two kinds of illegal activity. As the term is used here, "white-collar crime" refers to systematic illegal behavior carried on by individuals in the course of their regular business operations. This is the general meaning given to the term by its originator, E. H. Sutherland.[5] Professional "fringe" violators, on the other hand, are persons who engage in actions which are "deviant" within a particular professional group. The illegal actions in question involve the use of professional skills, such as abortion. Embezzlers are still a different breed, for they are persons who steal *from* their employers.

Types X and XI identify offenders who are engaged in crimes of violence. Type X describes behavior patterns of individuals who commit homicides, and Type XI outlines a kind of behavior which is less common and which is carried on by psychiatrically deviant persons.

Types XII, XIII, and XIV specify the characteristics of different sex offender roles. Type XII is represented by criminal individuals who engage in violent sexual assaults. Happily, these persons are infrequently encountered in the offender population or in treatment case loads. They engage in extraordinarily bizarre and violent sexual assaults which often culminate in homicide, and at the same time, they are therapy cases for which no ready solution can be found. Type XIII defines another form of sexual misconduct, child molesting and exhibitionism. Offenders in this category are also difficult therapy cases, but they differ in important ways from the members of Type XII. The individuals in the statutory rape category are, in turn, quite unlike the members of the other two types.

---

[5] Edwin H. Sutherland, *White Collar Crime* (New York: The Dryden Press, Inc., 1949).

Heroin users, Type XV, represent a final category of criminal that is relatively similar to the juvenile drug user identified in the delinquent typology.

The presentation departs somewhat from the format of the delinquent typology, in that five of the types will be described in abridged form. These five patterns of criminal behavior are analytically important but they do not loom large in the population of offenders in treatment settings. For example, "white-collar crime" is an important type of deviant behavior, but the participants in this activity are infrequently found in therapy situations. Hence a detailed discussion of white-collar criminals is somewhat irrelevant to the purposes of this book. Similarly, the "professional thief" is an important type insofar as the learning process involved in this behavior has implications for general causal theories in criminology. But, professional thieves are few in number and are seldom encountered in treatment case loads, so that a detailed discussion of them is not called for in the sections on treatment. Several other types are also mentioned only briefly, for reasons that will become apparent.

This typological scheme does not represent an inclusive system for there are forms of criminal behavior which are not included in it, such as racketeering or homosexuality. Also, certain forms of behavior, such as professional counterfeiting and professional forgery, are not specifically included. However, in these two instances, offenders who engage in these activities are very similar to the criminal labeled as the "professional 'heavy' criminal," even though violence and coercion are not normally employed in forgery and counterfeiting. These patterns are similar to that of the professional "heavy" because counterfeiters, forgers, and "heavies" exhibit similar social-psychological characteristics and social backgrounds.

By way of summary, the typology below represents a reasonable middle ground between gross systems of differentiation among offenders, such as "property" and "personal" criminals, and categorical systems which employ an extremely large number of types, such as a scheme based on specific offense labels. Although some of the type descriptions doubtless are defective and in error at specific points, most of these types do have empirical counterparts. At this juncture in the development of typological descriptions, not much more can be expected from any typological system.

I. Professional Thief

Professional theft is a highly skilled and esoteric form of crime involving such activities as "the wire," "the rag," "the pigeon drop," Spanish prisoner letters, shoplifting ("boosting"), and pocket-picking. These activities and the persons who engage in them have been described in detail by Sutherland, Maurer, and others.[6]

There is reason to believe that offenders of this type, who have never been extremely numerous, are rapidly disappearing in the United States. For one thing, the opportunities to "fix" cases with the police and to buy police protection and immunity from apprehension probably have declined markedly in this country in the past twenty years or so. In addition, certain forms of professional theft or "grift" have probably become obsolete because of changes in the structure of American society. It is probable that carnival grift has declined with the growth of metropolitan areas and the decline of traditional carnival operations in small towns. Finally, it may well be that naive victims have also become scarce, so that such activities as Spanish prisoner swindles have become more difficult to carry on.

The evidence regarding professional thieves indicates that these persons employ complex crime skills of a nonviolent kind in which essentially primary group relationships are established with a "mark" or victim. In turn, this relationship of confidence and trust is then systematically betrayed. The evidence also points to the importance of differential association with thieves as the means by which an individual comes to be a thief.

Relatively little is known about the backgrounds of potential professional thieves. However, recruitment into theft is in part a function of differential opportunities. Hence persons employed as taxicab drivers, bellboys, and bartenders may be the kinds of individuals most often recruited into professional theft by virtue of the fact that they work at occupations which bring them into contact with members of the criminal underworld. In addition, there is

---

[6] Edwin H. Sutherland, *The Professional Thief* (Chicago: University of Chicago Press, 1937); David W. Maurer, *The Big Con* (New York: Bobbs-Merrill Co., 1940); Maurer, *Whiz Mob* (Gainesville, Fla.: American Dialect Society, 1955).

some basis for supposing that a kind of personality pattern or organization of a "budding grifter" form is also involved here.[7] That is, recruits into professional theft may be chosen from among those individuals who are ingratiating, proficient in verbal skills, and who have manipulative skills in interpersonal relationships.

II. Professional "Heavy" Criminal

This typology distinguishes a number of criminal role-patterns involving property crime. Two of these distinctions are between "professional 'heavy' criminals" and "semiprofessional property offenders." In this particular case, the typology suggests the existence of two clearly distinct patterns which are, in fact, different from each other only in degree. The dividing line between professional and semiprofessional property offenders is somewhat arbitrary. On the whole, professional "heavies" are highly skilled, they earn large sums of money from criminal activity, and they work at this occupation full time. Semiprofessionals tend to be relatively unskilled, they are low paid for their criminal activities, and they work at crime on a part-time basis in some cases. Doubtless many offenders could be found who would fall clearly into one or another of these types. But on the other hand, there would be some criminals who might be difficult to classify, in that technical skill, amount of profit from crime, and involvement in criminality are matters of degree rather than dichotomous in character.

DEFINITIONAL DIMENSIONS

Offense Behavior. Professional "heavy" criminals engage in armed robbery, burglary, and other direct assaults upon property. They are highly skilled at crime, so that although the element of coercion and threat of violence is involved here, actual force is rarely employed. The *modus operandi* of professional "heavy" criminals involves a relatively lengthy period of detailed planning prior to the execution of the criminal offense. The actual burglary or robbery is then accomplished swiftly, with the offenders employing the element of surprise to avoid the risk of apprehension.

Interactional Setting. Most of the activities of professional "heavy" criminals are carried on as team or "mob" oper-

---

[7] Richard L. Jenkins, *Breaking Patterns of Defeat* (Philadelphia: J. B. Lippincott Co., 1954), pp. 148-58.

ations. Although robberies can on some occasions be carried out by a single offender, most burglaries and robberies by professionals utilize a number of crime partners. The crime partners are involved in specialized roles, so that one of the participants may be the "rod man" while another is the "wheel man," that is, a specialist in driving getaway cars.

Self-Concept. Professional "heavies" define themselves as criminals and as professionals in criminality. They exhibit pride in their specialized skills and view crime as a lucrative and satisfying way of life. Professionals draw clear distinctions between themselves and other offenders, whom they regard as amateurs.

Attitudes. The attitudes of the professional "heavy" toward the police range from scorn for inept policemen regarded as "clowns" to respect for competent police workers. In either event, the professional does not exhibit great hostility toward the police. The police are regarded as necessary persons who have a job to do. The professional "heavy" shows somewhat negative attitudes toward conventional work roles, inasmuch as crime seems to him to be a preferable way of earning a livelihood.

Role-Career. Professional "heavies" are normally from urban, lower-class backgrounds. Most of them began their criminal careers as predatory gang delinquents (Type I). This does not mean that most predatory gang offenders become professional "heavies," but rather that "heavies" are selected out of a large group of gang delinquents. The "heavy" usually goes through a process of increasing differential involvement with older professionals from whom he learns necessary crime skills. Persons who engage in professional property offenses tend to continue criminal activities into middle age, whereupon many of them ultimately "retire" into noncriminal occupations.

BACKGROUND DIMENSIONS

Social Class. See Type I, delinquent typology. Offenders of this type are from urban, lower-class backgrounds.

Family Background. See Type I, delinquent typology. As adults, professional "heavies" tend to be involved in conventional marital relationships.

Peer Group Associations. See Type I, delinquent typology. As adults, professional "heavies" are heavily involved in differential association with other professionals. Such association is necessary in order for a person to learn technical crime skills and to practice them. In addition, professionals tend to associate differentially with each other in noncriminal activities.

Contact with Defining Agencies. See Type I, delinquent typology. As adults, professional "heavy" criminals normally have minimal contact with the police, courts, and correctional institutions. The degree of skill employed in professional crimes is sufficient to minimize the risks of detection or apprehension. Consequently, professionals are rarely seen in correctional institutions.

III. Semiprofessional Property Criminal

DEFINITIONAL DIMENSIONS

Offense Behavior. Semiprofessional property offenders engage in strong-arm robberies, holdups, burglaries, larcenies, and similar direct assaults upon personal or private property. They employ crime skills which are relatively simple and uncomplicated. For example, strong-arm robbery does not involve much detailed planning and careful execution of the crime, but rather, the application of crude physical force in order to relieve a victim of his money. This type is referred to as semiprofessional crime, because even though technical skill is not characteristic of these offenders, most of them attempt to carry on crime as an occupation.

Interactional Setting. Many of the offenses of the semiprofessional offender are two-person affairs involving an offender and a victim, for example, strong-arm robbery and liquor store and gas station stickups. On occasion, semiprofessionals operate in collections of several crime partners as in instances of burglary and safe-robbery. In either event, the criminal act tends to be direct and unsophisticated, so that a complex interactional pattern is rarely involved.

Self-Concept. Semiprofessional property criminals view themselves as criminals. Additionally, the semiprofessional sees himself as an individual who has few alternatives to criminal behavior and as a victim of a corrupt society in which everyone has a "racket." Thus the semiprofessional is relieved from any sense of guilt regarding his criminality by deflecting blame onto "the system."

Attitudes. The attitudes of the semiprofessional offender toward the police tend to be more hostile and antagonistic than is the case with professional "heavies." Doubtless this is in considerable part a function of the greater number of contacts with police agents experienced by this offender. In the same way, the semiprofessional's views of the courts and correctional agents are more hostile than those of the professional "heavy." Semiprofessionals also denigrate conventional occupations as a way of life, holding that "only slobs work." They frequently show a rather diffuse set of bitter and resentful attitudes toward, not only the police and correctional agents, but toward their parents, social agencies, schools, and other groups as well.

Role-Career. Semiprofessional property offenders represent the more usual outcome of patterns of predatory gang delinquency, as contrasted to the professional "heavy" adult outcome. That is, most adult semiprofessional offenders exhibit juvenile backgrounds of predatory gang behavior. In turn, many juvenile gang offenders continue in criminality as semiprofessionals. As an adult, the semiprofessional rapidly accumulates an extensive "rap sheet," or record of crimes and institutional commitments. Because of the low degree of skill involved in the criminality of the semiprofessionals, the risks of apprehension, conviction, and incarceration are high. Many semiprofessionals spend a considerable part of their early adult years in penal institutions where they are likely to be identified as "right guys" or antiadministration inmates. It does not appear that conventional treatment efforts are successful in deflecting many of these persons away from continuation in crime. On the other hand, many of them ultimately do withdraw from crime careers upon reaching the early middle-age period.

BACKGROUND DIMENSIONS

Social Class. See Type I, delinquent typology. Most semiprofessional property offenders continue their lower-class social and residential affiliations in adulthood.

Family Background. See Type I, delinquent typology. In adulthood, semiprofessional offenders usually become involved in marital arrangements, but these are often rather unstable. Among other things, marital instability is engendered by the lengthy periods of incarceration experienced by these offenders which effectively remove them from normal marital participation.

Peer Group Associations. See Type I, delinquent typology. Adult semiprofessional offenders sometimes associate with other criminals of the same type in the commission of criminal offenses. More important, semiprofessionals associate differentially with other criminals in noncriminal contexts. One factor in this differential interaction stems from the pariah status accorded "ex-convicts" in American society. Interaction with other criminals has important consequences for the offender, for such associations provide him with a supportive social system in which shared rationalizations for crime are found and in which shared "antisocial" attitudes are communicated.

Contact with Defining Agencies. The numerous contacts with police no doubt contribute to the hostility expressed by semiprofessionals toward law enforcement agencies. Similarly, the usual outcome of contacts with correctional agents, including treatment workers, is reinforcement of negative attitudes on the part of the offender. It does not appear that correctional therapy produces rehabilitation in most cases. However, it would be an error to assume that continuation in crime is attributable mainly to negative effects of contacts with defining agencies. After all, the semiprofessional acquired hostile views relatively early in life. Additionally, the semiprofessional is a product of a general social milieu in which hostility toward the police and correctional programs is relatively generic in form.

IV. Property Offender—"One-Time Loser"

DEFINITIONAL DIMENSIONS

Offense Behavior. This category refers to offenders who commit a single property crime, frequently one which is relatively serious in nature such as grand theft. It excludes embezzlers, who also frequently commit only a single, isolated criminal act. "One-time losers" normally show little skill in criminality so that arrests are frequent.

Interactional Setting. The criminal acts of one-time losers are often carried out by the offender acting alone. In those cases in which several crime partners are involved, all of these persons are likely to be amateur offenders.

Self-Concept. Individuals of this type exhibit noncriminal self-images. The offender usually readily admits that he has been involved in a serious deviant act, but he maintains that it was an atypical act and that he is not a "real criminal." When seen in a correctional institution, he maintains that he is different from most of the inmates in the institution. In turn, he is seen as different by the inmate group. "One-time losers" are regarded as "square Johns" by other prisoners, that is, as aliens in the criminalistic subculture of the prison.

Attitudes. These offenders verbalize prosocial sentiments. In prison, this offender is likely to be planning to resume a law-abiding career upon release. In most cases, he was working at some conventional occupation before his arrest. His attitudes toward conventional work roles are the same as those of law-abiding citizens. Similarly, individuals of this type are usually married and they exhibit conventional attitudes regarding marital activities.

Role-Career. The one-time loser property offender usually shows no delinquency record and no prior criminal record other than minor law violations such as "drunkenness" or "disturbing the peace." Such persons are frequently placed on probation, and they usually complete the probation period satisfactorily. Some who have committed a property offense involving a large financial loss to the victim are sentenced to prison. Their adjustment there is satisfactory, they are infrequently involved in conduct infractions, and they earn early paroles. They complete the parole period satisfactorily and do not re-enter the offender population.

BACKGROUND DIMENSIONS

Social Class. These violators are from several social class levels, but the most common is lower-middle class. Many one-time losers are persons who earn modest incomes from skilled or semiskilled occupations and who are normally from nonslum areas or from relatively rural, small towns.

Family Background. Most individuals in this type are from relatively stable and conventional family backgrounds. Behavior of this kind cannot be linked to any critical kind of family background situation.

Peer Group Associations. There is nothing particularly unusual or striking about the peer associations of one-time losers, either as juveniles or as adults. These offenders receive no peer group support or encouragement for criminal acts.

Contact with Defining Agencies. Contacts with defining agencies are not causally significant except perhaps in a minor but positive way. These offenders share the same interpretation of their criminal acts as do law enforcement agencies. The individual views crime as an atypical act for him. Although he may develop rationalizations which excuse this atypical, "bad" act, such rationalizations are not powerful enough to counteract other prosocial attitudes. Accordingly, these offenders are not likely to repeat their deviant activities, quite apart from any rehabilitative program in which they might participate.

V. Automobile Thief—"Joyrider"

This adult type represents only a slightly older version of the juvenile delinquent pattern described as Type V. Some older juvenile joyriders are prosecuted as criminals in a criminal court rather than as juveniles in a youth court. Such individuals then turn up in penal institutions for young felons, that is, adult reformatories. The majority of those offenders who are dealt with in penal institutions apparently succeed on parole and do not return to the adult offender population.

VI. Naive Check Forger

DEFINITIONAL DIMENSIONS

Offense Behavior. Naive check forgers engage in unsophisticated forms of forgery. They normally pass "NSF" ("Not Sufficient Funds") checks on their personal checks and written on their own bank accounts. In some cases, personal checks signed by some fictitious name are passed. But in neither instance does the forger resort to such skilled activities as passing fraudulent payroll checks. Naive check forgers normally have no prior record of delinquency and a record of only minor adult crimes. The naive forger often passes a bad check a number of times: that is, naive forgery is not a "one shot" form of crime.

Interactional Setting. Check passing is an activity carried on by the offender acting alone. Checks are passed in liquor stores, supermarkets, and other retail business agencies. Not infrequently the check forger passes "NSF" checks at a business location where he is personally known, such as at a neighborhood bar.

Self-Concept. Naive check forgers do not view themselves as "real criminals." They tend to exhibit stereotyped rationalizations of the form: "You can't kill anyone with a fountain pen" or "No one is hurt by forgery because supermarkets make great profits and they don't miss a little money lost through bad checks." Although the forger admits that passing bad checks is outside the range of conventional and acceptable behavior, he argues that there are special circumstances which have compelled him to commit these acts.

Attitudes. Naive check forgers exhibit attitudes which are generally prosocial but which are somewhat atypical of law-abiding citizens. The check forger indicates commitment to conventional work roles and marital activities, but he exhibits dissatisfaction, bitterness, and resentment concerning his own participation in such activities. He often shows a pattern of occupational and marital instability which precedes involvement in forgery.

Role-Career. The role-career of the naive check forger normally begins in adulthood and is not preceded by delinquency. Onset of the role-career is preceded by difficulties in employment, marriage, and general social participation. The check forger gets involved in forgery after he has become significantly isolated from stable social ties. Once check forgery is embarked upon, repeated instances of it are not uncommon. The forger often is handled informally and outside the framework of criminal courts for his first episodes of forgery. Then, when he is dealt with in a court, he is frequently placed on probation. Probation violation rates are quite high for this class of offender, so that many of them ultimately make their way into correctional institutions.

BACKGROUND DIMENSIONS

Social Class. Check forgers are not exclusively from a single economic or class background. However, many of them would be categorized as middle class, for they have had relatively comfortable economic circumstances and have been employed at white-collar jobs or at similar occupational levels.

Family Background. There is little reason to suppose that naive forgers come from extremely disordered or unconventional family settings. It does not appear that check forgers have experienced parental contacts of a severe or atypical kind. Additionally, the adult family background of the check forger is relatively conventional. Many naive forgers are married, but disruptions in marital relationships often play some part in the development of check forgery. It does appear that the marital situation of the check passer has not been entirely harmonious prior to the forgery activities.

Peer Group Associations. There is no clearly significant role played by peer group associations in the case of naive forgery. Certainly the forger does not participate in a supportive subculture of forgers. Instead, it is commonly true that the naive forger discovers for the first time in prison that other offenders behave in ways similar to his own.

Contact with Defining Agencies. Check forgers tend to be dealt with informally for initial violations of the law and then to be handled in the least punitive way when dealt with through the courts, for example, probation. It may be that swift and rather dramatic action by defining agencies in the first instance of check forgery would be positive in its consequences. Stated differently, it may be that conventional procedures now employed with check passers contribute to the continuation of this behavior. These may lead the forger to assume that forgery can be carried on with relative impunity. Perhaps a more traumatic and earlier confrontation with the defining agencies would result in a different career outcome in this case.

VII. White-Collar Criminal

The concept of "white-collar crime" has been mishandled and distorted in the period since that term was introduced by Sutherland. All sorts of criminal acts have been lumped under the term. The only thing many of these share in common is that they are carried on by persons of above average income. Although

Sutherland himself contributed to the ambiguous character of the term through some of the examples he cited of white-collar crime, he nonetheless did have a fairly clear and specific definition in mind. For the most part, he employed the concept to refer to those violations of law representing conduct counter to state and federal business regulatory statutes. Furthermore, he intended the concept to include only those violations of law within the economic order which were carried on as a part of regular business practices. Crudely stated, white-collar crime means those criminal acts in which employees steal or violate the law for the benefit of their employer (although the individual employee may benefit from these violations too). Such crimes as embezzlement represent stealing *from* the employer. The employer does not encourage or sanction such activities, and they are not properly classified as white-collar crime.

In the typology, three types of criminal behavior which have sometimes been lumped together are defined. The typology discusses white-collar criminals, embezzlers, and "fringe violators." The description of white-collar criminals to follow is abridged, for such persons rarely receive treatment. Embezzlers, on the other hand, are represented in correctional case loads, as are "fringe violators," but in lesser numbers.

The white-collar criminal category is comprised of those persons in business and corporate organizations who violate state and federal regulatory statutes. The violations are usually processed by such federal regulatory agencies as the Federal Trade Commission, the Securities and Exchange Commission, and the Attorney General's office. Informal or civil court disposition of these cases is common, because of the difficulties of criminal prosecution. That is, partly because many of these activities are complex in character, it is often difficult to demonstrate that a clear-cut violation of law has occurred.

"Ignorance of the law" is not, in most cases, an important factor in white-collar violations. That is, the offenders were involved in activities which they recognized as illegal or probably illegal. What does appear to be significant in these cases is a process in which business and corporate groups have come to define violations of regulatory statutes as acceptable or necessary conduct. Many white-collar criminals acknowledge the moral superiority of regulatory provisions over prevailing business ethics, but legitimacy is withdrawn from these regulatory norms on the grounds that violation of such laws is necessary in order to survive in business, in order to regularize competition, and so on. In other words, it is likely that many white-collar violators would prefer to conform to the law, but at the same time, they define the economic situation as demanding deviant conduct. If this line of argument is correct, explanations seeking to locate the genesis of white-collar criminal acts in the backgrounds and personalities of the offenders would be misguided. Instead, white-collar criminals are normal, conventional persons who come to learn definitions of the situation favorable to violation of law in the course of involvement in business or corporate organization.

VIII. Professional "Fringe" Violator

DEFINITIONAL DIMENSIONS

Offense Behavior. Professional "fringe" violators are those members of legitimate professions who employ professional skills in the commission of crimes which are not regarded as legitimate activities within the profession. Illegal abortions by physicians represent the clearest cases, particularly in those instances of "abortion mills" in which the physician is involved in full-time, systematic practice of abortion. Also included would be those illegal practices that are occasionally found among members of the legal profession. This type does not include ordinary crimes committed by persons who incidentally happen to be professional persons.

Interactional Setting. Professional fringe violators are normally involved in two-person crimes involving the offender and a "victim." In the instance of abortions, no victim in the usual sense is involved, for the aborted female has sought out the services of the abortionist. Although fringe violators are regarded by other professionals as engaged in behavior which is beyond the pale, many of these offenders are at the same time abetted in their activities by other professional persons. In the case of abortion, for example, many abortionists commit these illegal acts upon females who have been referred to them by other physicians who are themselves unwilling to perform abortions.

Self-Concept. Fringe violators regard themselves as legitimate professional persons and not as criminals. Although the offender acknowledges the illegal character of his actions, he normally offers some explanation or rationalization by which he attempts to square criminality with his noncriminal self-image.

Attitudes. Fringe violators exhibit conventional, prosocial attitudes. Many abortionists would argue that they are performing a service which is technically illegal but which is necessary. In turn, they maintain that the proper solution to the problem of abortion would be to modify the legal statutes which define such acts as criminal.

Role-Career. In the nature of this form of criminality, fringe violators begin their criminal careers late in life. Some of them commit only a single law violation, others engage in several episodes of criminality, and still others are involved in the systematic practice of abortion and the like. Most of these law violations do not result in detection or prosecution. Among those offenders who are prosecuted, different outcomes develop. Some desist from further crimes of this kind, whereas in other cases, prosecution and incarceration fails to deter the offender from further deviant acts.

BACKGROUND DIMENSIONS

Social Class. By definition, professional fringe violators are middle-income, middle-class persons. Law violations of this kind are likely to be differentially common among professional persons in urban areas and less common among rural or small-town professionals.

Family Background. Professional fringe violators are in most cases from relatively conventional family backgrounds.

Peer Group Associations. Peer associations are relatively unimportant in this type of crime, except insofar as professional peers have failed to maintain the behavior of the offender within professional norms and standards. As suggested earlier, members of professional groups in which these kinds of violations occur tend to be somewhat ambivalent about certain illegal activities involving professional skills. This lack of strong moral censure for these acts plays some part in the behavior of fringe violators.

Contact with Defining Agencies. Fringe violators tend to have few contacts with defining agencies. It appears that for those professionals who are apprehended, convicted, and sentenced to institutions, such experiences have a relatively neutral impact. That is, in the case of those individuals who desist from further law violations, it is likely that they are responding more to concerns about their standing within the professional group than anything else. Regarding those offenders who commit further offenses, it is unlikely that they do so as a consequence of contacts with correctional agents or other defining agencies.

IX. Embezzler

DEFINITIONAL DIMENSIONS

Offense Behavior. This type involves persons who violate positions of trust by stealing from an employer. The category excludes those employees who pilfer small amounts of merchandise from an employer. The embezzler is an employee who converts a large sum of his employer's money to his own uses, usually through some form of alteration of business records.

Interactional Setting. The interactional setting of embezzlement is one in which the violator ostensibly performs a conventional occupational task, while, in secrecy, he also engages in criminal acts. The embezzler takes great pains to keep his illegal activities minimally visible. Normally, the criminal actions of the embezzler are unknown to the employer, to the spouse of the offender, and to other associates of the deviant.

Self-Concept. The embezzler exhibits a noncriminal self-image, but he shows relatively elaborate rationalizations for his conduct when discovered in embezzlement. These often include allegations that he was only "borrowing" the money, not stealing it. It appears that such rationalizations are contrived by the offender *before* he begins to embezzle. They allow him to square deviant activities with his self-image as a law-abiding person. When the embezzler is sent to prison upon conviction, he is likely to argue that unlike the other inmates, he is not a "real" criminal.

Attitudes. The embezzler is characterized by conventional, prosocial attitudes. The offender indicates that he acknowledges the "bad" character of such acts, but he has rationalizations which excuse him from culpability for these "bad" and "evil" actions.

Role-Career. The embezzler is normally a person without any delinquent or criminal record prior to involvement in embezzlement. One reason for this is, of course, that persons with criminal records are not able to obtain positions of trust in the first place. A great many detected embezzlers are dealt with informally by their employers or by bonding agencies, so that only a small and perhaps biased sample of them is handled within criminal courts. Those offenders who are convicted and sentenced to institutions tend to make a good adjustment in that setting. Upon release, further violations of the law are unlikely. However, it is probable that many paroled embezzlers find readjustment to civilian society somewhat difficult insofar as their criminal records create impediments for them. That is, a paroled embezzler is likely to have some trouble obtaining another position of trust.

BACKGROUND DIMENSIONS

Social Class. Embezzlers tend as a group to be persons from relatively comfortable, middle-class backgrounds.

Family Background. The parental background of the embezzler appears to be of little significance in the explanation of deviation. Embezzlers do not develop out of any specific parent-child interaction pattern. On the other hand, the offender's adult family pattern does have some significance, for some of his "nonshareable" problems, often described as "wine, women, and song" difficulties, relate to patterns of family activity. It is likely that many acts of embezzlement develop as attempts on the part of the person to sustain a standard of living and to live according to a pattern of expectations for which his legitimate income is insufficient.

Peer Group Associations. The peer associations of embezzlers are of little significance in the development of this behavior. Such offenders do not learn how to embezzle or attitudes favorable to embezzlement from their associates. It may be that peer associations play some part in embezzlement in that the offender is unable to communicate about certain "nonshareable" problems with his peers.

Contact with Defining Agencies. Contacts with the police, courts, and correctional agencies do not seem to be highly significant for embezzlers. In prison, the embezzler is regarded by other inmates as a "square John." He associates differentially with other "square Johns," and such associations tend to reinforce the offender's conception of himself as a law-abiding citizen.

X. *Personal Offender—"One-Time Loser"*

DEFINITIONAL DIMENSIONS

Offense Behavior. This type includes offenders who are involved in major crimes of a personal and normally violent nature. Murder, negligent manslaughter, and serious assaults are the forms of behavior included here.

Interactional Setting. Personal offender, "one-time losers" are normally engaged in offenses which take place with a victim who is well known to the offender. Homicide in which the victim is the offender's spouse is the classic case. In cases where the offender and victim are members of the same family group, the criminal act is often the culmination of a long period of tense relationships. In some instances of wife-murder, the offender has been involved in wife-beating for a long time. Finally, the person administers a beating to his wife which turns out to be fatal.

Self-Concept. One-time loser, personal offenders exhibit noncriminal self-images. Frequently the violator himself is involved in reporting his offense to the police, due to the fact that after it has occurred, the individual is contrite, guilty, and repentant.

Attitudes. The attitudes of the one-time loser are conventional and prosocial. In prison, these persons are designated by other inmates as "square Johns," that is, as prisoners who are aliens in the criminal subculture.

Role-Career. Most personal offenders show no extensive delinquency record or previous pattern of criminality. On occasion, the offender has been involved in a pattern of minor offenses such as drunkenness and wife-beating. Criminals of this type receive long prison sentences. When they are released on parole, as many are, their adjustment is normally quite satisfactory.

BACKGROUND DIMENSIONS

Social Class. One-time loser, personal criminals do not come from one specific social class background. However, those who are from lower-class backgrounds have often been involved in aggression preceding the major violent episode, partly because of the subcultural approval of interpersonal violence in lower-class groups.

Family Background. It does not appear that there is a specific family background of parent-child interaction which leads to a "violence-prone" personality type. The early family backgrounds of these persons are quite varied. On the other hand, the adult family situation is much involved in the illegal behavior of the person. Cases of extreme violence normally develop out of a marital situation in which tensions have existed for a long time between the victim and the offender.

Peer Group Associations. The peer affiliations of the personal offender apparently have little significance in the development of violent behavior.

Contact with Defining Agencies. The contacts of the one-time loser, personal offender with defining agencies are of neutral significance. The person shares the same definition of his behavior as do the defining agencies. He tends to agree that he should be punished for his deviant act. Correctional institutions appear to have little effect, positive or otherwise, upon such individuals.

XI. *"Psychopathic" Assaultist*

This type is the adult counterpart of the delinquent pattern, Type VII. Adult offenders of this kind commit a variety of offenses, against both property and persons. Property crimes are frequently accompanied by violent acts which seem clearly out of proportion to the demands of the situation. That is, the "psychopathic" assaultist engages in robbery-assaults in which his coercive and violent actions are essentially "senseless." Offenders of this type are likely to be diagnosed as "psychopaths" when they turn up in correctional institutions. Such persons appear to be the product of the same causal background as delinquents of Type VII. In prison, the offender is defined as an "outlaw" or "gorilla" by other inmates. Such a designation is placed upon a prisoner who is feared by other inmates because of that offender's asocial and violent disposition. Criminals of this type are frequently recidivists who spend short periods of time outside of prison and long terms in correctional institutions.

XII. Violent Sex Offender

DEFINITIONAL DIMENSIONS

Offense Behavior. Violent sex offenders engage in attacks upon female victims which are ostensibly sexual in character. The assault is usually accompanied by acts of extreme and bizarre violence such as slashing of the victim, cutting off of breasts, and other activities. This behavior is in no sense conventional statutory rape in which the "victim" is a willing participant in sexual intercourse but is below the age of consent. Violent sex assaultists employ extreme forms of aggression against the victim, sometimes culminating in homicide. In some cases, normal sexual acts are not a part of the actions of the person.

Interactional Setting. Violent sex assaults are two-person affairs between a victim and an offender. Victims are chosen in several ways. Some are casual pickups, and others are ambushed or surprised by the offender; in either case, the victim has not been in interaction with the offender for any lengthy period of time prior to the commission of the criminal act.

Self-Concept. Violent sex offenders think of themselves as noncriminal, law-abiding citizens, but they are likely to exhibit some self-awareness that they are "different" from other persons.

Attitudes. The attitudinal structure of the violent sex assaultist is conventional, except in the rather private area of sexual attitudes. These are attitudes which are not highly "visible" or likely to be noticed prior to the commission of a violent sex act.

Role-Career. Most violent sex assaultists have no delinquency record or history of involvement in criminality. On occasion, the violent sex offender has been involved in episodes of "peculiar" conduct, such as minor stabbings of females. The offender is normally apprehended after the commission of the crime, convicted, and sentenced to prison. He normally is incarcerated for a lengthy period of time so that recidivism is unlikely in many cases.

BACKGROUND DIMENSIONS

Social Class. Violent sex criminals seem not to be the product of any single social class background. The etiological factors which lead to this form of criminality are not class-linked in any important way.

Family Background. Although there is considerable confusion about the causal backgrounds which lead to this form of behavior, certain patterns of parent-child interaction are significantly involved. It is likely that the violent sex assaultist is the product of a family pattern of repressive sexual notions, seductive mother-son interaction, or similar conditions.

Peer Group Associations. Patterns of peer group interaction have no specific significance for behavior patterns of this kind.

Contact with Defining Agencies. This violator's contacts with defining agencies apparently are of neutral significance. Such contacts appear not to be harmful, but neither does any treatment seem to have an impressively positive effect.

XIII. *Nonviolent Sex Offender, "Rapo"*

DEFINITIONAL DIMENSIONS

Offense Behavior. This category includes offenders involved in exhibitionism, child-molesting, and incest. A comment is in order regarding the term, "nonviolent." It is true that on occasion, the victims of child-molesters are killed by the offenders. However, this is frequently the result of a panic reaction in which the individual fears that the victim will report him and is not an act motivated by some interest in homicidal behavior or violence. Thus persons in this category who commit homicides differ in two ways from persons in Type XII. The former commit sex acts against physically immature victims and they show no basic motivational component of violent and aggressive interests.

Interactional Setting. The interactional settings in which these crimes occur vary somewhat. In the case of exhibitionism, "victims" are usually persons unknown to the offender, chosen somewhat randomly. Exhibitionism tends to occur at places where female observers are likely to be present—at schools, parks, and the like. In the instance of child-molesting, some victims are unknown to the offender and chosen rather randomly. But others are youngsters who are well known to the deviant—neighborhood children,

children of friends, children of relatives, and the like. Finally, in the case of incest, the victim is obviously well known to the offender.

Self-Concept. The self-image of the nonviolent sex offender is noncriminal in form. Such offenders vehemently deny that they are "real" criminals. Some of them also deny that they did, in fact, commit the acts for which they are imprisoned. Others admit that they engaged in the acts for which they have been charged, but for reasons quite different from the apparent ones. Incest offenders, for example, sometimes maintain that they were not engaging in conventional sexual intercourse with their daughters, but rather that they were carrying out the parental role of "education." They claim not to have experienced any kind of sexual relief from their behavior. By this kind of reasoning, they seek to divest their sexual acts of sexual interpretations. Denial of involvement in sex crimes and avowal of righteous religious sentiments is a common characteristic of nonviolent sex criminals.

Attitudes. The attitudes of nonviolent sex offenders are for the most part conventional and prosocial.

Role-Career. Most criminals in this category are without delinquency records or backgrounds of other criminal activities. Persons who are engaged in this kind of sexual deviation are usually apprehended. In turn, they are usually convicted and then sentenced to long prison terms. Those who are released on parole appear to get reinvolved in such activities in a number of cases.

BACKGROUND DIMENSIONS

Social Class. This form of crime is not class-linked, so that such offenders come from a variety of social class origins.

Family Background. It does not appear that the early parental backgrounds of nonviolent sex offenders are of major significance. But these background experiences may play some contributory role in that the offender is characterized by a timid, retiring personality which resulted from early experiences. However, it appears that the more significant family variables by far have to do with the adult marital situation of the offender. In most cases, a pattern of long-term sexual inadequacy on the part of the individual seems to precede involvement in sex crimes, particularly exhibitionism and child-molesting. In turn, sexual inadequacy appears to be a part of a larger constellation of husband-wife characteristics in which the husband is dominated by a physically and socially more aggressive spouse. The husband has been troubled by the "man or mouse" question, in which he has experienced chronic, nagging doubts about his adequacy as a male. In the case of incest offenders, the family situation is somewhat different. In this kind of behavior, it appears that in many cases the spouse has discouraged the offender from sexual overtures toward her. Not infrequently, the offender's wife has given tacit encouragement to the person engaging in sexual acts with one or more of his daughters. Not uncommonly the incest violator comes to the attention of the authorities by means of reports from persons outside of the offender's family rather than by a complaint from the wife of the offender.

Peer Group Associations.   Peer group interaction patterns are not of major importance in the development of this kind of behavior, except insofar as the associates of the person have contributed to his sense of inadequacy through joking or ridicule directed at him. Such experiences may play a contributory role in the development of behavior patterns of this kind, but they do not play a central part in such activities.

Contact with Defining Agencies.   Nonviolent sex offenders rather frequently get into the hands of the defining agencies. These organizations tend to share the same extremely negative views of such offenders as do citizens generally. Doubtless such notions are communicated to the offender, so that he experiences considerable difficulty in preserving any kind of self-image as a "normal" person. In prison, nonviolent sex offenders are assigned the status of "ding" and "rapo." These terms refer to the lowest social positions occupied by inmates. All of these experiences create difficulties for the criminal, but it is also probable that he would encounter great problems of identity-protection even if he were to receive rather different reactions from the defining agencies, given the general scorn, revulsion, and hostility directed at him by the lay public.

XIV. Nonviolent Sex Offender—Statutory Rape

DEFINITIONAL DIMENSIONS

Offense Behavior.   Persons in this category are adult males who engage in sexual intercourse with minor females. The "victim" is a willing and voluntary participant in the sexual activities.

Interactional Setting.   Statutory rape cases develop in a variety of ways. Some offenders are persons such as sailors who are apprehended "shacking-up" with a minor female in a downtown hotel, for example. Other cases involve adult males who have been carrying on a long-term relationship with a minor female and who have been apprehended for sexual acts with that person. In either instance, the essential character of statutory rape is that two individuals have entered into a cooperative, voluntary sexual relationship which happens to be illegal because of the age of the female. The girl in question is usually dealt with in a juvenile court in cases of statutory rape which result in detection.

Self-Concept.   Statutory rapists regard themselves as law-abiding citizens. They usually view themselves as unlucky persons who were simply doing what everyone else is doing, but who got caught. There is, of course, considerable truth in that claim.

Attitudes.   The attitudes of statutory rapists tend to be conventional and prosocial.

Role-Career.   These persons usually are without any prior record of delinquency or adult criminality. They are essentially law-abiding citizens who have fallen into the hands of the police and courts for technically illegal but culturally widespread acts. Many apprehended and convicted statutory rapists are placed on probation, where they are good risks. Those who are sent to correctional institutions make good adjustments and tend to play the role of "square Johns" in the institution.

BACKGROUND DIMENSIONS

Social Class.   There is little reason to suppose that statutory rape is a class-linked form of behavior. However, there may be some tendency for law-enforcement agencies to take more stringent actions against detected lower-class offenders than they take against other statutory rapists.

Family Background.   The family backgrounds of statutory rapists are usually normal and conventional, lacking in any kind of major interactional problems among family members.

Peer Group Associations.   The peer group affiliations of statutory rapists are conventional ones. They are usually involved in peer associations in which sexual activities are highly regarded, but this is in no way an atypical kind of peer group value.

Contact with Defining Agencies.   Contacts with defining agencies are relatively neutral in effect. Quite probably, some offenders feel some degree of hostility toward the police and courts because they view themselves as merely "unlucky" rather than deviant. But it is doubtful that this hostility leads to any reorganization of the person's self-image or to continuation in criminality.

XV. Narcotic Addict—Heroin

Many adult drug users are the adult counterparts of the delinquent type, Type VI, described earlier. That is, they are persons who began drug use as juveniles and who have continued in a pattern of heroin addiction in adulthood. However, the routes to drug addiction are more varied for adults than for juveniles. Some adult drug users became addicted through medical treatment. More commonly, some drug users are individuals who were introduced to the use of narcotics through participation in some noncriminal, deviant subculture such as that of jazz musicians. Accordingly, the type description below describes some of these addicts better than others, as far as causation is concerned. Note however that persons who have entered into narcotic behavior patterns from several different causal processes tend to become relatively similar when they engage in habitual drug use.

DEFINITIONAL DIMENSIONS

Offense Behavior.   The principal offense behavior of the narcotic addict is possession and use of opiates, usually heroin. However, given the criminal nature of drug use and the fact that narcotics must be obtained illicitly, drug addiction is usually accompanied by other forms of crime. Among male users, various kinds of property crime are resorted to in order to obtain funds for a supply of drugs. These offenses sometimes include burglaries of doctors' offices and cars in order to obtain drugs directly; on other occasions, crimes such as stickups are committed in order to obtain money for the purchase of drugs. Among female addicts, drugs are obtained through thefts and commonly through the proceeds from prostitution.

Interactional Setting.   Most of the criminal offenses of

drug addicts are acts carried on by the user alone, rather than in concert with other narcotic users. This tends to be true both of drug use and narcotics-related crimes. Although addicts associate differentially with other addicts, they engage in drug use itself individually and secretively.

Self-Concept. Although narcotic addicts recognize that drug use is defined as illegal and criminal in nature, they view themselves as a rather special kind of criminal. They argue that narcotic use is not really a criminal act similar to most forms of crime. Instead, it is viewed as a relatively innocuous personal vice which should not be regarded as criminal in nature, in the same way that the use of alcohol or tobacco is not an illegal act. Consequently, although addicts define themselves as "hypes" and addicts, they see themselves as the victims of a capricious and unjust legal system.

Attitudes. The role-related attitudes of narcotic users vary somewhat from one addict to another. Some degree of disdain for conventional work roles, marital roles, and the like is exhibited by many of them. However, it is the member of such subcultures as that of jazz musicians who exhibits the most pronounced hostility toward conventional social roles. This person exhibits considerable antagonism toward "squares" and "square" behavior patterns.

Role-Career. Some addicts begin the use of "heavy" drugs during the adolescent years, whereas others enter into the drug subculture as adults. Regardless of the age at entry into this behavior pattern, the evidence suggests that drug use rapidly becomes a way of life that is usually continued for long periods of time. The usual life history of addicts shows a recurrent pattern of drug use, commitment to an institution or drug hospital, release and relapse into further drug use, re-entry into treatment, release and relapse, and so on. With few exceptions, contemporary measures directed toward rehabilitation appear to be notably unsuccessful.

BACKGROUND DIMENSIONS

Social Class. The routes to drug use are several, so that it does not appear that drug users are recruited from any single social class position, although persons from lower-class situations are quite common in the addict population. This is particularly true of users who began the use of drugs as juveniles.

Family Background. The family backgrounds of addicts tend to vary in terms of the different routes to drug use. Persons who become involved in narcotics through medical treatment, or who get into drug use as members of some deviant subculture such as that of jazz musicians, appear to be the products of relatively conventional family backgrounds in many cases. On the other hand, juvenile drug users who move into the adult addict population tend to be from more disordered family settings.

Peer Group Associations. Except for the medically addicted narcotic user, peer group interaction patterns play an extremely important role in the development of drug use. Most addicts originally get involved in drug use in interaction with addicted peers. These persons define drug use as harmless and pleasant, and they provide the neophyte with rationalizations for drug use, with information about sources of narcotics, and so forth. Once addicted, the addict then becomes dependent upon other users. Drug users as a group provide each other with mutual aid and also with definitions of treatment, "cures," and so forth. It seems likely that one impediment to conventional attempts to resocialize the addict is his continued association with persons who argue that "once an addict, always an addict."

Contact with Defining Agencies. Doubtless the addict's contacts with the defining agencies serve to emphasize the pariah status of narcotic users in American society. These contacts are productive of considerable hostility on the part of the addict directed toward these persons he sees as harassing him. But it seems unlikely that contacts with the defining agencies play a major causal role in drug use.

Diagnostic Rules

This chapter would not be complete without some indication of diagnostic procedures or rules that would be involved in the application of the preceding typologies to treatment diagnosis. The first point to be made was initially voiced in Chapter One, which is that diagnosis, whether of patterns of criminality or some other problem, is not a mechanical process but a skill. In particular, expertise of the highest order is needed in the interviewing of individuals which precedes the statement of a specific diagnosis. Different interviewing techniques elicit different kinds of information from offenders. An inexperienced interrogator is likely to obtain from the subject information which that person thinks the correctional worker wants to hear. Such material may not be accurate. On the other hand, a skilled interviewer is more likely to draw out accurate information from the person, so that his diagnosis is likely, in turn, to be more valid. Although this text is not directly concerned with techniques of interviewing, it should be recognized that effective diagnostic work depends upon skillfully obtained facts about offenders.

Diagnostic activities involve other skills as well. In the last analysis, a diagnosis is an *informed judgment* made by some worker. It is a judgment that a specific individual characterized by a number of peculiarities and unique features falls within some diagnostic pigeonhole, defined in terms of a limited number of general attributes. In this regard, diagnoses of offenders are similar to judgments concerning the mentally disordered. Both attempt to place complex, varied individuals within categories specified in a set of diagnostic nomenclature. For example, consider "paranoid" personalities. The psychiatric syndrome called "paranoia" is one which involves such things as persecutory delusions, which are defined in general terms rather than in detail. In actual diagnostic practice, psychiatrists encounter patients who do not uniformly exhibit the same patterns of delusions or related characteristics. The psychiatrist must ignore many of the details in individual cases and look for some general correspondence between the behavior of a patient and an abstract pattern defined in a psychiatric typology. Treatment classification of offenders operates in the same way. The correctional worker is required to make informed estimates that particular law violators more closely resemble one general pattern than another in a diagnostic system.

An additional diagnostic problem centers about the fact that perfect correspondence between the characteristics in a diagnostic type and the attributes of specific persons is rarely found. Humans are more complicated than descriptions in textbooks, and in addition, those individuals who fit within a type do not show exactly the same characteristics in terms of the dimensions of a typology. Diagnostic schemes deal in averages, for they identify characteristics that are *usually* found appearing together among offenders of some kind. However, in real life, some individuals within a type diverge from the description provided in a typology. For example, not all gang delinquents come from disordered home situations, even though this is a common background of gang members. Accordingly, diagnosis sometimes involves decisions to the effect that a specific individual is sufficiently similar to a particular category in a taxonomy to be identified as a member of that type, even though that person does not show all the characteristics specified in the type description. It is nearly impossible to specify rules in the abstract of the form "Offenders must have *n* number of characteristics to be included within Type *A*." Decisions of this sort are best made in actual diagnostic situations when all the evidence regarding a particular person is at hand.

It must be clear from the foregoing remarks that diagnoses are equally dependent upon (1) skilled, knowledgeable, trained diagnosticians and (2) valid diagnostic typologies. The argument of this text is that the typological devices in this chapter are sufficiently clear and detailed so that offenders can be placed within the types with a reasonable degree of reliability by trained workers. In general, the actual process of classification would proceed as follows. First, a tentative judgment that an individual belongs in a particular type would be made from an examination of the offense behavior and career of that person. This information is usually available in some abundance in the records of the offender. Additional data bearing upon the illegal activities of the person could be elicited from him through interviews. Next, further observations would be gathered regarding the social-psychological characteristics of the person. These are not now routinely collected in the conventional recording and data-gathering procedures in corrections, but there is no reason why they could not be obtained. Finally, evidence regarding the social class background, family history, and other information about the individual would be obtained from existing records and interviews with the person. At this point, the diagnostician would be called upon to assess the entire body of materials and to arrive at a specific judgment or diagnosis, confirming or altering the original decision about the type in which the person belongs. In either case, the last step in diagnosis is the location of the individual within some "problem" category. There is nothing novel about this general procedure, for this is what correctional workers now do in preparing presentence reports, admission summaries, and other diagnostic reports. Many of them may not recognize that this is how they operate and they may claim that they deal with each individual as a wholly unique person; but if so, such workers are unaware of how they actually function. The major difference between the procedure outlined here and conventional correctional decision-making is that the latter tends to be carried on in terms of *implicit* diagnostic schemes, rather than with an explicit, formal diagnostic instrument. That is, the correctional employee usually gathers together a body of information about an offender from which he attempts to draw out an interpretation that the person's misbehavior is a consequence of some sort of causal process. In so doing, the worker is guided by his recollections of previous cases which seem in some way to be similar to the case at hand. This text recommends the substitution of more standardized and explicit estimates through formalized diagnostic categories for unsystematic judgments based upon implicit typologies of offender patterns.

Summary

Two typologies have been presented in this chapter. Although the typological assertions are brief, they do provide a compact model of diagnostic typologies. They can be employed as first approximations to well-articulated schemes.

The next chapter takes up a typology of treatment procedures. In succeeding chapters, the diagnostic patterns are to be linked to the treatment forms specified in Chapter Four.

four

ON THE NATURE
AND
FORMS
OF TREATMENT

Introduction

This chapter begins by reiterating that this text is a primer on treatment theory. Just as the last chapter made no attempt to draw together all the theory and empirical evidence regarding types of offenders, this one does not try to provide a detailed and comprehensive review and analysis of the vast body of materials regarding treatment tactics in corrections. Instead, it discusses the basic characteristics of therapy as distinct from activities which are not rehabilitative in nature. In addition, the major features of a small number of general forms of treatment such as individual psychotherapy and group therapy are outlined. In actual practice, these general forms of therapy have been conducted in a number of specific ways. For example, some group treatment ventures have been directed by nonprofessional correctional employees in camp settings, whereas other group efforts have developed in probation settings, institutions, and in other situations. This chapter makes no effort to provide a full description of all these specific variants of group therapy.

What is treatment? A provisional answer would be that therapy for correctional "clients" consists of explicit tactics or procedures deliberately undertaken to change those conditions thought to be responsible for the violator's misbehavior. Treatment implies some rationale or causal argument to the effect that the criminal behavior of the individual stems from some particular set of factors or conditions. In turn, the steps which are taken to "change" or rehabilitate the offender are designed to alter some or all of the conditions specified in the treatment rationale as causally responsible for the person's undesirable behavior.

Before considering the details of treatment in terms of the specific aims of therapy, the nature of the conditions which must be modified if the offender is to be rehabilitated, and the like, it is necessary to return to an examination of the distinctions made in Chapter One among treatment, adjuncts to therapy, and humanitarian reforms as distinct sets of activities. This chapter seeks to clarify the character of treatment through a kind of exclusionary process, such that several lines of activity which are *not* therapeutic should be dealt with first.

Treatment and Humanitarianism

The goal of correctional treatment in the United States has developed parallel to an increased emphasis upon humanitarianism. The view that lawbreakers should be rehabilitated has arisen alongside of the view that they should be handled humanely. However, the implementation of humanitarian proposals in corrections has been more prominent than the development of treatment programs. At any rate, these two different sets of objectives have become bound up together so that considerable confusion exists in the public mind (and sometimes even in the thinking of correctional persons) concerning the differences between treatment and humane gestures. The latter are frequently assumed to be rehabilitative or therapeutic as well, although there is little reason to suppose that such activities do have rehabilitative consequences.

Humanitarian reform designates those changes that have been

introduced into corrections in recent decades which serve to lessen the harshness or severity of punishment. In many respects, the juvenile court movement, in which informal and less punitive procedures have been substituted for more severe actions directed at offenders under the age of eighteen, is a case in point. Now, the author is strongly in favor of humanitarianism in corrections. Let there be no mistake on that point. But humanitarianism should be and can be defended on moral grounds, in terms of the proposition that the sins of offenders are not so heinous as to demand long sentences; incarceration in small, dark cells; inadequate food; and similar forms of deprivation. The experience of "doing time" for even a short period of time in a penal institution operated under markedly humanitarian principles seems sufficient punishment for criminality of nearly any kind. The deprivation of the individual's liberty alone is an experience that is severe enough to satisfy the demands that he be made to suffer, without such additional gratuitous deprivations as isolation, inadequate diets, and so forth. In the same way, the lesser restrictions of liberty imposed under probation can be defended as sufficient punishment for the violations of law engaged in by persons who are normally placed on probation.

An incisive case for maintaining a clear separation between humanitarian reforms and therapy has been made by Korn and McCorkle. They point out that

It is the tragedy of modern correction that the impulse to help has been confused with treatment and seems to require defense as treatment. One of the more ironic difficulties with this position is that when one makes "rehabilitation" the main justification for the humane handling of prisoners one has maneuvered oneself into a position potentially dangerous to the humanitarian viewpoint. What if humane treatment fails to rehabilitate—shall it then be abandoned? The isolated survivals of flogging and other "tough" techniques which still disgrace American penology remain to remind us that this is no mere academic question. The bleak fact is that just as the monstrous punishments of the eighteenth century failed to curtail crime, so the mere humane handling of the twentieth century has equally failed to do so.[1]

[1] Lloyd W. McCorkle and Richard Korn, "Resocialization Within Walls," *Annals of the American Academy of Political and Social Science*, No. 293 (May 1954), 94-95.

Parenthetically, the issue in corrections is *not* one of punishment *versus* treatment. Insofar as the state invokes sanctions of some kind against persons who are defined as law violators, sanctions which are experienced by them as deprivations, such individuals are being punished for their transgressions. At the outset at least, nearly every law violator who is processed through the legal machinery of social control is an unwilling participant in these operations. The various penalties handed out to violators are coercive in nature—the offender does not voluntarily pay fines, serve jail sentences, report to a probation officer, or "do time" in an institution. Moreover, the legal basis for such coercive actions by the state is that the individual has violated the law and that, as a consequence, he must suffer certain penalties. The complication in all this is that in recent decades, the view has arisen that one consequence the offender should suffer is therapy. He should be put into some program designed to change him in some way so that he will not breach the law a second time. However, this does not alter the fundamental point that there is no basis in law for the state to act against a person solely because the individual is in need of treatment or behavioral change. The state has no power to intervene in the behavior of a neurotic individual in order to change that person in some way. In effect, being "treated" as a criminal is simply one form that punishment can take.

As long as the state continues to define a group of individuals in society as lawbreakers and as long as the state continues to differentially exercise sanctions against such persons, punishment will continue to exist. Consequently, the question then becomes: How much punishment of some particular form is just and equitable? The humanitarian answer in recent decades has been that traditional penalties have been too harsh, inequitable, and unjust. The newer view has developed that not all offenders should be segregated in special institutions, that instead, some should receive a lesser amount of deprivation of liberty through the mechanism of probation. Similarly, this position has held that punishment through incarceration within an institution is sufficiently harsh, so that it is neither necessary nor reasonable to physically abuse the inmate or to degrade him in some additional manner.

A closely related question in the treatment-punishment dialogue is this: To what extent is it possible to use treatment as one form of punishment of offenders? This matter has already been confronted in Chapter One, where it was argued that although some severe obstacles exist to the achievement of therapeutic goals within a punitive structure, nonetheless, rehabilitation is possible. Chapter Five takes up the matter of obstacles to treatment in considerable detail.

To return to the matter of humanitarian reform, consider the following example of humanitarian change. Traditionally, the visitor privileges accorded inmates in institutions have been quite restricted. One rationale for restricting the number of visitors the prisoner could see in a certain time period was that the fewer the visitors, the fewer the contraband problems, custodial dangers, and so forth. Not only were visitors few in number but also visits were held under extremely unfavorable circumstances. For example, in one western reformatory prisoners formerly entertained their visitors in the rotunda area of the institution. The members of the inmate's family were subjected to such sights as a group of chained, newly arrived "fish" hobbling through the sallyport and rotunda of the institution! In the past few years this same reformatory has liberalized the visiting policies. Inmates are allowed many more visitors per month and they see these persons in a specially constructed, pleasantly appointed "Visitor's Room." Both the convicts and guests are now spared the experience of clanging cell doors, chained inmates, and other reminders of prison life.

Changes of this kind may have positive repercussions for the institution. Perhaps increased visiting privileges reduce institutional tensions, although it is also possible that some prisoners actually suffer more when the number of outsiders they see is increased. It is not inconceivable that the inmate's sense of unworthiness is accentuated by these experiences. But in either event, there is little reason to suppose that persons who have numerous visitors during their stay in a prison will by that fact alone be less likely to commit crime. This is not to say that reforms of this kind should be discouraged, but neither should such changes be identified as therapeutic in character.

One tangential comment is in order regarding visiting rights. From time to time, in the name of treatment, proposals are made in the United States that conjugal visits be allowed inmates. Mississippi has the only state prison system which now allows such visits.

Doubtless many would agree that imprisonment, which forces heterosexual, married inmates to dwell in a theoretically celibate, one-sex society for an extended period of time, is harsh punishment indeed. It could be argued that it would be morally justifiable to allow prisoners to periodically engage in sexual interaction with their wives under a system of conjugal visits. Perhaps such arrangements would also reduce certain tensions that are endemic in prisons. But whatever the arguments pro and con such visits, it should be recognized that this is not a treatment procedure. There is no link between criminal conduct and abstinence from sexual activities (some Freudian theorists notwithstanding).

The illustration of visiting privileges is only one of a large number of similar changes which have been brought about in many of the more progressive state correctional systems. Other reforms include the construction of new cell blocks to replace crowded, dark "bucket cells" (cells without toilets); modified seating arrangements in institutional mess halls so that prisoners eat "family style" at small tables; increased forms of inmate entertainment such as movies, athletic events with outside teams, and so forth; discontinuance of such procedures as "lock step," prison stripes as wearing apparel, numbers on prison uniforms; wider use of probation; and so forth.

Not all the developments in corrections in the past several decades have been concerned with humanitarianism. Steps have been taken in a number of states to implement the growing emphasis on treatment as a correctional goal. Many of these steps have been *adjuncts* to treatment, centering around the creation and development of programs such as classification, educational or vocational training, and the like. In many institutional settings, these activities are pointed to as "treatment" in contrast to other operations which are identified as "custodial."

Endeavors such as these are different from humanitarian acts, but they are not treatment programs. For example, the rationale behind programs of inmate classification or reception-diagnostic centers does involve more than simply an interest in reducing the severity of serving time. The justification is that a thorough study and diagnosis of an inmate is a requirement for both effective treatment and custodial assignments. Accordingly, well-developed classification programs collect detailed information about newly arrived prisoners which is summarized and interpreted in a document usu-

ally called the "Admission Summary." This document is used by
the institutional classification committee in order to make custodial
and therapy assignments for each inmate. Seen in this light, the
process of classification (including periodic reclassification) represents the administrative arrangement through which the process of
diagnosis as outlined in this text is carried out in an institutional
setting. However, diagnosis or classification is only the starting
point of treatment. Once a decision is reached that an offender
should be treated in some specific way, this judgment must then
be implemented. The implementation of the therapy recommendation constitutes therapy. Unfortunately, in many institutional programs, classification often ends with a diagnosis based on an elaborate data-gathering process, without further steps being taken to
put the treatment recommendations into effect.

Other programs such as vocational training, education, religious
activities, recreational participation, and prerelease planning are
all examples of adjuncts to therapy. None of these are treatment
per se, for none of them deal directly with some therapy problem
presented by the inmate. For example, vocational training may
contribute to the eventual rehabilitation of an offender who is subjected to such a program, insofar as that experience provides the
prisoner with good work habits and vocational skills. But it is
likely to have some impact only when it is accompanied by some
kind of direct resocialization experience in which the inmate is led
to modify his negative attitudes toward work. This is another way
of saying that criminals engage in law violations, not because they
are unemployed or unemployable, but because they have acquired
attitudes which devalue the importance of conventional work-ca-
reers. The same point holds for educational activities and similar
ventures. Offenders may well be helped to make a successful law-
abiding adjustment by receiving some educational assistance, but
only insofar as they are changed in certain ways through involvement in therapy.

None of the foregoing should be read as implying that adjunct
programs are of no use. Quite the contrary, for a well-developed
system of treatment needs a number of adjunct activities in order
to maximize the probability of successful rehabilitation of offenders.
Nonetheless, a clear distinction should be maintained between direct therapy efforts and these various adjuncts to treatment.

The Nature and Forms of Treatment

ON THE NATURE OF TREATMENT

The provisional definition of treatment with which this chapter began identified therapy as some kind of explicit activity designed to alter or to remove some conditions operating on offenders which are responsible for their misbehavior. That definition is so broad and general that it probably would not provoke any controversy. It is when discussion moves on to ask questions and to provide answers regarding the details of therapy that disagreements are likely to develop.

The conceptualization of treatment provided here will not satisfy everyone. For example, the conception of motivation, and in turn of therapy, to be utilized places little emphasis upon such "hidden" personality dynamics as latent homosexuality and kindred elements as motivating forces in criminality. The lack of attention to views of that kind stems from the general assessment of such notions as empirically false or essentially untestable. As indicated in Chapter Two, most of the evidence collected to date concerning hypotheses about personality abnormality and deviant conduct is negative in character. Nonetheless, beliefs of that kind die hard, so that there are many persons in correctional organizations who are guided by such etiological hypotheses in treatment. Perhaps such frameworks are useful in correctional therapy when employed by persons with extended training in that kind of behavioral theory. Such interpretations may be useful in practice, so that some individuals who are treated within this behavioral perspective may show improvements in behavior or adjustment. Successful therapy is in considerable measure a function of the interpersonal skills of the therapist as well as the specific theory employed by the agent.

On this point, let it be understood that this book does not argue that only one picture of motivation and therapy can be articulated. Alternative views of treatment are possible. In addition, it may be that the framework here is not the only one that would produce results in corrections. But, to sneak in one affirmative claim along with this equivocation, there is more hard evidence in support of the etiological position of this book than there is for a number of competing views of causation and therapy. And, insofar as effective treatment is contingent upon valid behavioral theory, this point of view has more in its favor than some of the alternatives that are available.

The discussion of motivation and therapy in this chapter is necessarily abbreviated. Since an entire volume could easily be written on the issue of motivational elements in deviant conduct, the material that follows should not be viewed as a substitute for a diligent study of the literature on motivational patterns, socialization experiences, and kindred matters in deviant and nondeviant conduct.

So much for disclaimers. To get back to the business at hand, what is the "something" that treatment is designed to modify? Or, put differently, what leads persons to engage in criminality, and how can they be directed toward nondeviant behavior? Fundamentally, the view here is that criminal and delinquent acts are a function of *definitions of the situation* internal to the actors who engage in these acts. This conception is close to that of Sutherland's theory of "differential association" in which criminality is attributed to "definitions favorable to violation of law." [2] Definitions of the situation designate self-definitions of persons and attitudes toward criminality and allied matters, or in other words, belief systems or interpretive frameworks by which individuals "make sense" out of sensory perceptions and by which they direct their behavior.

The basic point regarding definitions of the situation and therapy is that the objective events which occur to individuals are subject to a variety of different responses and interpretations. Objective reality and the social-psychological worlds of particular persons are not the same thing, although in other than extreme cases a reasonable degree of correspondence between the two does exist. On the other hand, when objective reality and the private world of the individual become too much out of tune, the person is likely to be singled out as "crazy," "paranoid," "a nut," or abnormal in some other way.

In any event, whether the private interpretive standards and beliefs of the individual are consonant with objective reality or not, his behavior is a function of this set of beliefs and notions. In a word, the actor behaves as he does because of his definition of the situation. Accordingly, if he is to be directed toward a different

---

[2] Edwin H. Sutherland and Donald R. Cressey, *Principles of Criminology*, 6th ed. (Philadelphia: J. B. Lippincott Co., 1960), pp. 77-80.

kind of behavior, certain of his definitions must be modified. What this means in detail is that certain aspects of his self-image, attitudes, and beliefs must be altered.

Consider several examples of common definitions of the situation among lawbreakers. Take first the case of drug addiction. Doubtless the reasons why persons initially engage in drug use are variable but they all probably have to do with definitions by actors that drugs are a permissible "kick" or that narcotics may help them adjust to social situations which they perceive as difficult and harsh or other beliefs of this sort. In turn, once individuals become involved in addiction, their belief that "once an addict, always an addict" and their views that drug use is a relatively innocuous personal vice represent definitions of the situation which motivate them to continue the use of narcotics. Importantly, too, these claims and beliefs are shared among groups of addicts as subcultural definitions of the situation, rather than existing as idiosyncratic views of specific persons.

Another illustration can be found in the case of embezzlement. Cressey has shown that this behavior is the result of persons coming to define themselves as having "nonshareable problems." According to Cressey, the potential trust violator must also contrive a set of justificatory arguments or rationalizations for embezzlement *before* the act takes place, in order to square his conception of himself as a "trusted" person with the fact that he is about to commit a deviant act.[3] Cressey's findings indicate that violation of financial trust is a behavioral act which develops only insofar as individuals are able to work out a new interpretation of the situation replacing their former one that stealing is "bad."

The final example of definitions of the situation involves the criminal type which Chapter Three labeled the "semiprofessional property offender." These individuals are involved in criminality, in part at least, because they regard themselves as having little opportunity to earn money in legitimate ways and because they define themselves as victims of a society that has "ganged-up" on them and in which "everyone has a racket."

One line of elaboration upon definitions of the situation has to do with the question of where these are located and how they are

---

[3] Donald R. Cressey, *Other People's Money* (New York: The Free Press of Glencoe, Inc., 1953).

generated. It should be clear enough from the foregoing that they are internal to actors, so that in the last analysis therapy is directed at persons. Yet at the same time, many of the definitions, criminalistic and otherwise, of individual persons are shared ones. For example, certain attitudes and beliefs regarding the police are class-linked and common to most members of a particular social class. Some others are more narrowly restricted to small groups to which the individual belongs, and still others are truly individualistic and idiosyncratic in form.

As a general statement, it can be said that interpretive frameworks are the product of social interaction patterns. Many definitions are acquired early in life from socialization experiences. In turn, they remain with the individual throughout his lifetime, so that they represent part of the characteristics which lend predictability to his behavior. But some beliefs and views that are acquired by the actor relatively early in life subsequently are dropped or unlearned as the person's life circumstances and reference groups change. Conversely, some of the important definitions employed by the adult are ones that have been assumed relatively recently, as illustrated by the rationalizations of the embezzler. Some interpretations arise out of specific interactional activities and have a short life span. Indeed, in some cases it is almost as if conventional definitions are suspended temporarily rather than replaced by new ones. Most homicides illustrate this point, in that these events usually involve a quarreling husband and wife or other pairs of individuals who are in intimate social interaction with each other. The act of murder is often the culmination of a violent and drunken argument, in which the killing of the victim is inadvertent. The offender frequently reports himself to the police and confesses the act. Most of his actions suggest that he has not renounced norms prohibiting murder.

The fact that some temporal variations in definitions of the situation are more difficult to modify than others, owing to the differences in the time and place of origin and the like, has an implication for treatment. In a few extreme examples, certain definitions are so central a part of the personality organization of the person as to be almost wholly unamenable to modification. As one case in point, the beliefs of "overly aggressive" offenders centering around a view of other people as basically mean and untrustworthy represent major anchorage points of the self-other notions of the individual. The therapist should not be surprised to find that a law violator clings tenaciously to notions of this kind. Then at the other polar extreme, some definitions are of recent origin and are only tenuously held by the actor so that they can be modified rather easily.

One general comment which probably needs little repetition is that offenders are characterized by various patterns of definitions rather than by a single set of beliefs, attitudes, and the like which set them off from noncriminals or nondelinquents. The typological descriptions in Chapter Three were concerned with the different views exhibited by offenders and with the sources of these variations. Also, because definitions vary, as do the experiences producing them, no single kind of therapy activity can be expected to accomplish treatment.

The role of unconscious elements in human personality and criminality is also involved in criminal motivation and frames of reference. Queries about the place, if any, of unconscious motivation can be answered in several ways, depending upon what is intended by the concept of the unconscious. It might be argued that individuals act out of unconscious motivation in that the sources or origins of present definitions are to be found in earlier life experiences. It might also be claimed that unconscious motivational elements exist in that individuals are not usually aware of the definitions that they employ, nor are they cognizant of the origins of these interpretations. Thus the person who exhibits various verbal indicators of feelings of inferiority and status-anxiety, such as chronic sarcasm, may lack awareness of his feelings and may not realize that such self-notions developed from early family experiences. In this sense, his behavior could be said to be unconsciously motivated. There can be little quarrel with these views of unconscious motivation.

However, the notion of unconscious motivation is often taken to mean something quite different. In conventional psychoanalytic theory in particular, unconscious motivation refers to motivational elements that are somehow buried in the deep layers of personality. They are unrecognized by the actor, and more importantly, they are not accessible to study except through some kind of intensive "depth" probing by a skilled analyst. Also, in this view of things, it is commonly argued that behavior is frequently the result of motivational forces quite different from the apparent ones. In the case of criminality, this kind of theory holds that acts such as larceny are frequently generated by unrecognized desires to commit homosexual acts, incest, or other "forbidden" actions which the person's psyche will not allow him to perform. Criminality is a substitute for acts which the individual is secretly motivated to commit.

What of this conception of motivation? First, the difference between this view and the previous one is a matter of degree. This text does not involve a complete and unequivocal rejection of some of the specific claims about unrecognized forces in behavior which appear in the psychiatric literature on deviance. However, the extreme versions of this line of thought, in which deviation is seen as a response to latent homosexuality, incest fantasies, and other motives which flow out of some mysterious reservoir of motivational energy, are eschewed. This book will simply avoid such hypotheses, without any attempt to defend their omission, for a full defense would take the discussion too far afield.

The emphasis in this delineation of the nature of treatment has been upon the necessity of basing therapy upon knowledge about the forms of criminalistic deviance and the etiology behind them. Stress has also been placed upon the diversity of behavioral roles in the population of offenders, so that not one but a number of treatment tactics are required in order to deal with them. Now, there is a somewhat different view about treatment at present which underscores the importance of certain correctional organizational patterns as basic for changing deviants into law-abiding citizens. In this conceptualization, attention is given to identifying the elements of a "therapeutic milieu" for achieving resocialization. In brief, the claim is advanced that the critical ingredient in successful therapy centers about the development of a situation in which offenders are encouraged to exert pressure upon each other to reform themselves. In this view, the correctional problem can be compared to military training in which a military organization is faced with the problem of making soldiers out of recruits. Perhaps it would do well to put most of its effort into the development of a program of military socialization and less into consideration of the diverse social backgrounds of the recruit raw material. It might be possible to contrive a military training program that would uniformly create soldiers out of these recruits from diverse backgrounds. Indeed, military systems do manage to attain this goal through a standardized kind of training. In the same way, perhaps a correctional machinery can be devised which will unite diverse sorts of offenders into an "anticriminal society."

Attention to the form of treatment organization is not contradictory to the position advanced above. The latter part of this chapter devotes a good deal of space to the discussion of treatment milieus, and much of the emphasis in the chapters to follow is upon the need to develop certain kinds of correctional situations for the achievement of rehabilitative goals. In effect, the view that stresses the need for tactics based on knowledge about types of offenders and etiology is one side of the coin. The other side quite properly notes that successful treatment demands a particular kind of therapeutic climate. However, this book argues that because lawbreakers are such a heterogeneous lot, no one kind of rehabilitative organization can be found that will work equally well with all of them. For example, certain recent organizational innovations in the treatment of drug addicts to be discussed later in this chapter seem to have far-reaching implications for other kinds of offenders. But there are other violators who require a different kind of treatment in a different setting because they are behaviorally unlike narcotics addicts. The military analogy may, in this respect, be misleading. The problems of correctional treatment may be qualitatively different from the tasks of soldier-making, in that offenders are more varied and less malleable than recruits.

A TYPOLOGY OF TREATMENT FORMS

Although specific tactics of therapy vary markedly, with various forms shading into others, it is possible to lump most of them into two general classes: (1) psychotherapies and (2) environmental therapies. The two categories represent the treatment parallels of the two basic viewpoints regarding causation, the psychogenic and sociogenic orientations.

Different kinds of psychotherapy involve discrepant hypotheses about the nature and causes of deviant activity, but all of them operate from the basic premise that the causes of the individual's present actions are to be found inside the person. In turn, if the sources of behavior are inside the person, his psyche must be altered to change him. Normally, psychotherapy follows some procedure designed to reveal the internal workings of the person to the therapist and to the patient. Once this pattern is revealed, it is then believed that the way is opened for the patient to modify his unfavorable action patterns, normally through some guidance from the therapist. The client is viewed as a machine that is "wired" in a defective manner, so that he needs to be rewired. The therapist is to serve as the electrician.

Although theories of behavior on which psychotherapy is based acknowledge that the internal characteristics of the patient are the product of his life experiences, interactional patterns, and group associations, nonetheless, once they are formed, little attention need be given to the social relations of the patient. This implicit assumption sets off psychotherapy from the environmental forms of intervention. The latter do not deny that the patient's problem may be partially internal to the individual, or stated differently, that he carries response tendencies inside himself. But environmental tactics assume that many of the problems of the person are *shared* ones, so that they are tensions and difficulties which are common among certain groups of individuals. Furthermore, environmental therapies assume that many significant problems of adjustment are relatively accessible to treatment, are apparent to the person, and are not buried deep in the "inner layers of personality." Finally, they usually proceed from the premise that problems are related to the ongoing interaction and associations in which the subject is immersed, so that to change him, the pattern of associations must be altered. The individual must be removed from his present interactional circumstances and introduced into new groups, or the members of his present associational networks must be changed into new sorts of social beings.

These two basic forms of treatment can be divided into six major subtypes, to which discussion now turns. The subtypes are also briefly summarized in Figure 3.

Patterns of Psychotherapy

INDIVIDUAL "DEPTH" PSYCHOTHERAPY

Individual "depth" psychotherapy is not all of one kind, for among other things, psychotherapists vary in educational backgrounds and therapy techniques. Some psychiatrists vary among themselves in terms of conceptual orientations, some are clinical psychologists, and others have still other training. Nevertheless, different brands of depth psychotherapy usually involve allegiance to Freudian or neo-Freudian psychoanalytic behavioral theory and to psychoanalytic therapy techniques. The essentials of this kind of therapy include the following premises:

1. Most causes of personal maladjustment are rooted in early life experiences, particularly those involving parent-child interaction;
2. these causes are only dimly understood, at best, by the patient;
3. a skilled analyst or therapist can discover the causes of maladjustment through the therapeutic relationship;
4. the patient will experience "catharsis" or emotional relief when he is led to understand the source of his difficulties by the therapist.

The essentials of individual psychotherapy have been aptly summarized by one leading psychotherapist, S. R. Slavson, as follows:

One of the chief aims of psychotherapy is to release from repression the early resentments and hostility which are unavoidably attached to one's parents and to bring to consciousness the conflict between one's destructive impulses and the restraints of the conscious and unconscious superego. The psychotherapist's method of achieving this aim is to permit the patient to regress to the early stages in his development in which these conflicts originated. The patient is then encouraged to act out or talk out these early feelings, that is, to experience a "catharsis." [4]

One of the best brief statements on psychotherapy is represented by Jenkins' discussion in his book, Breaking Patterns of Defeat.[5] He indicates that

A psychotherapeutic relationship can be described as a controlled interpersonal relationship directed toward aiding the growth of the patient toward a more mature or satisfactory life adjustment. The therapist is expected to be able to submerge his own needs for the time being and to manage the relationship in terms of the needs and growth of the patient. This requires a high degree of emotional maturity and self-discipline, as well as a high degree of understanding.[6]

[4] S. R. Slavson, "Group Psychotherapy," Scientific American, Vol. 183 (December 1950), 42.
[5] Richard L. Jenkins, Breaking Patterns of Defeat (Philadelphia: J. B. Lippincott Co., 1954), pp. 220-39.
[6] Ibid., p. 221.

Jenkins goes on to list a number of elements of psychotherapy. The first of these is a sense of emotional security which the patient develops from interaction with the therapist. He argues that this feeling of emotional well-being is exceedingly important and that it derives out of the acceptance and understanding shown the patient by the therapist. This relationship of security gives the client the courage to acknowledge and confront various problems which he has earlier been unable to face.

Respect for the integrity and self-determination of the individual, or respect for the patient's identity, is a second element of psychotherapy listed by Jenkins. He notes that the problem of respect for the patient's identity is both an end of therapy, and often, a stubborn obstacle in the way of treatment. The subject may resist attempts to change him, even though he is concerned about attaining an improved pattern of adjustment, because change represents a threat to the self-image he has built up. Jenkins notes several ways in which a skilled therapist can handle this difficulty.

The relief of pent-up emotional tension or "catharsis" is a third element of psychotherapy. Jenkins notes that many persons who seek psychotherapy have been concealing or suppressing strong emotional feelings, so that the therapist acts as a safety-valve, allowing the individual to "blow off steam" in a protected, nonthreatening situation. This reduction of tension may then lead, through therapy, to analysis of the tension-producing situation and, ultimately, to better adaptation to stress by the patient.

Other elements of psychotherapy involve (1) reduction or stimulation of the patient's sense of responsibility for his actions and (2) attenuation or stimulation of the guilt-anxiety of the person. In some cases, individuals who seek therapy are overburdened with self-condemnatory feelings, an exaggerated sense of responsibility for perceived personal shortcomings, or crippling anxiety and guilt. One aim of therapy is to reduce these feelings of responsibility and guilt. In other instances, patients take too little responsibility for their actions, tending instead to shift blame to others. In these occurrences, some attempt must be made to encourage the growth of a healthy sense of personal obligation on the patient's part. Again, Jenkins indicates some measures to be taken to achieve these ends.

A sixth component of psychotherapy concerns the reduction of feelings of inferiority or inadequacy of patients. The promotion

PSYCHOTHERAPY

Type	Treatment Goal	Nature of Therapist	Number of Clients or Patients	Length of Treatment Period	Frequency of Treatment	Appropriate Treatment Circumstances
1 Individual "Depth" Psychotherapy	Uncover individual problems, lead patient to insight, develop new patterns	Psychiatrist, clinical psychologist, psychiatric social worker	Only one patient in each therapy case load or experience	Depends upon severity of problems, but frequently extensive	Normally, treatment should be intensive, i.e., several times per week	Private, quiet surroundings such as private office of therapist
2 Group Psychotherapy	Same as individual therapy, but also, get person to see other's problems	Same as above, but patients are therapy agents, too, to some extent	Small group, fifteen persons or less	Depends upon severity of problems, but shorter than individual psychotherapy	Same as above	Private surroundings where patients not observed by outsiders
3 Client-Centered Therapy	Uncover individual problems, patient is led to analyze himself, change	Person trained in eclectic procedures of client-centered work	Only one patient in each therapy case load or experience	Shorter time than "depth" therapy, often a few weeks or so	Usually intensive, i.e., several times per week	Private, quiet surroundings such as private office of therapist

figure 3 SUMMARY OF PATTERNS OF TREATMENT

146

ENVIRONMENTAL THERAPY

Type	Treatment Goal	Nature of Therapist	Number of Clients or Patients	Length of Treatment Period	Frequency of Treatment	Appropriate Treatment Circumstances
4 Group Therapy	Discover group pressures to problem behavior, develop new norms	Initially, some person called "therapist," but ultimately, group members	Small group, fifteen persons or less in most cases	Depends upon problem to be solved, but usually fairly long, i.e., one year	Fairly intense, once per week or more frequently	Private surroundings where patients are not observed by outsiders
5 Milieu Management	Develop new behavioral norms in more general living group than therapy group	Initially, some person(s) named as therapist, but ultimately, entire group	Living group or associational group of larger size than group therapy	Fairly lengthy to extremely long-term, may extend over several years	Treatment tends to be continuous, rather than interwoven with nontreatment	Stable living group situation such as apartment or some similar arrangement
6 Environmental Change	Develop new behavioral norms in wider social environment than above	Usually, no specific person as therapist, in long run, environment	Usually, large group, often many members of large social environment	Fairly lengthy to extremely long-term, may extend over several years	Treatment tends to be continuous rather than interwoven with nontreatment	Social environment to be changed, such as community area

figure 3 SUMMARY OF PATTERNS OF TREATMENT (Cont.)

147

of personality patterns in which the adjustment problem of the patient and solutions to it are incorporated into the personal organization of the individual is another. The patient must come to recognize his difficulties and to build up a fund of solutions to them, but this recognition must also be integrated with the person's basic values and general psychological frame of reference.

Beyond these characteristics of psychotherapy, Jenkins also discusses a number of other considerations, such as the need for the patient to actively and cooperatively participate in the process, requirements of proper planning, the need for rapport, and so forth.[7]

One final set of extremely incisive remarks by Jenkins concerns the role of personality theory in psychotherapy. He declares that

Various superstructures of theory have been developed by the therapeutic schools of Freud, Adler, Jung, Rank, etc. Entirely disproportionate stress has been laid upon the superstructures of theoretical formulation under which much psychotherapy is carried out. Bitter controversy has raged about the correctness or incorrectness of certain formulations. The battles which have raged and are still raging in this regard tend to obscure two very vital and fundamental facts:

1. Any one of these theoretical formulations represents a schematization of human behavior to make it more intelligible. As a schematization, it necessarily leaves out much. It is therefore a partial statement only. Different schematic simplifications of a phenomenon so complicated as human life may each have elements of truth and usefulness.

2. Since the main criterion by which theoretical formulations are judged is their usefulness in a therapeutic relationship, we have a highly pragmatic criterion. The value of a theoretical formulation lies in the extent to which it is useful in aiding the patient to see things from a new viewpoint, break out of a pattern of defeat, and achieve a pattern of success. There is no single interpretation by which alone this can be accomplished. In a given situation any one of several alternative interpretations may be used to help the patient break the vicious circle. The essence is a new synthesis in the patient which brings about a capacity to forge a new pattern for living. To the extent that we accept therapeutic usefulness as a criterion for truth, to that extent we must expect to find that truth is multiple, not unitary—that there are alternative formulations of truth. . . .

[7] *Ibid.*, pp. 222-39.

Two disadvantages of adherence to a highly developed theoretical superstructure are worthy of note. Because of the unfamiliar language and the unfamiliar way in which relationships are stated, the patient is at a disadvantage in contributing synthesis himself, at least until he has been through a relatively long and expensive period of psychotherapy. A second disadvantage is that too frequently the therapist tends to treat this theoretical superstructure, not as a series of useful formulations of typical or frequent situations, but as a full-fledged system of eternal truths about personality development. As a result, he may feel it necessary to force the patient's problem into a particular mold, regardless of whether or not this treatment promotes or obstructs its understanding.

The question may be asked as to how far the able therapist needs such a highly developed theoretical superstructure, and as to how far the temptation to use a theoretical superstructure rigidly limits the work of the therapist not so able. He who uses it most flexibly has the least need of it. It seems safe to predict, at least, that the development of better therapists will be accompanied by the greatly reduced emphasis upon the complexities of the theoretical superstructure, by a larger fraction of insights contributed by the patient himself, hence by a more flexible, varied, and eclectic use of interpretations.[8]

It is clear from the preceding that the process of psychotherapy is a relationship between a patient and therapist which in many ways approximates normal relationships in the socialization process. The aim is to bring about the managed progress of the person toward a state of improved mental health and adjustment so that he can better manage his own affairs. It endeavors to achieve, in a deliberate and accelerated fashion, results similar to those that flow out of normal socialization experiences.

Psychotherapeutic techniques have been most widely applied to individuals experiencing adjustment difficulties who seek the help of a therapist, rather than to such deviants as criminals who do not normally define themselves as having problems. Still, psychotherapy has frequently been suggested as the main form of treatment that should be administered to criminals and delinquents. Several important questions are immediately apparent regarding the use of psychotherapy with law violators. For one, what kinds of criminals or delinquents need psychotherapy? Certainly this is an inappropriate form of treatment for many offenders, but at the same time, it may be that it would be efficacious with other types of lawbreakers.

8 *Ibid.*, pp. 234-35.

Chapters Six and Seven identify those offender types for whom psychotherapy is relevant, so that at that point, further consideration will be given to the justification for the use of psychotherapy with certain criminalistic deviants.

A second question about psychotherapy in correctional treatment has to do with the special difficulties that complicate the treatment task, arising out of such factors as the initial resistance to therapy characteristic of many offenders, the antitreatment values of the inmate culture in institutions, the generally unfavorable physical environment for therapy that is often found in probation settings and institutions, and kindred problems. Many of these obstacles to rehabilitative efforts are discussed in the next chapter. In the several chapters in which forms of therapy are linked with offender patterns, techniques for handling the special problems of treatment in correctional settings are noted.

GROUP PSYCHOTHERAPY

Prior to the discussion of group psychotherapy, notice must be taken of the recent history of group treatment procedures in the United States. In the period since World War II particularly, a great deal of interest and attention has focused upon treatment programs for deviants of all sorts which are carried on in group settings. These have been called variously "group psychotherapy," "group therapy," "guided group interaction," "group counseling," and other terms as well. Much of the commentary about group programs implies that there is a single general form of therapy under discussion, so that terminological preferences aside, group treatment is of a unitary sort.

Nothing could be further from the truth. There are two distinct kinds of therapy involving the "group" label: *the first, group psychotherapy, is essentially individual therapy in a group setting; the second is "group" therapy in the true sense, and it is designed to change groups, not individuals.* Even though the differences between these two kinds of treatment are not always clearly perceived, major differences do exist. The aims of the programs differ, the role of the therapist differs, the nature of the group activities differs, and still other contrasts can be identified.[9]

[9] Donald R. Cressey, "Contradictory Theories in Correctional Group Therapy," *Federal Probation*, Vol. 18 (June 1954), 20-26.

True group therapy is discussed as one of the environmental therapies later in this chapter, but at this point some indication should be given of its general outlines. This treatment stratagem focuses upon groups as the "patient." It assumes that specific persons exhibit unfavorable attitudes, self-images, and the like because of the associational network in which they are involved. Because the person's interactional associates are extremely meaningful to him, any attempt to change the person without altering those groups with which he associates is likely to fail. Accordingly, group therapy proceeds on the premise that entire groups of persons must be recruited into therapy groups and changed. In addition, it is argued that treatment in which an individual's close associates are participants is likely to have more impact upon a specific person than some other form of treatment. Group therapy encourages the participants to put pressure on each other for behavioral change and to get the group to define new conduct norms. In a real sense, individual participants in group therapy are at the same time patients and therapists. The person who is formally designated as a therapist frequently comes to play a secondary role in the therapeutic process as it develops over time. In summary, group therapy represents a kind of primary group relationship in which behavioral change is attempted through the same mechanisms by which attitude formation and behavioral change take place in conventional primary groups.

Although there may be points of similarity between group therapy and group psychotherapy, these are two relatively distinct approaches to treatment. The focus of attention in group psychotherapy is *not* upon groups but rather upon specific persons. The group is regarded as a convenient vehicle through which a number of individuals can obtain psychotherapy simultaneously. Not infrequently, group psychotherapy is joined in practice with individual therapy so that patients get a double dose of treatment. For a brief statement of the aims of group psychotherapy, see the quotation from Slavson on page 144. Continuing the quotation, Slavson declares:

Now it is no simple matter to obtain regression. The patient will allow himself to regress only if he feels that he will not be disapproved or punished. The great value of group therapy is that it facilitates the regression and release of the patient. The members of the group have a catalytic effect upon one another. Their mutual support reduces each patient's defenses and fear of self-revelation. As a result the patients act out and reveal their problems more easily and therapy is speeded up. Transference, too, is greatly facilitated, because the group is a protection against the therapist and the parental and environmental authority of which he is the symbol.[10]

Slavson argues that group psychotherapy has the advantage of providing mutual support for the patients undergoing therapy. On the other hand, Jenkins suggests that in some cases, individual problems may be so painful that treatment in a group setting would inhibit the free flow of information from the patient.[11] Thus it appears that there may be some circumstances in which group psychotherapy would have advantages and others in which it would be disadvantageous as a treatment program. At any rate, the basic outlines of group psychotherapy are not very different from those of individual psychotherapy.

In real-life situations cases of group therapy or group psychotherapy frequently do not manifest the same sharpness of definition as in the preceding discussion. Indeed, there are undoubtedly many actual instances of therapy that are not clearly one or another of these forms. In practice, cases of group treatment shade off from one another, more or less approximating these polar opposites. Quite probably, most real-life group treatment activities fall closer to the "group" end of the continuum. For example, in group psychotherapy directed at mental patients, the persons who are assembled together for treatment represent something more than a simple aggregate of individuals. Insofar as they begin to "care about" membership in the therapy collectivity so that it becomes a reference group for them, insofar as they engage in criticisms and analyses of each other's personalities and conduct, and insofar as they adjust their actions in accordance with these responses of other group members, the rudiments of a social group have emerged. In turn, although these results may be seen by the persons in charge of the program as relatively incidental benefits, it is nonetheless likely that the emergent group processes do contribute in important ways to resocialization.

Departures from the polar type of true group therapy are also

[10] Slavson, *op. cit.*, 42.
[11] Jenkins, *op. cit.*, p. 238.

quite common. In many real-life cases, the aims of group therapy center about the creation of therapeutic group structures *in order to modify the attitudes and behavior of specific members of the group*. Indeed, it is hard to visualize a pristine version of group therapy in which the concern is wholly centered upon groups rather than upon individuals. In summary, the distinction between group therapy and group psychotherapy is a matter of degree. The former refers to programs which attempt to create social groups out of aggregates of patients or offenders to modify individual and group attitudes and behavior patterns. Group therapy also designates treatment ventures which place major emphasis upon the group as a therapeutic agent. Although the two kinds of therapy differ fundamentally in terms of the causal propositions about behavior on which they are based, they do not turn out to be completely unlike each other in operation.

One tangential comment about both individual and group psychotherapy is that release of hostility and "blowing off steam" have frequently been identified as one therapeutic end. However, treatment would be incomplete if it resulted only in the ventilation of hostility and other emotions. The release of pent-up emotional energy is not an end in itself; rather, it is encouraged so that patients can then be led to develop healthier ways of coping with tension-producing situations. It is not normally possible to completely remove an individual from situations of stress and tension, so that healthy adjustment involves some ability on the part of the person to overcome or adjust to stresses. The reason for this seemingly obvious remark is that "catharsis" has sometimes been equated with adjustment, as though the person's problems are solved when he becomes able to verbalize about them. But why should this be so? If the anxieties and hostilities of the patient are based upon his inability to handle various stress situations, if the "steam" which he blows off is the product of tensional, recurrent experiences, reduction and solution of these problems will be facilitated only by some solution of the underlying stresses and strains.

Questions similar to those raised under individual therapy must be considered regarding the uses of group psychotherapy in correctional treatment. What kinds of offenders would profit from group psychotherapy? Are there any special impediments to group psychotherapy in correctional settings? For example, one probably common problem is that care must be taken to separate therapy from other experiences in institutional settings. Inmates cannot very easily continue ventilating hostility outside the therapy group without getting into disciplinary predicaments. At the same time, any separation of therapy from other prison experiences is likely to imbue treatment with an air of artificiality. Matters of this kind are to be discussed in the chapters to follow.

CLIENT-CENTERED THERAPY

"Client-centered therapy" is usually associated with the name of Carl R. Rogers.[12] Rogers and a number of associates have been involved in the development of a theory and principles of client-centered counseling as well as in research regarding the effectiveness of this procedure, so that the term normally has a relatively specific and clear referent of particular activities. The essential ingredients of client-centered therapy have been described by Rogers in the following terms:

Client-centered therapy is built on two central hypotheses: (1) the individual has within him the capacity, at least latent, to understand the factors in his life that cause him unhappiness and pain, and to reorganize himself in such a way as to overcome these factors; (2) these powers will become effective if the therapist can establish with the client a relationship sufficiently warm, accepting, and understanding. From these two convictions it follows that in practice we do not try to do something *to* the client. We do not diagnose his case, nor evaluate his personality; we do not prescribe treatment, nor determine what changes are to be effected, nor set the goal that shall be defined as a cure. Instead, the therapist approaches the client with a genuine respect for the person he now is and with a continuing appreciation of him as he changes during the association. He tries to see the client as the client sees himself, to look at problems through his eyes, to perceive with him his confusions, fears, and ambitions. The therapist in such a relationship is not concerned with judging or making suggestions, but always strives to understand. In this atmosphere of complete psychological security the client can lay himself bare with no danger of being hurt. Protected by the conditions of therapy, he begins to reorganize the structure of self in accordance with reality and his own needs. We take this approach because we have found it to be a

[12] Carl R. Rogers, " 'Client-Centered' Therapy," *Scientific American*, Vol. 187 (November 1952), 66-74; Rogers, *Client-Centered Therapy* (New York: Houghton-Mifflin Co., 1951).

deeper and more effective method than any interventive procedures we might use to help the individual deal with life.[13]

Clearly, this is a different view of therapy and the role of the therapist than represented by the previously discussed forms of treatment. This approach is based upon a kind of personality theory which departs from the hypotheses on which depth therapies are based. To cite Rogers again, the personality framework of client-centered therapy follows this line of argument:

> As the work progressed, client-centered therapy developed a theory of personality which is based on the image that a person holds of himself. By this "concept of self" we mean the individual's perceptions of his own characteristics and his relations to others, and the values he attaches to these perceptions. This conscious scheme of the self has a regulatory and guiding influence on behavior. Anxiety and maladjustment occur when it is threatened by a dim awareness of experiences contradictory to it. We view therapy, therefore, as the process by which the structure of the self is relaxed in the safety of the relationship with the therapist, and previously denied experiences are perceived and then integrated into an altered self.[14]

This kind of personality theory has obvious points of similarity with the role orientation of this book. Both stress the importance of self-image patterns in the behavior patterns exhibited by individuals.

Rogers has summarized the results of much research which he and his associates have carried out on the procedures of client-centered therapy. Among other things, the research indicates that the treatment experience usually produces a decline of problem-oriented statements by the client over time, accompanied by an increase in his insight and an acceleration of his decision-making and planning. Patients also tend to reduce the number of negative self-judgments they make over the treatment period. Conversely, they tend to increase the number of positive self-reference remarks. They also show improvements in acceptance and respect for themselves as the experience proceeds. Finally, the evidence suggests that the positive changes brought about by therapy persist beyond the treat-.

---

[13] Rogers, " 'Client-Centered' Therapy," 66-67.
[14] *Ibid.,* 68-70.

ment experience, so that many clients are permanently improved in adjustment.[15]

Rogerian client-centered therapy is quite clear and specific in conceptual orientation; that is, the technique is based upon rather explicit notions of personality structure, and therapists have been trained by Rogers in accordance with this theory and set of procedures. Thus in the narrow sense, client-centered therapy refers to a rather well-developed kind of activity, which is somewhat different than depth psychotherapy. The latter category includes a variety of procedures which stem from variant personality theories and variant notions of psychotherapeutic procedure.

In this text, client-centered therapy designates somewhat more general procedures than those described by Rogers. The definition of client-centered therapy can be relaxed so as to include procedures which are relatively similar to, but not identical with, the Rogerian definition. Much of what is now frequently done with delinquents and criminals in such circumstances as probation or institutional case work is a kind of client-centered treatment. There are many correctional workers who operate with eclectic behavioral theories, who attempt to direct offenders toward an acceptance of their illegal behavior as a "problem," and who try to get them to restructure their attitudes and self-images in a nondeviant direction. Moreover, many of these agents attempt to put most of the therapy responsibility upon the offender, so that he is directed toward a self-analysis of his difficulties. Also, much of the theoretical literature of individual social case work is presented in terms similar to those of Rogers, even though the suggested procedures and approaches are not called "client-centered therapy." The case worker is enjoined to "respect the inherent worth of the individual," to assume that the "client has the capacity for constructive change within him," and so forth.[16]

The application of client-centered techniques to offenders would probably be most successful with correctional clients who are dissatisfied with their present self-images and who define themselves as having problems—in the same way that therapy with noncor-

---

[15] *Ibid.*, 70-74.
[16] For one example of client-centered principles applied to probation and parole, see David Dressler, *Practice and Theory of Probation and Parole* (New York: Columbia University Press, 1959), especially pp. 135-40.

rectional patients rests on such foundations. One question that arises, then, is whether or not there are such clients in correctional case loads. Persons are found who do verbalize considerable discontent with themselves and their illegal behavior, but not all offenders exhibit these characteristics. There are many who allege that they have no problems, that their behavior may be a problem to someone else but not to themselves. Conceivably, in some cases, assertions of this sort are used by the individual as a defense against gnawing feelings of dissatisfaction with himself and with his deviant role behavior. If so, his initial resistance to treatment may be overcome. In any event, there is a need to consider the kinds of offenders for whom client-centered therapy is most appropriate. This is a matter which will be taken up in Chapters Six and Seven.

Patterns of Environmental Therapy

The classification of psychotherapeutic techniques and approaches into three patterns was relatively crude. Within the depth psychotherapy category, many variations are found in the kinds of behavioral theory guiding therapists, in the training of therapists, and in other matters. The same point holds for the other two categories of psychotherapy as well. However, the following three classes of environmental therapy exceed the earlier three in roughness and crudeness.

The three kinds of environmental therapy distinguished here are group therapy, milieu management, and environmental change. Group therapy refers to a form of activity which is a relatively autonomous part of a larger whole of correctional experiences, such as treatment sessions within an encompassing institutional program involving religious activities, vocational training, educational operations, and so forth. Milieu management designates activities in which attempts are made to structure the totality of experiences in which the offender is immediately involved toward rehabilitative ends. Milieu management usually goes on in institutions in which nearly all parts of the operation are oriented toward the creation of a therapeutic group-living experience. Finally, environmental change refers to programs which try to effect alterations in some general, noninstitutional environment. Examples can be found in community reorganization programs, where the major focus of attention is upon modifications in the structure of social activities in the community area rather than upon specific changes in the behavior of delimited collections of individual offenders.

One difficulty with these distinctions is that real-life programs cannot be so cleanly separated into these categories. Some examples of group therapy can be found which are carried on within an institutional program that is quite unrelated to the treatment effort. It is also possible to find some examples of milieu management in which nearly all the events that occur within the organization are planned ones, so that they are all rationalized as part of an over-all therapeutic effort. But at the same time, group therapy efforts are sometimes found in institutional settings where partial attempts have been made to integrate other programs with the treatment activities so as to develop a therapeutic milieu. Accordingly, the problem then arises of precisely where these cases are to be placed in the three-fold classification.

Another problem with these distinctions centers around the third category, environmental change. In practice, many existing programs of environmental changes have as their principal aim prevention of illegality rather than the modification of deviant behavior which has already occurred. But there is no reason why efforts at environmental change could not also be directed toward behavioral change by persons who are already deviants. Such undertakings, based upon notions of "society as the patient," would be as significant for treatment ends as for preventive ones. However, the development of such programs is difficult. Suppose the assumption is made that society is the patient. If so, what is wrong with the patient? Where should curative actions begin? Unfortunately, precise knowledge regarding the dynamics of community and societal influences upon criminality is not abundant. Instead, sociologists have a kind of ambiguous faith in the assumption that there is *something* about social organization which creates deviant behavior, rather than a body of valid generalizations which pinpoint specific community and environmental influences as significant. Accordingly, environmental change programs are likely to be somewhat tentative and experimental until better evidence accumulates regarding particular conditions leading to deviance in communities. In the terms of the earlier metaphor, some "exploratory surgery" upon the societal patient may be required before the precise ailment is discovered.

Although these three patterns of environmental change therapies are crude in definition, they are adequate for the purposes at hand. More detailed commentary about each of these three is presented below. Additionally, in Chapters Six and Seven, further elaboration of these forms of treatment will be made in connection with discussions of specific types of offenders.

GROUP THERAPY

One lucid statement of the principles underlying group therapy has been made by Cressey in an article devoted to applications of Sutherland's theory of differential association to treatment.[17] To quote Cressey, the implications of differential association include the following principles:

1. If criminals are to be changed, they must be assimilated into groups which emphasize values conducive to law-abiding behavior, and, concurrently, alienated from groups emphasizing values conducive to criminality. . . .

2. The more relevant the common purpose of the group to the reformation of criminals, the greater will be its influence on the criminal members' attitudes and values. . . .

3. The more cohesive the group, the greater the members' readiness to influence others and the more relevant the problem of conformity to group norms. . . .

4. Both reformers and those to be reformed must achieve status within the group by exhibition of "proreform" or anticriminal values and behavior patterns. . . .

5. The most effective mechanism for exerting group pressure on members will be found in groups so organized that criminals are induced to join with noncriminals for the purposes of changing other criminals. . . .

6. When an entire group is the target of change, as in a prison or

[17] Donald R. Cressey, "Changing Criminals: The Application of the Theory of Differential Association," *American Journal of Sociology*, Vol. 61 (September 1955), 116-20; see also the more general statement by Cartwright on which Cressey's model is based: Dorwin Cartwright, "Achieving Change in People: Some Applications of Group Dynamics Theory," *Human Relations*, Vol. 4, No. 4 (1951), 381-92.

among delinquent gangs, strong pressure for change can be achieved
by convincing the members of the need for change, thus making the
group itself the source of pressure for change.[18]

Group therapy programs following these "group relations" principles can be viewed as contrived or managed operations that parallel "natural" social processes involved in attitude development and
change. They represent the practical application of some basic
principles regarding the origins of social attitudes. Group therapy
flows out of implicit or explicit assumptions that deviants behave
as they do because of the group associations in which they are involved. In the main, the attitudes and values of the individual
criminal or delinquent are the beliefs of his major reference groups.
If this is so, to turn him into a nondeviant, his group associations
must be changed. He must either be induced to enter new social
groups and to break off interaction with his former associates, or
attempts must be made to change the behavior and attitudes of
the existing groups with whom he now interacts. Group therapy
tries to accomplish the latter—to convert criminalistic groups into
noncriminalistic ones.

Group treatment can take several different forms, including efforts to work with natural groups. "Detached worker" ("street
worker") programs used with delinquent gangs in lower-class neighborhoods in American cities represent one example of this kind.
In these, treatment workers are assigned to work with delinquent
gangs "at large." They seek out specific delinquent gangs known
to already exist in the community and then attempt to infiltrate
the gangs or to become a kind of member of the group. They use a
variety of specific techniques to try to convert gangs into groups
oriented around prosocial norms and attitudes. The point is that
this form of group treatment begins with real-life collectivities that
have existed prior to the development of the preventive or rehabilitative program.

A second form which group therapy often takes in practice involves efforts to create anticriminalistic *groups* out of *aggregates* of
criminalistic persons. In institutions, a bunch of inmates are collected and assigned to a specific treatment "group." The members
of this therapy collection do not initially represent a true social

---

[18] Cressey, "Changing Criminals," 118-19.

group, even though many of them may be acquainted with each other. In many cases, at the outset, the principal thing these persons have in common is an interest in using the therapy experience for "deviant" ends, such as to impress the parole board and gain an early release from prison. But this mutual interest does not make them a group in the social sense. As therapy proceeds, the expectation is that the members will come to represent a group in the sociological sense, with shared norms, a status and leadership structure, and other associational properties which emerge in the course of treatment. In turn, such a group may develop allegiance to noncriminal norms and values so as to ultimately become an important prosocial reference group for each individual participant.

As group therapy, or guided group interaction as it is sometimes called, has developed in practice, small groups of offenders usually meet together over a period of time with some correctional person designated as the leader or therapist. In the beginning, that person is called upon to initiate discussions of various topics, to provide direction to the interaction, and in other ways to act as a leader. However, his aim is to rapidly become a group-centered therapist in the course of the meetings. He tries to become simply one member of a group, in which the other participants are as active or more active than he is. In effect, the attempt is made to evolve a real group with some consensus around the need for behavioral change, in which the offenders engage in problem-solving discussions and in which new, anticriminal norms develop.

Actual group therapy sessions frequently begin with random, hostile remarks and complaints by members which represent a sort of ventilation of feelings or "blowing off steam." But this is not an end or goal of therapy, as already noted. Instead, the ultimate goal is one wherein such remarks and statements by particular individuals come to be criticized, corrected, or modified by other group members. Hostility ventilation is seen as providing grist for group interaction which hopefully will eventually lead to the development of new, prosocial norms and attitudes.

One issue in the literature regarding group therapy is the question of what kinds of individuals are capable of initiating and directing such therapy. Distinctions are sometimes drawn between "group therapy" and "group counseling," on the basis that the latter is a less intense process than the former. Group therapy is regarded as more intensive (and presumably, more therapeutic) activity which can best be directed by persons with training in case work and behavioral science, whereas group counseling is seen as a more informal and less intensive process which can be carried on by untrained persons such as prison guards.[19]

This sort of terminological proliferation is unfortunate, for it diverts attention from the key question regarding the extent to which some form of activity is designed to create real groups with new attitudinal and normative patterns. If it has this purpose it is group therapy; if it does not, it is not group therapy. Basically then, group therapy and group counseling are words for the same thing insofar as they are efforts to contrive prosocial groups in order to change offenders into nondeviants.

Another disturbing feature of this group therapy–group counseling distinction is that an implicit assumption is usually involved that guards, cottage workers, and other relatively untrained correctional workers are not capable of carrying out intensive forms of treatment. According to this view, these must be restricted to clinicians, psychiatrists, or highly trained case workers. There is little evidence for such a presumption, so that it may well be that many prison guards could be as effective, or more effective, than so-called professional workers in treatment efforts, given that they were provided with a modest degree of behavioral knowledge through in-service training. After all, most correctional officers have one advantage as potential treatment agents not possessed by professionals in that they usually are from backgrounds similar to those of the inmate group. In a word, they "speak the con's language."

The point at issue here also applies to other kinds of therapy, such as client-centered individual treatment directed at "normal" offenders. In the case of many of the persons who find their way into correctional case loads, hypotheses that they are suffering from severe personality malfunctioning cannot be sustained. Many individuals in conventional correctional settings such as predatory and conflict gang delinquents, joyriders, semiprofessional property criminals, naive check forgers, and other types are law violators

---

[19] This sort of distinction is contained in Norman Fenton, *An Introduction to Group Counseling in State Correctional Service* (New York: The American Correctional Association, 1958). Fenton's volume represents one detailed effort to spell out procedural steps, specific tactics, and the like to be used by "nonprofessional" employees in correctional group counseling. Also see Fenton, *et al., Explorations in the Use of Group Counseling in the County Correctional Program* (Palo Alto, Cal.: Pacific Books, 1962).

with relatively normal personality structures but with deviant "definitions of the situation." As such, they may be amenable to several
forms of treatment which would attempt to create new definitions
to replace those interpretive views which lie behind their deviant
behavior. The relevant therapy needed probably does not require
the services of such highly trained rehabilitative agents as psychiatrists. Instead, it may be possible to provide reasonably intelligent, stable laymen with a modest amount of training sufficient to
make them effective rehabilitators. Quite obviously, this means
something more than giving guards or cottage workers some vague
directive such as "Get out there and rehabilitate prisoners." The
hypothesis is not that anyone can do treatment work, but rather,
that it would be possible to utilize many persons who are not now
usually implicated in therapy, provided that they are given some
training in group principles, criminal and delinquent causation,
and so forth.

Up to the present, most applications of group treatment have
been in institutional settings. An orderly group program can be
run there because inmates can be given directives to appear for
treatment at an appointed time. Fewer applications of group
methods have been made in such settings as probation and parole
agencies, although there is no apparent insurmountable obstacle
to the use of group methods in these areas of correctional activity.
It has already been noted that the "detached worker" or "street
worker" programs among delinquent gangs in working-class neighborhoods in American cities are examples of group therapy "at
large."

MILIEU MANAGEMENT

Milieu management is a form of treatment which is more
ambitious than group therapy but which pursues the same basic
goals. The term refers to efforts which usually go on in institutions
where nearly all parts of the program are coordinated to the goal
of rehabilitation. The core notion behind operations of this kind
is clear enough, namely, that the most effective kind of therapeutic
experience for offenders in institutions would be one in which the
situation in all its details represents an experiment in social living,
so that by learning how to adjust to the institution, the inmate
also learns how to manage himself in a law-abiding fashion in the

free community. Conversely, the argument is that therapy will be less effective if it must compete with a variety of antitreatment influences in the surrounding environment. For example, the efforts of social workers or psychiatrists on behalf of prisoners will probably not produce maximum behavioral change if the correctional officers are hostile to the treatment operation and if they go about actively promulgating negative definitions of therapy. Efforts to contrive a therapeutic milieu in this situation would be concerned with changing the guard's views of psychiatrists as "head-shrinkers" or "bug doctors," with involving the correctional officers and other nonprofessional personnel in the rehabilitative operation, and with a whole series of other modifications in this direction.

Much of the contemporary interest in milieu management in corrections has been stimulated by the growth of theory and research findings regarding "therapeutic communities" for mental patients. These have developed out of the accelerated awareness in the mental health field that many of the features of traditional mental hospitals militate against treatment of patients. Many observers have noted the rigid authority structures, the hardened status distinctions among employees, the antitreatment attitudes characteristic of ward personnel, and the existence of an informal social structure as well as the formal one in most state mental institutions. The corollary belief has arisen that the therapeutic career of the patient in the hospital is markedly affected by the various "nontreatment" events that occur to him there and that are a result of the institution's social organization. More and more concern has been voiced for programs which will either keep many mentally disordered individuals out of mental hospitals in the first place or which will materially alter the institutions toward therapeutic communities. Anyone interested in parallel programs for criminalistic deviants would be well advised to study the literature that has grown up around these matters, particularly in view of the relative paucity of commentary on therapeutic milieus in corrections.[20]

[20] A small sample of some of the more useful of these works, for correctional purposes, would include Maxwell Jones and others, *The Therapeutic Community* (New York: Basic Books, Inc., 1953); Jones, *Social Psychiatry in the Community, in Hospitals, and in Prisons* (Springfield: Charles C. Thomas, 1962); Alfred H. Stanton and Morris S. Schwartz, *The Mental Hospital* (New York: Basic Books, Inc., 1954); William A. Caudill, *The Psychiatric Hospital as a*

Several examples can be offered to show the form of milieu management in corrections. The Highfields project in New Jersey is one such example.[21] Here the former Lindbergh mansion at Highfields was taken over by the state as the site for a program which was initially experimental in form. A group of about twenty boys was assigned to the institution and was subjected to a therapeutic diet of "guided group interaction" combined with other structured activities.

The originators of the Highfields program were guided by some explicit theory of causation and treatment. The boys who were the subject of attention were viewed as individuals who had acquired antisocial attitudes and self-images through interaction with delinquent peers within a general context of social and community disorganization. Guided group interaction was employed to change their self-images from delinquent to nondelinquent. Personality change of this kind is attempted through group processes, where the influence of the group is used to free the boy from control by delinquent association.[22] The developers of the program argued that delinquent motivations and role-conceptions are the product of social experiences such as association with delinquent peers. It follows that the treatment problem is to modify these psychological concomitants of deviant behavior through a reversal of conventional group influences toward delinquency. That is, guided group interaction strives to create groups emphasizing nondelinquent perspectives.

However, the Highfields program involves more than guided group interaction meetings within a conventional institutional structure. Because the organization is small, Highfields has a minimum of fixed, formal rules, and the boys have trouble trying to "beat the system" by learning how to evade rules. Additionally, inmates work forty hours per week, usually as farm laborers at a nearby mental hospital. This work situation is set up to approximate, as nearly as possible, an employment environment that a boy

---

Small Society (Cambridge, Mass.: Harvard University Press, 1958); August Aichhorn, *Wayward Youth* (New York: Meridian Books, 1955); Bruno Bettelheim, *Love is Not Enough* (New York: The Free Press of Glencoe, Inc., 1952); Fritz Redl and David Wineman, *Controls From Within* (New York: The Free Press of Glencoe, Inc., 1952).

[21] Lloyd W. McCorkle, Albert Elias, and F. Lovell Bixby, *The Highfields Story* (New York: Holt, Rinehart and Winston, Inc., 1958).

[22] *Ibid.*, pp. v-vi.

might find in the outside community. The boys are paid for their labor, and they can be disciplined by their supervisor or even fired for poor work activities. The rationale is that because many Highfields wards come there with the view that "only suckers work," they must learn new definitions of the place of employment in their lives if they are to make a successful postrelease adjustment. This and other parts of the over-all program are intended to provide boys with opportunities to try out new social roles and behavior patterns. In summary, Highfields represents an institutional correctional system which has tried to develop and articulate connections between the formal therapy activities and other parts of the total operation.

A second illustration of milieu management would be the New Haven Borstal institution in British Columbia, Canada. This program is carried on in a physical plant not unlike that of Highfields in that both Highfields and the New Haven plant are former residential structures which have been converted to correctional uses. In the latter case, a group of about thirty boys reside there at any one time. The program in which they are involved is a blend of individual social case work treatment by a social worker, vocational training, and informal group counseling by the employees of the institution. Most of these persons are older, mature males who are ostensibly hired to supervise the vocational or work activities of the inmates. However, they also carry on a good deal of informal individual and group counseling with their charges. Here again, this program is one which tries to create a series of different but related experiences through which boys proceed and which are designed to have therapeutic consequences.

A third and final illustration of milieu management is represented by the institution known as "Synanon." [23] Unlike the first

[23] Lewis Yablonsky, "The Anticriminal Society: Synanon," *Federal Probation,* Vol. 26 (September 1962), 50-57; Daniel Casriel, *So Fair a House: The Story of Synanon* (Englewood Cliffs: Prentice-Hall, Inc., 1963); a thoughtful but discordant note regarding Synanon is sounded in David Sternberg, "Synanon House—A Consideration of its Implications for American Correction," *Journal of Criminal Law, Criminology and Police Science,* Vol. 54 (December 1963), 447-55. Among other things, Sternberg suggests that the goals of Synanon are more in the direction of long-term *protection* of addicts than they are toward "rehabilitation" involving early return of the person to full participation in the general society. He also suggests that direct applications of Synanon procedures to conventional correctional work might not be possible for a variety of reasons, including the nonvolunteer status of correctional clients.

two cases, this is a nongovernmental operation. Synanon is a private organization which originated about six years ago in Santa Monica, California. It is a residential program for drug addicts, located in an old building which was at one time a National Guard armory. The present activities of Synanon evolved from some informal associations between a collection of drug addicts and alcoholics with Charles E. Dederich, the "founder" of Synanon. Dederich has described the social climate that operates in Synanon in the following terms:

> We have here a climate consisting of a family structure similar in some areas to a primitive tribal structure, which seems to affect individuals on a subconscious level. The structure also contains overtones of a nineteenth-century family set-up of the type which produced inner-directed personalities. It is the feeling of the Synanon Foundation that an undetermined percentage of narcotic addicts are potentially inner-directed people. A more or less autocratic family structure appears to be necessary as a preconditioning environment to buy time for the recovering addict.

> . . . The autocratic overtone of the family structure demands that the patients or members of the family perform tasks as a part of the group. As a member is able to take direction in small tasks such as helping in the preparation of meals, housecleaning, and so forth, regardless of his rebellion at being "told what to do," his activity seems to provide exercise of emotions of giving or creating which have lain dormant. As these muscles strengthen, it seems that the resistance to cooperating with the group tends to dissipate.[24]

In an article by Yablonsky, from which the above quotation is taken, the program of Synanon is indicated as including some type of work activity, either inside the institution or in the outside community; a noon educational seminar; the Synanon or group therapy program; and daily interaction with hundreds of "squares" (nonaddicts) who visit the building regularly.[25]

In its basic outlines, the Synanon operation is very close to that of Alcoholics Anonymous, at least in certain respects. It is also quite similar to Cressey's group treatment model cited earlier. In Synanon, addicts have voluntarily banded together to help each other become cured. The experience record to date suggests that this program

---

[24] Yablonsky, *op. cit.*, 51.
[25] *Ibid.*, 51-52.

"works," in that it has resulted in a sizeable number of addicts staying "clean" (free from drug use) for extended periods of time. These results are in marked contrast to the high relapse or recidivism rates characteristic of conventional programs for the rehabilitation of addicts.[26]

One thing that is readily apparent about all these illustrations of milieu management is that they represent marked departures from traditional institutional programs. All of them are treatment endeavors involving a relatively small number of inmates or patients, and in the case of Synanon, the residents are all voluntary patients rather than captives. Although there might be some question about the optimal size of organizations in which milieu treatment can be carried out, it is quite probable that complete forms of treatment require a relatively small group of participants, somewhere under a hundred persons. The organizers of Highfields report that when they attempted to deal with more than twenty inmates at a time, some important negative consequences to the program developed.

Korn and McCorkle have developed a description of the treatment process for "adaptive," "normal" offenders in conventional, large-population penal institutions which represents a somewhat circumscribed version of milieu therapy.[27] "Adaptive" offenders are common in both juvenile and adult correctional facilities, as they are frequent among gang delinquents, semiprofessional property offenders, and other offender types.[28] Adaptive violators are persons who are pursuing conventional goals by deviant means and who have been relatively successful in these endeavors. As a result,

[26] Rita Volkman and Donald R. Cressey, "Differential Association and the Rehabilitation of Drug Addicts," *American Journal of Sociology*, Vol. 69 (September 1963), 129-42. In this article, they show that the Synanon program closely parallels Cressey's notions of the form of criminal treatment implied by differential association theory (see p. 159 of this book). Also, they present evidence indicating that the success rate for persons staying longer than 7 months in the Synanon program is 86 per cent. That is, 86 per cent of those persons participating in the program for more than 7 months have stayed "clean" (free from drug use).

[27] Richard R. Korn and Lloyd W. McCorkle, *Criminology and Penology* (New York: Holt, Rinehart and Winston, Inc., 1959), pp. 540-52. This book should be examined by anyone interested in some valuable commentary on treatment, for it contains probably the best textbook discussion of therapy produced so far. See especially pp. 532-78.

[28] Richard L. Jenkins, "Adaptive and Maladaptive Delinquency," *The Nervous Child*, Vol. 2 (October 1955), 9-12.

they enter any sort of therapeutic relationship intent upon manipulating and exploiting the therapist in order to obtain various situational objectives. They are not initially motivated to seek help because they do not see themselves as having real problems.

Korn and McCorkle identify seven stages in the treatment of inmates of this kind. Presumably these stages would occur in either successful client-centered or group-centered therapy. Stage 1 is called "The Struggle for Control," in which the offender tries, unsuccessfully, to establish a manipulative relationship with the therapist. When the inmate fails to define the worker as a "dupe" or "sucker," he then tries to put him in the role of oppressor or "son of a bitch." Somewhere along here, the subject enters the second stage, in which he withdraws from therapy but attempts to manipulate other workers in the institution, such as work supervisors, teachers, or guards. At this point, it is vital that the entire institution be able to thwart the prisoner in this kind of attempted adjustment, while at the same time, allowing him sufficient freedom to try to establish an exploitive adjustment. In other words, he must not be prevented from trying to "beat the system," but he must be made to fail at the attempt.

Korn and McCorkle maintain that when the inmate encounters repeated failure at his endeavors to adjust to the institution on his terms, to "play it cool" and to do "easy time," he enters Stage 3 in which he tries to carve out a martyr role for himself. He begins to engage in flamboyant and disruptive behavior. At this point, he should be transferred to the segregation unit. He would not be abused in any way there so that he could not become an "heroic sufferer," but he would be prevented from playing a role as a visible inmate hero-martyr.

After a time, the inmate would enter the fourth stage of despair, as he experiences repeated frustration of his system-beating efforts. Still later, the stage of self-doubt emerges, in which the person begins to see that his efforts at antisocial adjustment are getting him nowhere. At some point in this period, the therapist would begin to help the offender toward new perspectives, although much of this would be the product of the person's own efforts. Then at still a later point, the inmate would be released from segregation and would enter the sixth stage, where his new orientation would be tested in the prison community. The final stage of therapy involves termination of treatment, which might be handled by transferring the "rehabilitated" prisoner to a minimum security institution.[29]

Now, there is reason to ask whether this therapy process identified by Korn and McCorkle depends too much upon psychological devices and negative conditioning in the form of frustrating experiences and not enough upon positive pressures toward conformity emanating from peers and staff members. Be that as it may, the program which they identify qualifies as a version of milieu management in that it depends for its success upon a coherent, integrated, and systematic set of prison or training school experiences which undermine the inmate's confidence in manipulative modes of adjustment. It is not sufficient that the prisoner is not able to "con" the case worker—he must fail in efforts to manipulate any and all other officials too.

It is likely that the establishment of this kind of milieu is fraught with difficulties, and the creation of a more diffuse, positive therapeutic community within traditional prisons would probably encounter even greater problems. What are some of these obstacles that develop when milieu programs are attempted in large organizations? One problem centers around disciplinary incidents involving inmates and staff members, interpersonal problems among prisoners, and escapes. Suppose that someone were to attempt to convert a conventional reformatory holding a thousand or so prisoners into a full-blown therapeutic milieu. That person would immediately be faced with the fact that among the inmates there are some who are uncooperative and hostile individuals, prone to violence and escape attempts. Even though such prisoners might be a minority in the institution, their numbers would still be sizeable. As a result, considerable attention must be given to containing these individuals within the penal facility, while at the same time repressing their aggressive behavior. In turn, the more time spent on custodial activities, the less which remains for treatment efforts.

Even if it were somehow possible to remove most of the more violent and intractable inmates from the situation by segregating them elsewhere in another facility, important impediments to the development of a therapeutic community would still be found. Given a population of prisoners numbering a thousand or more, and given a small number of employees to deal with them, almost

---

[29] Korn and McCorkle, *Criminology and Penology*, pp. 542-52.

inevitable pressures develop in the direction of "block handling" of men. The fact of population size alone means that programs and decisions must be routinized. Schedules must be set up in which clots of individuals perform actions according to established routines. These routines take forms such as the following: "all prisoners in Cell House B line up for the evening meal at 5:00 P.M. and leave the mess hall at 6:15 P.M. All inmates in Cell House B shall be locked in their cells at 6:30 P.M." In short, the spontaneity and flexibility characteristic and necessary in milieu forms of programs must be sacrificed to the demands for conformity among prisoners and for institutional security.

This is not to say that steps toward a therapeutic milieu in large institutions are impossible. Rather, the point of these remarks is that on logical grounds alone, it might be argued that all treatment efforts which involve group therapy (or other kinds of treatment such as psychotherapy) should be structured within a generally therapeutic milieu. But from a practical standpoint, it is rather doubtful that such a recommendation can be fully implemented. Existing correctional institutions cannot all be torn down and replaced with small living units designed for milieu treatment. Instead, rehabilitative ventures will continue to be carried on, in part at least, within existing, large facilities. Although some important steps might be taken to transform these places into systems in which the general institutional climate is more conducive to therapy, there are some limits to the extent to which this can be accomplished.

On the other side of this issue, there are certain modifications which could be made, and in some cases which have been made, in large custodial institutions toward a therapeutic milieu. One of these is the development of inmate councils in which a small group of inmate representatives is given some consultative role to play with the administrative officials in the determination of policy. Another innovation in recent years involves exploratory, experimental reductions or changes in some traditional prison routines. For example, some institutions have tried out new policies in which inmates are allowed to move to and from evening recreational programs in spontaneous small groups rather than in long, single lines under guard. These innovations seem to indicate that although the system demands some degree of routinization, it is possible to become too guided by routine and mass scheduling. Untoward incidents have not accompanied some of these program innovations.

The creation of reception and orientation operations is yet another development in the direction of a treatment-oriented facility. Finally, some modification of the institution's social climate could be obtained through alterations in the treatment programs. Specifically, group counseling in which correctional officers conduct therapy sessions as a part of their job responsibilities is one such step. One consequence of guard-directed therapy might well be the development of a shared definition of the organization as treatment-oriented. This is in contrast to the common situation at present in which "treatment" is regarded both by the prisoners and the correctional officers as an incidental and trivial operation tenuously grafted onto the organization.

One relatively novel suggestion for milieu program development in institutions ought to be considered, namely, the use of offender "patients" as therapists. Deviants also represent a potential source of effective therapists in other settings, such as probation, but it is in custodial institutions that such roles might be most easily implemented. In turn, the use of inmates as rehabilitative agents would be a move toward the creation of therapeutic communities.

How could "clients" be employed as therapists? In a correctional facility program, the general outlines of such an endeavor are reasonably clear. Certain prisoners would be selected to serve as therapists at an advanced point in their institutional careers. In turn, under supervision by a staff member, they would be given the assignment of conducting individual or group treatment sessions. Group activities of this kind would be similar to Alcoholics Anonymous in format, as the latter operates without any kind of group leadership by a professional therapist. The difference between a system utilizing inmate-therapists and conventional group treatment centers on this leadership role. The latter activity usually operates under the direction of a staff member, even though the inmates in the group contribute in important ways to the therapeutic undertaking. But in the former pattern, certain prisoners would assume the leader role normally played by a professional staff member.

To whom would the benefits, if any, of inmate-managed therapy accrue? In theory at least, these undertakings would be therapeutically significant for both the inmate-therapist and the treatment subjects. The prisoner doing the job of therapy would be engaged in experiences which powerfully reinforce his emerging conception of himself as someone who can "make it" as a law-abiding citizen. In effect, by acting as a therapy agent, the prisoner would be engaging in some crucial role-playing experiences with the institution. At the same time, the inmates making up the treatment group would presumably be benefitting from the therapy. In turn, at some advanced point in their resocialization experience, many of them might be converted into rehabilitators.

At least one attempt has actually been made to incorporate inmates into treatment activities as therapists.[30] In the Intensive Treatment Program in operation at the California Institution for Men at Chino, some of the group therapy given to the experimental subjects is being administered by inmate "social therapists," as they are called. The program in question is one involving young, first-offender felony cases. An experimental (treatment) group, along with a control group not receiving the intensive therapy, is to be studied during a two-year parole period to assess the effects, if any, of correctional treatment conducted in a special therapeutic milieu within the host institution. The unit in which this special project is being conducted is isolated from the rest of the facility. Also, the staff members in the program are involved in unconventional role-patterns, in that they wear no uniforms and perform both treatment and custodial assignments. The therapy subjects participate in daily community meetings of prisoners and staff and in social therapy groups of twelve or so men five times per week.

The history of this project presents an illuminating demonstration of the possibilities for the use of offenders in treatment work. In addition, the chronology of events illustrates some of the difficulties that crop up in efforts to innovate new procedures within ongoing correctional structures. The use of inmate therapists started with the selection by the administrators of ten prisoners to serve as "social therapists." Over the subsequent seven months, these individuals engaged in a variety of troublesome actions, such as using their new roles as a "front" behind which they went about various

---

[30] Dennie L. Briggs, "Convicted Felons as Social Therapists," *Corrective Psychiatry and Journal of Social Therapy*, Vol. 9 (3rd Quarter 1963), 122-27; Briggs and John M. Dowling, "The Correctional Officer as a Consultant: An Emerging Role in Penology," *American Journal of Correction*, Vol. 26 (May-June 1964) 28-31.

illegal activities. All ten were finally "fired" from the treatment job and returned to regular prisoner assignments. Following that development, the inmates established new criteria for the selection of therapists. At the time of Briggs' report, four prisoners were serving as therapists, apparently quite effectively.

It seems debatable that many communities would tolerate experiments in probation, parole, or other situations outside of penal facilities, in which "bad guys" are employed to rehabilitate other "bad guys." Nonetheless, a powerful case could be made on theoretical grounds for efforts of that kind. The basic argument would be twofold, for perhaps the therapeutic activity would have positive repercussions upon both the treater and the treated. At any rate, notions of this kind ought to be explored in the search for efficacious strategies of behavioral intervention.

ENVIRONMENTAL CHANGE

The dividing points among the different forms of treatment identified so far are not entirely abrupt, and this is certainly the case with the demarcation between milieu management and environmental change. However, the first involves tactics aimed at changing a specific, narrow social situation such as the organizational and social climate of a correctional institution, whereas the second refers to efforts which are considerably more comprehensive in scope. Environmental change designates endeavors to alter or remove features of natural social environments, such as urban community areas, which are believed to be directly or indirectly implicated in the production of criminal or delinquent behavior.

The focus of attention in environmental change is often more upon *rate-producing* factors in criminality than it is upon alterations in the attitudes and behavior of specific deviants or upon eradication of the forces impelling them to deviation. Environmental programs frequently center around such things as improvements in community social organization and do not directly involve lawbreakers in a first-hand effort to change them. As a result, it might be argued that the inclusion of environmental change with the previously discussed forms of treatment violates the conception of treatment with which this chapter began. According to that earlier statement, the term treatment should be applied to those actions specifically intended to alter criminalistic characteristics of persons.

There are two arguments for the discussion of environmental change programs in this book. The most obvious one is that programs of this kind are in existence in some number, so that to ignore them would be to create a misleading impression of the forms taken by rehabilitative programs. Correctional activities are not confined to probation, institutional, and parole settings. Also, some of these efforts have joined diffuse community tactics with specific procedures aimed at deviant persons or groups, so that such programs are not completely unconcerned about individuals. However, the most important defense of environmental change as a form of treatment is that in the last analysis, if these endeavors have positive effects which lead to reductions of rates of deviance, those effects are to be observed upon specific individuals. In other words, environmental change activities represent a circuitous approach to the alteration of deviant roles. In effect, the intention of efforts of this kind is to bring about changes in antisocial sentiments of members of the community. Even though particular individuals are not singled out for attention, the fact remains that community modification actions are intended to produce changes by a large number of persons, both deviant and otherwise. After all, it is not possible to change rates without changing people, for rates are compounded out of the behavior of individuals.

Most of the efforts toward environmental change to date have been preventive in orientation, geared to nipping fledgling delinquent careers in the bud; treatment activities were not designed to change persons already known to be law violators,[31] and rehabilitation of existing offenders has usually been viewed as an indirect by-product. But there is no apparent reason why environmental modification programs could not be directed at treatment as well as prevention. Such efforts would be extremely difficult and complicated, but this is no less true for preventive programs than for treatment undertakings.

One well-known and pioneering example of environmental

---

[31] For a summary of many of these, see Helen L. Witmer and Edith Tufts, *The Effectiveness of Delinquency Prevention Programs*, U.S. Children's Bureau Publication No. 350 (Washington, D.C.: U.S. Government Printing Office, 1954); Sutherland and Cressey, *op. cit.*, pp. 590-624.

change which was structured to achieve both preventive and therapeutic ends is the Chicago Area Project.[32] This program has the
dual objectives of preventing delinquency and crime in certain
Chicago neighborhoods and also of rehabilitating parolees in the
areas. One summary of the goals and assumptions of the Chicago
Area Project is the following:

> The Chicago Area Project operates on the assumption that much of
> the delinquency of slum areas is to be attributed to lack of neighborhood
> cohesiveness and to the consequent lack of concern on the part of many
> residents about the welfare of children. The Project strives to counteract
> this situation through encouraging local self-help enterprises through
> which a sense of neighborliness and mutual responsibility will develop.
> It is expected that delinquency will decline as youngsters become better
> integrated into community life and thereby influenced by the values of
> conventional society rather than those of the underworld.[33]

The etiological theory involved in the Area Project is that delinquent and criminal values arise from lack of means or lack of
access to success goals, predominately monetary ones, experienced
by the majority of persons in lower-class, underprivileged slum
areas. As a consequence of this frustration, the attachment to conventional norms by some persons is eroded away. Some of these individuals begin to utilize deviant and illegal techniques to attain
success goals. At the same time, a general situation of personal
isolation exists in these areas in which people refrain from med-
dling in the affairs of others. The result is a community area lacking in social cohesion and embodying conflicts of values, and in
which criminal and noncriminal norms exist in the same area, so
that tolerance of deviant behavior is widespread. Symbiotic connections between carriers of criminal culture and ostensible nondeviants are commonplace, such as the links between junk dealers
and predatory delinquents or among policemen, "policy" gambling
figures, and "respectable" citizens.

Proceeding upon this version of slum "disorganization" theory,
the Chicago Area Project views the key to prevention as involving

[32] See Witmer and Tufts, *op. cit.*, pp. 11-17; Sutherland and Cressey, *op. cit.*,
pp. 610-11; Solomon Kobrin, "The Chicago Area Project—A 25-Year Assessment,"
Annals of the American Academy of Political and Social Science, Vol. 322 (March
1959), 19-29.

[33] Witmer and Tufts, *op. cit.*, p. 11.

self-help activities on the part of noncriminal citizens in slum areas. High-status residents are encouraged to utilize their leadership potential in the program, for only in this way will a sense of neighborhood cohesiveness develop. As a corollary of this approach, outside leadership of community efforts is kept to a minimum. The core of this self-help effort is the neighborhood center, which is a recreational and educational facility, staffed mainly by community residents. However, the Area Project involves a number of other related activities as well, such as discussion groups on child problems and so forth. In summary, the Chicago Area Project is a program which strives to develop an "antidelinquency society" in slum communities so that pressures toward delinquent and criminal conduct will be reduced in these areas.

A more recent example of environmental change is found in the Midcity Project,[34] a delinquency control venture carried on in a lower-class district of Boston between 1954 and 1957. It proceeded upon a sophisticated and complex theoretical rationale, so that in this sense, the project provides an excellent example of the direction in which treatment ventures might generally be moving.

The several kinds of activities constituting the Midcity undertaking all flowed out of a "total community" philosophy regarding control and inhibition of illegal actions among juveniles in working-class urban neighborhoods. The central thesis on which this project was based is that delinquent behavior is generated, encouraged, and facilitated by a number of structural features of the community, rather than primarily by personality disturbances among adolescents. These premises led to action programs directed at the community, family units, and delinquent gangs. These three societal units were regarded as importantly involved in the genesis and stimulation of delinquent actions by juveniles.

The community segment of this program involved two major parts. Attempts were made to "beef up" community citizens' groups so that they might be able to take more effective action against local difficulties of one sort or another. In addition, efforts were made to obtain improved cooperation among various professional agencies in the community having dealings with adolescents, such as churches, schools, and police and probation departments. The intention of

[34] Walter B. Miller, "The Impact of a 'Total Community' Delinquency Control Project," *Social Problems*, Vol. 10 (Fall 1962), 168-91.

these several lines of work was to bring together a number of formerly separate, diffuse, and overlapping services so that their efforts might lead to maximum results.

In the area of family services, the Midcity Project directed attention toward "chronic-problem" families in the area. That is, a number of families with long records of involvement with different social welfare agencies were given an intensive dose of psychiatric case work intended to make them less dependent upon agencies for assistance in problem-solving.

The major effort of this project centered about delinquent gangs and involved the detached-worker stratagem which has been utilized in New York City and elsewhere. This part of the project was particularly well developed, for all the workers were professional persons with degrees in social work. In addition, each agent handled only a single group, so that he was able to engage in intensive interaction with his gang. Finally, each worker had psychiatric consultation available to him, so that he was armed with more methods than usual among detached workers.

The Midcity Project was a demonstration effort, planned to operate for a specific, limited time period and to serve as an illustration of the efficacy of the "total community" approach. Unfortunately, the project failed to achieve a significant reduction in delinquency. The impact of the undertaking was measured in three different but related ways.[35] Trends in disapproved forms of customary behavior, such as certain sexual activity patterns, were studied, as well as trends in illegal behavior and court appearance rates for the delinquent gang members included in the project. When evaluated in these terms, the project appeared *not* to have achieved any significant reduction in delinquency.

In his discussion of this project, Miller points out that some parts of the Midcity Project were more completely "tested" than were others, in that some of the segments were developed to a greater extent than were others. The negative impact findings apply most emphatically to the citizens' council operation and to the street-worker activities, for these were the most highly developed. Miller also points out that the project did accomplish certain important results, even though it failed to achieve delinquency reduction. For one, the establishment of the project had a calming effect

[35] *Ibid.*, 176-86.

upon the community, which had been fearful and excited about a presumed wave of delinquent behavior. In addition, neighborhood social organization was left in a more highly-developed state than when the project began, so that the area was better prepared to deal with community problems, including delinquency, in the future.

Miller's interpretation of these findings is that certain lower-class values and interests are so compelling and pervasive in character as to outweigh or minimize the influences of programs such as the Midcity Project.[36] Undeniably, community action programs in working-class neighborhoods do face formidable obstacles in cultural and social structure, so that short-term programs cannot be expected to make much of a dent in crime and delinquency. Perhaps the investment of energy in such efforts must exceed some minimum figure, such as five years of activity, before results begin to occur, before a "take-off" point is reached. Thus it is possible that the negligible impact of this specific program was a function of insufficient effort, rather than of a misdirected or erroneous rationale. However, such a line of argument could easily be turned into a "dodge" to explain away all negative findings. Stated differently, it is possible that in particular programs such as the Midcity Project, significant results would not occur no matter how long they were carried on, in that they stem from a basically faulty rationale. Only time and more research will tell which of the possibilities is the correct one.

Other kinds of environmental change activities in addition to those that have been discussed can be visualized. Some of these have already been attempted, such as programs designed to increase the recreational outlets available to teenagers in high delinquency areas. Also, there are a number of current theories of crime and delinquency which have implications for community action. For example, suppose that Cohen's arguments regarding delinquent subcultures and the status problems of working-class boys are made the basis of programs of change.[37] Concerted efforts might be made to modify the social climate of schools and other community institutions in lower-class areas, so as to reduce the amount of invidious status discrimination leveled at working-class boys. Or take

[36] *Ibid.*, 185-86.
[37] Albert K. Cohen, *Delinquent Boys* (New York: The Free Press of Glencoe, Inc., 1955).

another case, the "opportunity structures" theory of Cloward and Ohlin.[38] The environmental changes implied in this theory are relatively clear, namely, a series of modifications in the prevailing structure of opportunities such as in employment or education for lower-class boys. Another program stemming from the Cloward and Ohlin argument might be one which attempts to communicate an accurate picture of available legitimate opportunities to working-class youths, for many of them may be unaware of the actual opportunities that are presently available to them. A multimillion dollar project in New York City called "Mobilization for Youth," which has developed from a theoretical base of Cloward-Ohlin theory, is underway.[39] This project is an exceedingly ambitious and multi-dimensional one, involving thirty separate "action" programs in the four major areas of work, education, community, and group service.

One of the dominant orienting themes of Mobilization for Youth is that lower-class youngsters must be provided with genuine opportunities to behave in nondeviant ways, or in Cloward-Ohlin terms, with legitimate opportunity structures, if they are to be prevented from engaging in deviant behavior. Mobilization for Youth is also predicated upon the assumption that local residents must be implicated in prevention programs. Effective control of delinquent behavior cannot take place solely through the operation of programs imposed upon the community from the outside. In short, the view is that an organized, anticriminal community must be developed in order to create pressures toward nondelinquent juvenile behavior.

Following from the above notions, Mobilization for Youth is constituted of a number of specific programs of action in the areas of work, education, community, and group services, carried on in a section of New York City's Lower East Side. One of the major parts of the total program concerns the "world of work," in which an "Urban Youth Service Corps" provides paid employment for several hundred unemployed, out-of-school youths. The participants are employed in neighborhood conservation endeavors and a num-

[38] Richard A. Cloward and Lloyd E. Ohlin, *Delinquency and Opportunity* (New York: The Free Press of Glencoe, Inc., 1960).

[39] This program is reported in detail in *A Proposal for the Prevention and Control of Delinquency by Expanding Opportunities* (New York City: Mobilization for Youth, Inc., December 1961); it is reported briefly in *A Report on Juvenile Delinquency* (Washington, D.C.: Hearings of the Subcommittee on Appropriations, 1960), pp. 113-16.

ber of other kinds of work activities. This youth corps is intended to create work skills and prowork attitudes on the part of boys who are initially almost unemployable because of their lack of these skills and attitudes. Also in the work segment, a "Youth Jobs Center" acts as a coordinated agency which attempts to find permanent employment for boys who have completed a work experience in the Urban Youth Service Corps.

Mobilization for Youth also involves many activities in education, including teacher visitation programs and a laboratory school to demonstrate effective methods of teaching lower-income students. Another educational project is called the "Homework Helper" program, in which academically successful lower-class high school students are hired to tutor elementary school students.

The community part of the Mobilization for Youth project involves efforts to strengthen a pre-existing community organization, the Lower East Side Neighborhoods Association. A variety of specific tactics are also employed to create social organizations among formerly unaffiliated, isolated community residents. In the same way, indigenous operations such as store-front churches, not usually a part of neighborhood organization efforts, are to be drawn into collaborative area development efforts.

Another feature of Mobilization for Youth concerns assistance of various kinds to "problem" families in the project area. Local "helping stations" called "Neighborhood Service Centers" are established in four Lower East Side areas. These were created to help families obtain social services, redress housing complaints, and so forth.

Finally, in the group service section of the Mobilization for Youth project, the program is involved in supplementing services to delinquent gangs now provided by the New York City Youth Board. Thus detached-worker activities are a part of the total program, although not operated specifically by Mobilization for Youth. Another group effort centers around three "coffee shops" which are cultural centers set up in store fronts to serve as more desirable substitutes for conventional neighborhood hangouts. Finally, relatively young children in the project area are to be drawn into an "Adventure Corps" which is designed to provide appealing nondelinquent activities and experiences for delinquency-prone youngsters.

The Mobilization for Youth program is an imaginative undertaking, as well as a theoretically sophisticated one. As such, it provides a model for community-level prevention efforts. Research evaluation of the program is to be undertaken, although no evidence is yet at hand regarding the effectiveness of the project. In this regard, it should be noted that the multifaceted character of Mobilization for Youth, which is probably its major virtue as a preventive venture, works real hardships upon efforts to evaluate the undertaking. Given the many different components that are included, it may become exceedingly difficult to untangle the specific contribution, if any, that each part has made to an end result, such as reduced rates of deviant behavior. Programs such as this truly indicate the complexity of behavioral change, and they illustrate as well some of the extraordinary difficulties in correctional evaluation research.

These several programs illustrate what could be done in environmental modifications. Doubtless other changes could be visualized as well. The possibilities of environmentally oriented programs certainly have not been exhausted, for such projects have been restricted to lower-class or "subcultural" gang delinquency. Quite probably there are other forms of crime and delinquency in which environmental tampering would make sense. But one major difficulty of such programs at present stems from the empirical indeterminateness of prevailing theories regarding social structural and community factors in crime and delinquency. Some existing theories are just that, speculative arguments not supported by any hard data. Then, too, it is probably true that existing theories regarding environmental pressures are oversimplified in statement, even if they do possess elements of truth. For example, it is perhaps the case that working-class delinquency stems from a number of interrelated environmental pressures rather than from some single set, such as the lack of legitimate opportunity structures. Some working-class youths may be involved in misbehavior out of motives arising from perceived defects of status, others may be motivated to engage in law violations as an illegitimate opportunity structure, and still others participate for reasons identified in other, alternative theories of gang delinquency. This would seem to be a distinct possibility in the instance of working-class gang delinquency, in view of the fact that a number of these alternative formulations are variants on a common theme—lack of opportunity. That is, Cohen argues that gang delinquency develops as a consequence of one kind of lack of opportunity, whereas Cloward and Ohlin and others discuss other forms of defective opportunity structures as causal in delinquency. Perhaps life in lower-class settings is characterized by a range of invidious and frustrating experiences partially identified in each of the theories. There is no logic which demands that a behavioral outcome such as gang delinquency must be attributed to only one set of factors. An equally plausible possibility is that several different, identifiable, and related processes lead to the same outcome. This is not a question to be settled by fiat, but instead, it is an issue which can be properly adjudicated only by a test utilizing empirical evidence.

The foregoing is not to be confused with an antiscientific position to the effect that no stable causal processes in illegal behavior can be identified in operation. This book is committed to the presumption that etiological generalizations can be discovered, but it is another matter to assume that there must be only one specific causal sequence for each behavioral outcome.

If there are interrelated community pressures and factors operating in delinquency and criminality, the question then arises: "Where should attempts to change the criminogenic influences begin?" At the present juncture, programs of environmental modification may have to be directed at several collections of factors, rather than at one particular set which has been singled out in some etiological theory.

Before departing from this subject, a few remarks should be made about the shape of things to come. Specifically, considerably more attention will probably be directed toward a variety of environmental alteration efforts than has been characteristic in the past. The recent several decades in the United States have involved some profound changes in American life which cry out for more programs centering upon environmental modification of the broadest possible scope. These changes have been summed up in the widely discussed phenomenon of "the exploding metropolis."[40] As the population has become collected in large cities and suburban areas, two Americas existing side by side have emerged. One of these is the "affluent society" of abundant consumer goods and comfortable life styles, inhabited by skilled workers, white-collar employees, professionals, and the like, and located most usually in the suburbs

---

[40] Editors of Fortune, *The Exploding Metropolis* (Garden City, N.Y.: Doubleday and Co., Inc., 1957).

or in certain areas of the central city.[41] This is the world of the "haves," of the favored citizens. But there is also an "Other America," to borrow Harrington's phrase.[42] The major features of that portion of society according to Harrington are as follows:

> Now the American city has been transformed. The poor still inhabit the miserable housing in the central area, but they are increasingly isolated from contact with, or sight of, anybody else. Middle-class women coming from Suburbia on a rare trip may catch the mere glimpse of the other America on the way to an evening at the theater, but their children are segregated in suburban schools. The business or professional man may drive along the fringe of slums in a car or bus, but it is not an important experience to him. The failures, the unskilled, the disabled, the aged, and the minorities are right there, across the tracks, where they have always been. But hardly anyone else is.[43]

Harrington does not mean to simply draw attention to life in the slums as the other America. There is nothing new about the existence of slums—they have been around for a long time. The distinguishing feature of this new pattern developing in metropolitan areas is that present-day residents of the slums have extraordinary liabilities facing them in any effort they might make to escape from the slums—liabilities which were not encountered by traditional slum residents of yesterday. The new slum dweller is trapped there, unlike his predecessors who moved out in successive waves as they were able to gain entry into better jobs and higher incomes. These days the slum residents are most frequently minority groups such as Negroes or American Indians.[44] They are solidly walled into their ghettos by discrimination in housing. Even if they could obtain housing elsewhere, most of them could not afford it, because they are untrained, poorly educated, and in other ways deprived. The most appropriate emotion for them would per-

[41] John K. Galbraith, *The Affluent Society* (Boston: Houghton-Mifflin Co., 1958).

[42] Michael Harrington, *The Other America* (New York: The Macmillan Company, 1962); for a brief, incisive statement on the causal contributions to delinquency of the changes singled out by Harrington and others, see Jackson Toby, "The Prospects for Reducing Delinquency Rates in Industrial Societies," *Federal Probation,* Vol. 27 (December 1963), 23-25.

[43] Harrington, *op. cit.,* p. 4.

[44] Editors of Fortune, *op. cit.,* pp. 92-114.

haps be rage or despair, not hope or optimism. Regarding the kinds of individuals collected in slums, Harrington says:

> Thus the new form of the old slum. If the ethnic slum had been a narrow world of a single religion, language, and culture, it was also a goad to the outside world. This new type of slum groups together failures, rootless people, those born in the wrong time, those at the wrong industry, and the minorities. It is "integrated" in many cases, but in a way that mocks the idea of equality: the poorest and most miserable are isolated together without consideration of race, creed, or color. They are practically forbidden any real relationship with the rest of society.[45]

Any attempt to work out all the criminological ramifications of these trends in urban life and in social, economic, and ethnic patterns would take this book too far afield. Moreover, the precise details of the causal connections between residential, economic, and ethnic discrimination and deviant behavior are not entirely clear. Still, it can hardly be denied that links do exist—that those who reside in the other America represent prime candidates for entry into criminality, political radicalism, and other deviant behavior patterns. It is also possible that motivations to engage in deviant conduct are going to become increasingly more difficult to contain or control if the sense of difference and unjust inequality widens between those who "have" and those who "have not." Put another way, the relative deprivation experienced by members of the other America may well be on the increase, as a result of the diffusion of more facts about the affluent segment of society to this group through the mass media. On this general line of commentary, Merton, Cloward and Ohlin, and others to whom this book has already alluded have much to say.

One obvious implication of this discussion regarding changes in American society is that crescive declines in criminality, particularly of predatory kinds, are not to be expected. Continued high levels of illegality should persist, partly as a simple function of an increasing population. Given a sustained modest rate of population growth, correctional problems will almost inevitably continue to increase. But more than that, exacerbation of the crime and delinquency

---

[45] Harrington, *op. cit.*, pp. 144-45.

problem can be predicted as an outcome or accompaniment of the changes in American life noted here.

If it is true that much criminality and delinquency in American society is carried on by those who perceive themselves as deprived, neglected, and generally disadvantaged, changes in their life circumstances would be required to change the behavior of these individuals. This is the sort of thing that several of the examples of environmental change examined above attempt to accomplish. But perhaps the real task for the future is not so much one of accelerating the pace of relatively circumscribed environmental modification programs, such as Mobilization for Youth, valuable as they might be in themselves. Perhaps instead the most significant strategies for reducing rates of crime and delinquency would be indirect. Who can say that some impressive declines in delinquency would not eventually flow from an effective program of urban redevelopment which provides decent, low-cost housing to the residents of the other America? [46] Perhaps progress on that front would do more to create anticriminal communities out of urban slums than any other approach. Conversely, who can say that delinquency prevention programs that work with groups of individuals who have been forced out of one slum undergoing redevelopment into another, even more wretched, area are likely to be particularly effective? The forced evacuation and displacement of low-income persons from one slum into another, a kind of urban "musical chairs," has of course been the history of urban redevelopment.

In the same way, it is quite conceivable that efforts to find employment for slum dwellers represent only a partial solution at best to problems of crime and delinquency. Massive governmentally sponsored programs of job retraining, stimulation of new industries and job opportunities, and other actions of that sort not specifically designed to deal with criminality may represent the best hope for the future. Along the same line, another development of major

---

[46] These remarks should not be read as indicating that crime and delinquency will simply go away if slums are eradicated and so forth. Rather, the argument is that slum clearance is one of a number of steps which are needed as first stages in efforts to evolve a greater degree of community organization and other anticriminal influences in neighborhoods. Also, the difficulties of sustained efforts at urban renewal and redevelopment should not be minimized. For one commentary on some of the problems of renewal, see Martin Millspaugh, Gurney Breckenfeld, and Miles L. Colean, *The Human Side of Urban Renewal* (New York: Ives Washburn, Inc., 1960).

significance for the reduction of criminality might be one having to do with attenuation of racial barriers in employment and housing. The civil rights revolution of the 1960's could indirectly be a major force in crime reduction, in the event that the revolution succeeds. If on the other hand, dramatic progress is not made fast enough in the assimilation of the other America into the mainstream of national life, conceivably very little could be done to stem the tide of many kinds of crime. Perhaps one of the most important steps that could be taken to reduce delinquency and crime would be to heed the warnings of such persons as James Baldwin, who argues that time is running out for the perpetuation of racial inequality.[47]

The essence of the Baldwin thesis is that the discontent of American Negroes has reached an intensity such that civil disorder and violence may develop between Negroes and whites unless the conditions producing these tensions are rapidly removed. Baldwin and others note a hardening of Negro attitudes toward whites. They observe with alarm the rise of groups such as the Black Muslim organization with its "devil theory" of race relations. This growing concern is well founded. Already it appears that the growth of Black Muslimism in prisons has led to prominent incidents of Negro-white conflict. There is good reason to wonder about the difficulties that such feelings of estrangement and victimization on the part of urban, slum area Negroes are likely to produce for programs of environmental change in the future. At the time this book is being written, the future of matters of this kind is clouded. The one thing that is not in doubt, however, is that the next several decades are pregnant with dangers and problems which promise to complicate crime and delinquency prevention or reduction.

One final comment regarding environmental change programs is this: It seems clear that such modifications are more relevant to some forms of deviant behavior than to others. Most persons would agree that environmentally oriented activities make good sense in treatment of gang delinquency but are less germane in that of naive check forgery, sex offenses, embezzlement, and other specific forms of criminality. Thus in the discussions of treatment strategy for particular offender types, kinds of environmental change will be recommended in some cases but not in others.

[47] James Baldwin, *The Fire Next Time* (New York: Dial Press, 1963).

Summary

This chapter has identified six more-or-less distinct forms of treatment. In Chapters Six and Seven, the six types will be connected to the offender patterns specified in Chapter Three. In a number of instances, more than one form of intervention will be suggested for particular offender roles, in that it does not appear to be the case that only one form of treatment would bring results with specific types of individuals. For example, gang delinquents would probably be influenced positively by group therapy, but they might also respond favorably to some kind of milieu treatment or environmental program. The choice of program in such instances often comes down to certain contingencies such as the time and place at which a gang offender is available for treatment. In the same way, alternative recommendations will be made for other types as well. Before moving on to this matter, some consideration must be given to a number of obstacles to the implementation of treatment recommendations. Some of these have been touched upon in this chapter. However, Chapter Five represents a more systematic overview of some of these obstacles.

five

OBSTACLES

TO

TREATMENT

Introduction

This chapter is devoted to the examination of two general sets of obstacles to treatment efforts in corrections. The first of these is termed "bread and butter" problems of correctional practice. "Bread and butter" problems refer to those complaints, which are discussed almost endlessly in correctional journals, at correctional meetings, and in other places, centering around inadequate financial resources, low salaries, excessive case load size, and kindred problems. The second set is comprised of a number of difficulties which seem almost inherent in the social organization of correctional programs, such as basic conflicts in the assigned functions of institutions, the antisocial inmate culture, and so forth. These impediments have until recently been less recognized than the "bread and butter" ones. But in the past fifteen years an impressive body of theory and research data has accumulated dealing with what might be labeled "the sociology of correctional organization." The significance of these organizational problems is that they may continue to thwart rehabilitative efforts in corrections, even if the more immediate and clearly recognized "bread and butter" difficulties were removed or modified.

Like the preceding four chapters, this one is a brief overview. No attempt is made to provide a complete résumé of all the literature dealing with either kind of correction problem. The commentary to follow represents a brief introduction to a large body of correctional literature.

"Bread and Butter" Problems

There is no purpose to be served by listing all the "bread and butter" complaints that have been voiced in the past several decades regarding deficiencies in the correctional field. The plain and overriding fact is that corrections has been a "shoestring" operation. However, a partial enumeration of these complaints would include the following: First, corrections traditionally has been plagued by inadequate administrative structures. Too often correctional administrations have been part of the political "spoils system" in which untrained and disinterested individuals have been appointed to important administrative posts. As a result, the wardens of penal facilities have often been the least competent persons to exercise leadership within those institutions. Similarly, parole boards have been staffed with political appointees of questionable competence. Such persons serve for relatively short periods of time, for they are often removed from office when a new governor is elected. They are then replaced by new incompetents who are members of the victorious political party. Consequently, correctional administrations have tended to be subject to instability and lack of consistency in program development. Penal history in many states has been cyclical in form, so that periods of reform have been followed by reversals of progressive developments. Over an extended period of time, many correctional systems show little evidence of long-term improvements.

Lack of financial support has often gone hand in hand with defective correctional organization. Very often, state legislatures have been consistently tightfisted in providing funds for the support of correctional reforms, so that monetary outlays have been the minimum necessary to keep a simple custodial operation going. On those infrequent occasions when unusual allocations of money have been made, they have often gone to provide more cell spaces to relieve situations of chronic overcrowding or for some other purpose of this kind. Adequate financial support has rarely been granted for the implementation of some program of treatment.

Inasmuch as maintenance of the *status quo* has been the dominant orientation of legislators, deficiencies in addition to those already noted frequently characterize corrections. Customarily, rehabilitative efforts have had to contend with physical settings that are not conducive to progressive programs. Most of the correctional plants in operation in this country at the present time are at least sixty years old, and many of them are over a hundred years old. These prisons and reformatories have grown in "Topsy" fashion over the years, with new buildings being added to existing, obsolescent physical plants. Such places have severe custodial problems built into them, so that excessive time has to be given to the maintenance of security and order. Indeed, even the most enlightened prison staff would have difficulty managing a comprehensive treatment program in many of the prisons in this country.[1]

The lack of financial support for programs has also meant that salaries at all levels of correctional employment have been inadequate to attract a corps of trained, intelligent, and dedicated individuals. Or, if competent persons take positions in corrections, many of them soon move on to more lucrative kinds of work, so that personnel turnover is excessive. Given the salaries that prevail in many states, the wonder is that any able individuals are to be found working in correctional settings.

Excessive case loads are still another concomitant of defective organizations and inadequate financial resources. Although there is room for argument concerning the optimum size of parole, probation, or other correctional case loads, there can be little doubt that existing case loads are far from that optimum figure. Probation officers are commonly found handling case loads in excess of 200 probationers. Obviously, even the most highly trained probation officer would find a work load of this size nullifying his efforts at rehabilitation.

---

[1] Some indication of the defective and obsolete physical structure of many United States prisons can be found in U.S. Bureau of Prisons, *Handbook of Correctional Institution Design and Construction* (Washington, D.C.: U.S. Bureau of Prisons, 1949); Harry Elmer Barnes and Negley K. Teeters, *New Horizons in Criminology*, 3rd ed. (Englewood Cliffs, N.J.: Prentice-Hall, Inc., 1959), pp. 328-86.

This list of deficiencies could be greatly expanded, but enough has been said to indicate that existing programs frequently fall far short of the mark as far as rehabilitative efforts are concerned. As Schnur has indicated, it does not make much sense to ask whether the "New Penology" is a success, for the "New Penology" for the most part still exists only in textbooks.[2]

In all probability, the lag in the implementation of the rehabilitative goal of corrections stems in considerable part from the image of offenders as "bad" persons who willfully violate criminal laws. Little effort has been expended to create a public conception of lawbreakers as sympathetic figures. Moreover, there is serious question as to whether any effort in corrections parallel to the "mental health" movement can be entirely successful. It may be that the common view of law violators as individuals who deliberately chose to be "evil" and "bad" will continue to be a major perspective conditioning the programs which arise to deal with them. If this be the case, "bread and butter" problems, particularly financial ones, will probably continue to plague rehabilitative efforts. Adequate financial support is likely to be withheld on the grounds that the social rejects who are the focus of rehabilitative programs do not deserve to be "coddled." This prediction gains additional weight from the fact that most states presently operate with financial resources inadequate to meet all the demands made upon them. Considering the competing appeals for greater monetary support for education, public welfare, highway construction, and other segments of state government operations which go on in state legislatures, corrections is likely to receive less than what correctional authorities defined as their "fair share." After all, correctional managers do not have a popular "product" on which to base fund appeals and, parenthetically, even the "product" is presently ambiguous. There is not much evidence which can now be marshaled to show that there is a "payoff" to treatment efforts in the way of decreased crime rates, lower recidivism, and so forth.

The brief and general description of the state of corrections

[2] Alfred C. Schnur, "The New Penology: Fact or Fiction?" *Journal of Criminal Law, Criminology and Police Science,* Vol. 49 (November-December 1958), 331-34; for some evidence suggesting that the "New Penology" has not been fully implemented in England either, see Terence Morris, "In The Nick," and Alan Little, "The Borstal Boys," *The Twentieth Century* (London) (Winter 1962), 22-34, 35-57.

sketched above is more-or-less accurate for particular state and county systems. California exhibits these characteristics to a lesser degree than almost any other state, and conversely, that state shows the greatest progress toward a comprehensive correctional treatment program. For one thing, California has had over twenty years of consistent administrative leadership by Richard McGee, Heman Stark, and many others. The state has also had an administratively sound organizational structure which is relatively free from political interference. The correctional authorities in that state have consistently been supported in their efforts by the governor and other state government leaders. As a consequence, California has responded to the increased number of offenders in its charge by constructing a number of new penal institutions for both adults and juveniles. These facilities have been staffed with trained, reasonably well-paid, career-oriented employees, and ambitious programs of treatment have been developed for all juvenile and adult inmates. In addition, a number of experimental therapy programs have been organized in institutional and parole settings. Research evaulation of these operations has become an established part of the correctional effort in both the Department of Corrections and the California Youth Authority. Finally, county juvenile court and adult probation systems have shown parallel movement toward progressive, ambitious treatment efforts. All of these changes have meant that California serves as a model for other states, so that numerous visitors appear in the state each year to observe the workings of the system. Also, a number of other states have periodically "raided" California for administrators, which is another reflection of the growth and progress of the over-all system.

However, it would be a mistake to attribute the improvements in the California system to an overwhelming and articulate public demand for such changes. Instead, it appears that these developments have been accomplished in spite of general public disinterest and apathy. A recent investigation of public knowledge of programs in California suggested that most citizens have only a dim awareness of correctional matters other than such things as where criminals are executed in the state, the identity of notorious, well-publicized criminals, and the like.[3] Few persons were able to identify different

[3] Don C. Gibbons, "Who Knows What About Correction?" *Crime and Delinquency*, Vol. 9 (April 1963), 137-44.

penal institutions and few of them demonstrated any detailed understanding of what happens to offenders in institutions or at other points in the correctional process. Perhaps even more surprising was the finding that some important gaps in knowledge existed in the case of correctional "professional" employees as well.

Some evidence of the deficiencies in contemporary corrections has been shown by Schnur. Several years ago, he pointed out that about 27,000 persons were employed in state and federal penal facilities to manage some 165,000 inmates—a ratio of one employee for every six prisoners. Only small numbers of these employees were assigned to activities that could be called treatment; most of the workers are custodial officers. Moreover, only a small proportion of the persons designated as treatment personnel were actually involved in therapy activities. According to Schnur, "more people, however, are employed to shuffle papers than to implement the new penology."[4] For example, only 23 psychiatrists were available full time to treat 165,000 inmates, so that the ratio of prisoners to psychiatrists was 7,026 to 1. If each convict received the same amount of psychiatric help, he would get 82 seconds of therapy per month.

A more recent study of the same general kind has been reported by Johnson.[5] Johnson found in a 1961 survey of 47 state correctional systems that persons with M.S.W. degrees were employed in only 14 states. Eighteen states indicated that no "social workers" were employed in their programs. Additionally, in those remaining states reporting the utilization of social workers, this occupational category was defined broadly so as to include persons who did not have training in social work practice and techniques. Further, the definition of social work was stretched so as to subsume a variety of institutional activities not conventionally thought of as social work.

The deficiencies of corrections are also highlighted in a study by Diana, who investigated the kind and amount of assistance given to juvenile probationers in the Alleghany County (Pittsburgh), Penn., juvenile court.[6] He found that the average number of contacts be-

---

[4] Schnur, *op. cit.*, 332.

[5] Elmer H. Johnson, "The Present Level of Social Work in Prisons," *Crime and Delinquency*, Vol. 9 (July 1963), 290-96.

[6] Lewis Diana, "Is Casework in Probation Necessary?" *Focus*, Vol. 34 (January 1955), 1-8.

tween probationers and probation officers was about 5 within a 16-month period. Moreover, these were for the most part quite superficial, so that only 14 per cent of the probationers received any sort of case work treatment. Diana also found an inverse relationship between frequency of probation contacts and later criminality, so that offenders who had the least interaction with officers were less recidivistic than boys who had received more frequent assistance. What this probably indicates is that there are many juveniles who are placed on probation who are not seriously delinquent, who need little attention from probation agents, and who turn out to be "self-correctors." Accordingly, the officer tends to work with more serious offenders, ignoring the "low risk" cases in his case load.

Another study parallel to that of Diana turned up similar findings. England found that a group of adult probationers had a recidivism rate of only 17.7 per cent, but that this low rate was unrelated to treatment.[7] Most of the offenders received only routine surveillance and superficial help from the probation workers. In England's view, the generally consistent high success rates for probation as a form of disposition are to be attributed principally to the fact that most of the persons placed upon probation are essentially "prosocial" and not in need of intensive resocialization.

Finally, a study by Hengerer of several juvenile probation departments suggests that most of what goes on in probation is something other than treatment.[8] The workers examined in that study spent most of their time in writing reports, in driving from one place to another, and in similar operations. They had large case loads and little time in which to provide therapy to their wards.

The preceding remarks indicate that "bread and butter" obstacles to treatment are generic in corrections, so that even the most "pro-

---

[7] Ralph W. England, Jr., "What is Responsible for Satisfactory Probation and Postprobation Outcome?" *Journal of Criminal Law, Criminology and Police Science*, Vol. 47 (March-April 1957), 667-76; see also his "A Study of Postprobation Recidivism Among 500 Federal Offenders," *Federal Probation*, Vol. 19 (September 1955), 10-16. See also a more recent report which presents similar findings regarding federal probation work: Albert Wahl and Daniel Glaser, "Pilot Time Study of the Federal Probation Officer's Job," *Federal Probation*, Vol. 27 (September 1963), 20-25.

[8] Gertrude M. Hengerer, "Organizing Probation Services," *National Probation and Parole Association Yearbook, 1953*, pp. 45-49; see also Gibbons, "Probation: Theory and Reality," *Canadian Journal of Corrections*, Vol. 1 (January 1959), 10-18.

gressive" state systems suffer from excessive case loads, inadequate salaries, and other problems. Existing systems range from reasonably adequate to those grossly underequipped with the monetary, physical, and administrative prerequisites for rehabilitation. It does no good to pretend that things are otherwise, that the situation is generally conducive to massive therapy efforts. The correctional recruit should enter into this occupational area with a realistic appreciation of the prevailing state of affairs. It is probably better for the neophyte to know at the start that therapy efforts are frequently handicapped in a variety of ways than to have to learn this painful fact after undertaking a correctional career. He should be told that unbridled optimism regarding the prospects for rapid implementation of the "New Penology" is not in order. But at the same time, the experience of California and certain other states demonstrates that the deficiencies of the correctional field can be reduced. Although California is a long way from the correctional millennium, that state does have a system more congenial to therapy efforts than was true two decades ago. The same can also be said of certain other states, such as Washington, Wisconsin, New York, and New Jersey. Thus the above should not be interpreted as a counsel of despair. Instead, within the limitations now imposed by "bread and butter" difficulties, some measure of effective treatment is possible.

Problems of Social Organization

The past decade has seen a remarkable growth of theory and research findings in an area of sociological investigation which might be termed "the sociology of correctional organizations." This work is concerned with the discovery of the social patterns and processes characteristic of correctional structures. These institutions have been viewed as particular cases of "total institutions" and as one subtype of the larger class of formal, complex organizations.[9] The focus of most of this work has been centered upon correctional organizations *as* organizations. The interest has thus been more

[9] Erving Goffman, "On the Characteristics of Total Institutions: The Inmate World," and "On the Characteristics of Total Institutions: Staff-Inmate Relations," in Donald R. Cressey, ed., *The Prison* (New York: Holt, Rinehart & Winston, Inc., 1961), pp. 15-106.

upon the dimensions of these systems which are common to, or shared by, complex organizations of various kinds, rather than upon "bread and butter" issues. These works have important and direct implications for rehabilitative ventures in corrections even though they have not been concerned primarily with therapy. They suggest that certain structural problems and contradictions exist which are likely to persist and to complicate the implementation of rehabilitative goals.

This chapter makes no attempt to provide a detailed and comprehensive catalogue of the burgeoning literature in this area of investigation.[10] Instead, only a skeleton analysis is put forward here,

---

[10] A large sample of this material would include Donald Clemmer, "Leadership Phenomena in a Prison Community," *Journal of Criminal Law and Criminology*, Vol. 28 (March-April 1938), 861-72; Clemmer, *The Prison Community* (Boston: Christopher, 1940), reissued by Holt, Rinehart and Winston, Inc., 1958; Richard A. Cloward, Donald R. Cressey, George Grosser, Richard McCleery, Lloyd E. Ohlin, Gresham Sykes, and Sheldon Messinger, *Theoretical Studies in Social Organization of the Prison* (New York: Social Science Research Council, 1960); Cressey, "Professional Correctional Work and Professional Work in Correction," *N.P.P.A. Journal*, Vol. 5 (January 1959), 1-15; Cressey, "Contradictory Directives in Complex Organizations: The Case of the Prison," *Administrative Science Quarterly*, Vol. 4 (June 1959), 1-19; Cressey and Witold Krassowski, "Inmate Organization and Anomie in American Prisons and Soviet Labor Camps," *Social Problems*, Vol. 5 (Winter 1957-1958), 217-30; Cressey, "Achievement of an Unstated Organizational Goal: An Observation on Prisons," *Pacific Sociological Review*, Vol. 1 (Fall 1958), 43-49; Cressey, ed., *The Prison* (New York: Holt, Rinehart & Winston, Inc., 1961); Joseph W. Eaton, *Stone Walls Not a Prison Make* (Springfield, Ill.: C. C. Thomas, 1962); Sethard Fisher, "Social Organization in a Correctional Community," *Pacific Sociological Review*, Vol. 4 (Fall 1961), 87-93; Johan Galtung, "The Social Functions of a Prison," *Social Problems*, Vol. 6 (Fall 1958), 127-40; Peter G. Garabedian, *Western Penitentiary: A Study in Social Organization*, doctoral dissertation (Seattle: University of Washington, 1959); Oscar Grusky, "Role Conflict in Organization: A Study of Prison Camp Officials," *Administrative Science Quarterly*, Vol. 3 (March 1959), 452-72; Grusky, "Organizational Goals and the Behavior of Informal Leaders," *American Journal of Sociology*, Vol. 65 (July 1959), 59-67; Frank Hartung and Maurice Floch, "A Social Psychological Analysis of Prison Riots," *Journal of Criminal Law, Criminology and Police Science*, Vol. 47 (May-June 1956), 51-57; Norman S. Hayner, "Washington State Correctional Institutions as Communities," *Social Forces*, Vol. 21 (March 1943), 316-22; Hayner and Ellis Ash, "The Prisoner Community as a Social Group," *American Sociological Review*, Vol. 4 (June 1939), 362-69; F. E. Haynes, "The Sociological Study of the Prison Community," *Journal of Criminal Law and Criminology*, Vol. 39 (November-December 1948), 432-40; Elmer H. Johnson, "Sociology of Confinement: Assimilation and the Prison Rat," *Journal of Criminal Law, Criminology and Police Science*, Vol. 51 (January-February 1961), 528-33; Richard McCleery, *The Strange Journey*, Vol. 32 (Raleigh: University of North Carolina Extension Bulletin, March 1953); Lloyd W. McCorkle and Richard Korn, "Resocialization Within Walls," *Annals*

made up of observations about the characteristics of correctional organizations which are most relevant to implementation of treatment. However, to place the specific observations in this chapter within a wider perspective, a few general, prefatory comments are in order regarding this line of criminological inquiry.

One point is that to date, no comprehensive, general theory of correctional organization has developed. Instead, the area of investigation is made up of a body of specific and not entirely interrelated lines of speculation and research on facets of correctional organization. The investigators of these matters show a shared interest in a general substantive topic rather than in a common theory upon which their different efforts have proceeded. For example, a substantial measure of work has been done upon the social world of prison inmates, but it has not been based upon a single, unifying set of hypotheses regarding the culture of prisoners.

Another feature of this activity is that theoretical statements have multiplied faster than substantive research findings, so that the subject area is presently characterized by a number of unresolved theoretical issues for which relevant data have not yet appeared.

---

of the American Academy of Political and Social Science, Vol. 293 (May 1954), 88-98; Lloyd E. Ohlin, Herman Piven, and Donnell M. Pappenfort, "Major Dilemmas of the Social Worker in Probation and Parole," *N.P.P.A. Journal,* Vol. 2 (July 1956), 211-25; Norman A. Polansky, "The Prison as an Autocracy," *Journal of Criminal Law and Criminology,* Vol. 33 (May-June 1942), 16-22; Howard W. Polsky, "Changing Delinquent Subcultures: A Social-Psychological Approach," *Social Work,* Vol. 4 (October 1959), 3-15; Polsky, *Cottage Six* (New York: Russell Sage Foundation, 1962); Hans Reimer, "Socialization in the Prison Community," *Proceedings of the American Prison Association, 1937,* pp. 151-55; Clarence C. Schrag, "Leadership Among Prison Inmates," *American Sociological Review,* Vol. 19 (February 1954), 37-42; Schrag, "A Preliminary Criminal Typology," *Pacific Sociological Review,* Vol. 4 (Spring 1961), 11-16; Gresham M. Sykes, "Men, Merchants and Toughs: A Study of Reactions to Imprisonment," *Social Problems,* Vol. 4 (October 1956), 130-38; Sykes, "The Corruption of Authority and Rehabilitation," *Social Forces,* Vol. 34 (March 1956), 257-62; Sykes, *The Society of Captives* (Princeton, N.J.: Princeton University Press, 1958); George H. Weber, "Conflicts Between Professional and Non-Professional Personnel in Institutional Delinquency Treatment," *Journal of Criminal Law, Criminology and Police Science,* Vol. 48 (May-June 1957), 26-43; S. Kirson Weinberg, "Aspects of the Prison's Social Structure," *American Journal of Sociology,* Vol. 47 (March 1942), 717-26; Stanton Wheeler, *Social Organization in a Correctional Community,* doctoral dissertation (Seattle: University of Washington, 1958); Mayer N. Zald, "The Correctional Institution for Juvenile Offenders: An Analysis of Organizational 'Character,'" *Social Problems,* Vol. 8 (Summer 1960), 57-67; Zald, "Power Balance and Staff Conflict in Correctional Institutions," *Administrative Science Quarterly,* Vol. 7 (June 1962), 22-49.

One case in point centers around the set of antisocial injunctions termed the "inmate code," said to characterize all prisons and kindred institutions. Two interpretations of the inmate code have developed, which might be termed the "functionalist" and "diffusion" arguments. In the former, the prisoner normative system is alleged to be functional in solving certain adjustment problems of inmates, whereas in the latter, the code is regarded as a set of norms which certain convicts import into the institution from the outside world. More will be said about this controversy at a later point in this chapter. But note that this is a critical quarrel because the implications of these two views for the development of treatment are quite different. Accordingly, research findings on this point are sorely needed.

As this area of inquiry has grown, differential attention has been paid to particular segments of correctional organization. There is a rather large body of theory and evidence concerning various facets of prison and reformatory social structure and organization, but most of this material has accumulated from observations in a few maximum security institutions. It may well be that there are important organizational differences among penal facilities with different kinds of inmate inhabitants, among those with varied physical plants, and among those of different size. Reformatories which handle relatively young felons might show a greater incidence of troublesome, unstable inmate behavior than would a prison where the captives would be more involved in "doing their own time." Similarly, other things being equal, facilities with obsolete architecture might be more custodially oriented than recently constructed, "functionally designed" institutions. Finally, organizational contrasts that are a function of size may well exist between such places as Southern Michigan Prison at Jackson, Michigan, with a population of about 7,000 inmates, and various prisons in the western United States with less than 1,500 prisoners. These are matters which need to be investigated.

So far, relatively little attention has been paid to institutions for juvenile offenders and female criminals, to probation settings within the juvenile court operation, or to parole and probation structures for adult offenders. Obviously, these are deserving of attention. Some brief commentary is included about these different correctional processes in the sections to follow, based on the scanty theory and research available.

PRISON ORGANIZATION

The general description of prison organization that follows is drawn from the existing literature and should be viewed as most descriptive of maximum security prisons and as more-or-less accurate for institutions that vary in the ways suggested in the preceding remarks.

Prisons are often thought of as autocratic in form, particularly by members of the general public.[11] Custodial officers *give orders* and inmates *obey* them. Prisoners are seen as totally managed, as persons whose opportunities for self-direction and individual action are almost completely circumscribed. Penal institutions are also commonly regarded as monoliths with a singularity of purpose in which all the responsibilities of all the members of the system are clearly and specifically defined. Prisons are well-oiled, smooth running, people-punishing, and people-changing social machines. In this view, there is clarity and consensus among all prison employees, from the warden down to the guards. All these individuals are in agreement regarding their tasks of maintaining, disciplining, and sometimes of treating inmates. Accordingly, prisons are sometimes believed to be models of autocratic and rational bureaucratic structures.

There are major distortions in this image of prisons, which normally depart rather markedly from the autocratic model. One basic problem faced by penal authorities in the management of offenders is that the inmates are not in the institution voluntarily and they do not accord legitimacy to the official norms or prescriptions of the organization. The situation of prisoners is different from that of persons in a military autocracy, for in the latter case, most of the members of the system have internalized the authority of the rules, albeit somewhat grudgingly. Most of them are motivated to conform to military regulations and procedures, even though they may regard conformity as personally unpleasant. The same cannot be said for many (but not all) prison inmates.

Autocratic rule over hostile and uncooperative inmates could theoretically be obtained at a price. Prisoners could be isolated from each other, they could be physically abused and coerced, and they could be put under continual and pervasive surveillance by

---

[11] For an analysis of prisons as autocracies, see Polansky, *op. cit.*

guards. In theory, they could be maintained under conditions of anomie and demoralization. However, these possibilities do not exist in actual fact. Restraints are imposed upon the regime administrators are able to construct which derive from the relatively recent humanitarian movement of penal reform. Prison officials are expected to deal with their charges in a humane fashion. They are obligated to minimize the physical and social isolation of inmates, rather than to maximize it, and they are forbidden to physically abuse or coerce prisoners. These are very real limitations, for institutions do come under periodic scrutiny by the outside world. Then, too, constant surveillance of prisoners by correctional officers to detect rule violations is impossible for two reasons: Most prisons are not physically constituted in such a way as to allow continual supervision and observation of convicts, and there are not enough observers. Although guards comprise the largest single class of employee, they are greatly outnumbered by the prisoners.[12]

Prisons have diverged further from an autocratic, rational model as "rehabilitation" has been added to their functions or responsibilities. The addition of the treatment role has introduced views into the institution to the effect that a coercive, restrictive social climate is inimical to therapy. Prisoners are seen as being in need of opportunities to ventilate hostility, to work out new patterns of adjustment, and so forth. Prisons have come to be regarded as serving ends similar to those of mental hospitals, but significantly, this new view is not usually shared by all members of the employee group. Such notions have frequently been brought into the institution by top administrators who attempt to impose them upon the custodial force. However, a large segment of the guard group is made up of veterans of the "old order" who have served for many years under a straightforward custodial system. These officers are supported by the force of tradition in their belief that the "old ways" are better, and they tend to be unreceptive to rehabilitative declarations by recently arrived administrators. Nonetheless, correctional institutions which are attempting transformation into treatment-oriented systems do exhibit a relaxed, less coercive social climate than do the more traditional penal facilities. Although

---

[12] For some incisive commentary on the limits of "total power" in prisons, see Sykes, *The Society of Captives*, pp. 40-62; Sykes, "The Corruption of Authority and Rehabilitation," *loc. cit.*; Clarence C. Schrag, "Some Foundations for a Theory of Correction," in Cressey, ed., *The Prison*, pp. 338-39.

there are serious questions regarding the extent to which prisons can be converted into therapeutic communities, efforts to do so weaken the authoritarian order of the institution and disrupt the relations among employees.

For reasons of this kind, prisons might be more accurately defined as partially disorganized, rather than model, autocracies. They exhibit less-than-complete organizational consensus by employees, and they tend to show defective communication patterns. Orders are supposed to move down a chain of command to guards, where the orders are implemented, while information on which decisions are made moves up the command line. But distortions frequently occur in message flow, particularly in the feedback of explanations behind orders to low-ranking members such as custodial officers. Consequently, prisons frequently show a degree of guard alienation from the institutional program.[13] Officers either do not understand the bases on which decisions and orders are formulated or they disagree with these directives. This lack of internal consensus among employees regarding the goals of the system is commonly found in treatment-oriented prisons, where the guards are often more similar to the inmates than they are to the higher administrators. That is, because they tend to view therapy operations as a threat to sound custody, they are in accord although for different reasons, with the prisoners' negative definitions of treatment programs.

Departures from the autocratic model in the actual operation of prisons can also be seen in the area of custodial operations, particularly in guard-inmate interaction. In theory, officers are expected to maintain social distance from prisoners and to give orders which inmates are presumed to obey because of their powerlessness to do otherwise. But as indicated earlier, prison guards do not have techniques of physical coercion available to them by which to obtain compliance from recalcitrant prisoners. Moreover, physical force would be self-defeating as a technique for managing inmates in the long run, even if it were legitimized. Guards are grossly outnumbered by inmates, so that their extensive use of force would produce convict reprisals, uprisings, and other negative consequences.

One technique contrived for the control of uncooperative prisoners has been to urge them to put themselves into voluntary isolation

---

[13] Schrag, "Some Foundations for a Theory of Correction," pp. 336-38.

from other convicts, to "do your own time," and to pursue incentives and privileges as rewards for conformity. In turn, if an inmate violates rules, privileges are withdrawn from him.[14] However, this mechanism has severe limitations. For one, deprivation of privileges tends to have little effect within the harsh environment of institutions because the prisoners are already severely deprived. They are cut off from sexual relations and from many kinds of freedom of action as to choice of clothing, companionship, and so forth. Thus, to be denied the privilege of attending a movie tends not to be viewed as a severe loss. Incentives such as reductions of the inmate's sentence for good behavior have been redefined by the prisoners as "rights" rather than as rewards, so that the administration tends to tamper with "good time" credits only in extreme cases. Furthermore, they are accorded to the inmate at the start of his sentence, rather than at points in his institutional career in the form of rewards for appropriate institutional conduct. Thus they do not operate as important incentives, and they are normally routinely awarded to nearly all inmates except those who have had institutional careers of an extremely troublesome and violent kind.

The modern prison must find some way of maintaining a reasonable degree of order without physical coercion and without manipulation of meaningful rewards for conformity. The solution of this problem of how to keep the peace with and among uncooperative inmates takes the form of "corruption of authority" in many prisons.[15] Corruption of authority, in turn, assumes several forms. One refers to liaisons, relationships, "deals," and other informal, *sub rosa* ties which develop between inmates and administrators and which are not defined as legitimate or proper within the formal definitions of prison procedures. Prison administrators and prisoner "elites" enter into informal relationships which provide special privileges to these leaders. In turn, they take over the job of coercing other inmates into minimally disruptive behavior. As Korn and McCorkle have indicated, "far from systematically attempting to undermine the inmate hierarchy, the institution generally gives it covert support and recognition by assigning better jobs and quarters to its high-status members providing they are 'good inmates.' In this and other ways the institution buys peace with the system by

[14] Richard A. Cloward, "Social Controls in the Prison," in Cloward, Cressey, Grosser, McCleery, Ohlin, Sykes, and Messinger, *op. cit.,* pp. 20-48.
[15] Sykes, *The Society of Captives,* pp. 52-62.

avoiding battle with it." [16] Being a "good inmate" in this context means refraining from direct assaults upon the administrative system. It *does not* mean "doing your own time," for elites are persons who interfere with other inmates, who control them, and who demand special privileges and favors from less powerful prisoners. They are covertly aided in these activities by the prison administration. Parenthetically, the wave of prison riots in the 1950's seems to be attributable, in part at least, to this arrangement. Riots seem to have developed as a response of elites to attempts by some prison administrators to weaken their position. As these officials attempted to take control of the institution away from prisoners, those inmates reacted by creating protest actions designed to re-establish the "old order." [17] The lesson to be learned from these disturbances is that the changes which are necessary to create a favorable treatment situation are not easily and painlessly achieved. Perhaps one index of the extent to which "therapy" has been introduced into an institution is to be found in the extent to which that prison has suffered a transitional period of unrest, violence, and the like.

A second form of corruption of authority extends to inmate-guard relationships generally, in which correctional officers obtain a measure of cooperation and obedience from inmates by discretionary action in which they overlook some conduct infractions. In turn, in a *quid pro quo* relationship, inmates are expected to create a minimum of visible trouble for the guards. In other words, the guard persuades convicts to behave by allowing them to deviate from rules in certain situations. This form of authority corruption stems from several factors. For one, correctional officers are not immune from general pressures to be "good guys." They probably find it difficult indeed to associate with inmates on extremely distant and aloof terms, for they quickly come to discover that prisoners are quite ordinary individuals and not monsters. More important, discretionary actions represent the most obvious available technique by which inmate disorder can be kept to a minimum by the guard. The officer who is without a club of some sort must persuade and cajole. Discretionary action represents his "carrot" by which he obtains conformity to major rules and regulations.

In the public view, the job of correctional officer is one fit for

[16] McCorkle and Korn, *op. cit.*, 91.
[17] Hartung and Floch, *op. cit.*, 53-57.

simpletons who need only follow explicit orders. In reality, it is probably one of the more difficult occupational tasks in American society. The job demands a high order of skill in manipulating and managing men. The officer must use discretion, but at the same time, he must be alert to the dangers of being drawn into situations where he buys cooperation from prisoners at too great a price. He must avoid being lured into *sub rosa* relations in which he takes contraband into or out of the institution or performs other illicit services for inmates. Discretion up to a point is required of the guard, but there is considerable risk that he will be manipulated by convicts into discretionary actions beyond the tolerance point of his superiors. Thus if he uses too much discretionary judgment, he may be fired or punished in some other way. To further complicate his situation, appropriate action is something to be worked out by each officer himself, for the most part unguided by advice and instruction from anyone else. Cressey has suggested that in prisons of either custodial or therapeutic orientation, the guard faces a situation in which his superiors are not able to give him explicit directives to follow as to precisely how and in what way he is to function in his discretionary role.[18] In the custodial facility, he is obliged to maintain orderliness but is not told how to accomplish this task. In the treatment prison, he is told to sustain order and to contribute to therapy at the same time. Here again, he is not instructed in the appropriate steps to take to accomplish these tasks, nor is he evaluated by his superiors in terms of the end product, rehabilitation of inmates. He cannot be measured in terms of resocialization of prisoners for there is no consensus concerning what a "cured" offender looks like. Moreover, the real test of whether or not an inmate has been rehabilitated takes place in the postrelease period. Accordingly, observations about therapeutic effectiveness are not available to the prison administrator.

The problems of prisons discussed to this point appear to be generic to treatment and custodial institutions alike. But there are some additional difficulties which seem to be peculiar to therapy-oriented prisons.

It would be an error to suppose that rehabilitative views quickly gain primacy and emerge as the dominant orientation in institu-

[18] Cressey, "Contradictory Directives in Complex Organizations: The Case of the Prison," 1-19.

tions where they have been introduced. The more usual outcome is an uneasy marriage of custodial and therapeutic activities, and often security considerations prevail in the operation of the organization.[19] In other cases, the rehabilitative goal pervades many facets of the prison, but in the face of resistance by some employee holdouts. The specific pattern which emerges probably depends in the main on how the treatment function is brought into the prison. If it is introduced by hiring middle-level employees such as social case workers, but is not supported by the warden and his aides, the common outcome is to find it perverted in practice to serve custodial ends. Thus psychiatrists are used in such institutions to "cool out" threatening inmates rather than to conduct therapy. In the same way, the treatment recommendations of other workers are subordinated to custodial decisions. The custodial force is able to control communication within the organization in this situation, so that the therapists are kept ignorant of, and removed from, the important operations of the prison. They are reduced to a form of prison "window dressing."

The outcome of the treatment-custody quarrel in prisons differs where the warden and other top-level administrators have introduced rehabilitation as an end or where they give allegiance to this goal. In this case, treatment workers are more influential in the operation of the institution and they make important policy decisions. But again, the situation tends to be an uneasy one in which functional harmony is less than complete. No clear format has yet been devised which spells out the nature of an effective therapy program operating within the limits of necessary security provisions. Treatment-oriented prisons tend to lack unambiguous definitions regarding the specific manner in which rehabilitative agents are to operate. As a consequence, many of these employees come to see themselves as rescuers, helpers, and protectors of inmates, rather than as rehabilitators. The worker who identifies his task as one of helping prisoners sometimes comes also to conceptualize his job as involving the protection of inmates from the custodial force. He comes to see himself as a mediator between offenders and guards, rather than as a co-worker with the correctional officer with whom he shares a common task. This kind of role-performance probably

[19] Donald R. Cressey, "Limitations on the Organization of Treatment in the Modern Prison," in Cloward, Cressey, Grosser, McCleery, Ohlin, Sykes, and Messinger, op. cit., pp. 78-110.

exacerbates the treatment-custody conflict in prisons. Additionally, it has been argued that the treatment agent who views his task as one of rescuing and helping inmates plays into the hands of the prisoners. He lends covert support to that group's attempts to "reject the rejectors" or to deflect blame away from themselves and onto "society." [20]

From the discussion so far, it is evident that the administrations of most prisons do not present a united front to the inmate group. Points of ambiguity exist within the organizations, conflicts between different administrative groups lie barely hidden and sometimes blossom into overt intraorganizational conflict, and other difficulties characterize prisons. However, little has been said so far about the inmate group. What is the nature of social life among prisoners in maximum security prisons?

One common but exaggerated view of convicts is that they are an aggregate of persons all standing in opposition to the administrative regime. Thus Sykes and Messinger have described an "inmate code" of normative prescriptions said to exist in all prisons. [21] By implication, allegiance to this code characterizes most convicts. The code consists of a collection of conduct definitions centering around directives to refrain from interfering with inmate interests, to avoid quarrels and conflicts with other prisoners or to "go no rap" with one's fellow captives, to be strong in the face of administrative pressure and punishment, and the like. The code defines the model convict, from the inmates' perspective, in terms which contrast markedly with the staff version of the good inmate. Prisoners are expected to cooperate with each other in covert and overt defiance of institutional expectations.

Several hypotheses have been advanced to account for this code. Sykes and Messinger maintain that the most likely explanation is functional, in which the code is seen as serving to reduce the "pains of imprisonment" found in custodial institutions. [22] These pains of incarceration include deprivations of liberty, goods and services, heterosexual relations, and autonomy, which are experienced as psychologically painful by offenders. According to these authors,

[20] McCorkle and Korn, op. cit., 88-89.

[21] Gresham M. Sykes and Sheldon Messinger, "The Inmate Social System," in Cloward, Cressey, Grosser, McCleery, Ohlin, Sykes, and Messinger, op. cit., pp. 5-19.

[22] Ibid.

"as a population of prisoners moves in the direction of solidarity, as demanded by the inmate code, the pains of imprisonment become less severe." [23] A compatible thesis is advanced by McCorkle and Korn, who hold that the code and prisoner solidarity in opposition to the authorities permits the inmate to "reject his rejectors" rather than himself.[24] That is, convicts are supported by their peers in a set of definitions and attitudes which hold that society is at fault for their criminality, so that they are not forced to turn blame inward upon themselves.

There is no question that an inmate code exists in prisons and that psychological pains do accompany the experience of incarceration. But that does not necessarily mean that the code is the product solely of pressures of confinement. It is conceivable that it exists in prisons, in part, because some inmates bring it into the institution from the outside. There are several pieces of evidence which support a "diffusion" interpretation of inmate norms. For one, Wheeler has shown that role-conflict and discrepancies in role-expectations between inmates and administrators are less than complete.[25] He found that prisoners had different expectations regarding the behavior of other inmates than did guards, but there were some offenders with views similar to those of correctional officers who approved of violations of inmate definitions. Additionally, Wheeler suggests that some of the conflict between prisoners and authorities is more apparent than real. His data show that prisoners judge other inmates to be more hostile to treatment and other institutional activities than they are in fact. This discrepancy between private sentiments and estimates of group views appears to be related to the greater visibility of the most antisocial persons in the prison. That is, individual prisoners gauge the degree of antiadministration sentiment among other offenders from observations about a biased sample of the total prisoner group. If this is the case, it may be possible to make modifications in the climate of penal facilities which would be conducive to treatment. Among other things, alterations in the communication patterns among the captives and their captors might provide for the dissemination of more accurate information about inmate opinions. In this way, the pro-

---

[23] *Ibid.*, p. 16.

[24] McCorkle and Korn, *op. cit.*, 88-89.

[25] Stanton Wheeler, "Role Conflict in Correctional Communities," in Cressey, ed., *The Prison*, pp. 229-59.

social prisoner might come to observe that there are other persons who support his prosocial frame of reference.

Wheeler has contributed a second kind of evidence supporting a diffusion interpretation of the inmate code. His findings from a number of Scandinavian prisons show that the pains of imprisonment are found in those places,[26] but there is no clear parallel to the inmate code or to prisoner solidarity observed in American institutions. Wheeler's interpretation of these results is that most prisoners in the Scandinavian institutions enter them from a society which contains a lower incidence of antiauthority attitudes than in the United States. Conversely, in American prisons, many offenders bring into the institution antisocial attitudes which are widespread among lower-class groups.

Observations regarding social types or argot roles in prisons also lend support to diffusion hypotheses regarding the inmate code.[27] Chapter Two presented four role types described by Schrag in some detail, along with the parallel set of argot roles indicated by Sykes, so that there is no need to cover that ground again. But the important point regarding social roles in prison is this: There are many prisoners who engage in some form of antiadministration, proinmate code activity, and these inmates are usually called "right guys." There are others who cooperate with the authorities, who uphold conventional norms and reject the inmate code, and who are termed "square Johns." In turn, antisocial inmates are usually from lower-class backgrounds with lengthy prior records and previous institutional commitments, whereas "square Johns" often show no prior criminal pattern and no history of previous incarceration. Now if the pains of imprisonment lead to the emergence of a prisoner code, and to allegiance to the code by convicts, how are prosocial "square Johns" to be explained? Certainly it could be argued that the first-offender, situational criminal would be the most traumatized by prison. On the other hand, the recidivism-prone, crime-wise, working-class prisoner should be least likely to experience a prison sentence as severe societal rejection. To state the point another way, the diffusionist view is that allegiance to

[26] Stanton Wheeler, "The Comparative Analysis of Prison Social Structure," paper read at the meetings of the American Sociological Association, September 1962.

[27] Schrag, "A Preliminary Criminal Typology"; Schrag, "Some Foundations for a Theory of Correction"; Sykes, The Society of Captives, pp. 84-108.

an inmate code by certain offenders is the continuation, inside the walls, of a pattern of "rejection of the rejectors" which originated at a much earlier point in their careers. In many cases, the point of origin probably lies in early experiences with the police, juvenile courts, and so forth. In addition, elements of the inmate code represent institutional manifestations of hostility to the police and other attitudes which are widespread in lower-class society. On the other hand, the first offender experiences the pains of imprisonment and societal rejection, but his preprison experiences and his involvement with prosocial reference groups outside the walls serve to insulate him from developing any serious loyalty to the inmate code. In addition, insofar as the situational first offender is a novice in crime, he is likely to be rebuffed in any attempt he might make to play the role of "real criminal" among the antisocial individuals in the prison.

Regardless of which of these arguments is most accurate, it is true that a code does exist and that inmate role patterns are found in prisons. In turn, the code and the existence of antisocial "right guys" (and asocial "outlaws" and pseudosocial prisoners as well) suggests that those inmates most in need of treatment are the very ones who are least motivated to seek it. Moreover, they may be deterred from entering into rehabilitative activities even if they privately were interested in doing so because they fear loss of status among their peers. One obvious implication of all this is that participation in therapy programs will probably have to be compulsory, not voluntary, so that prisoners will not have to face inmate accusers who charge them with deviation from the inmate code.

These observations about inmate society and other organizational features of prisons suggest a pessimistic evaluation of the rehabilitative potential of the prison. At the very least, they contain a number of implications for the implementation of treatment values in corrections. One of these is that the organizational patterns within which specific penal facilities are placed, now existent in some states and localities, must be replaced with stable and professional administrative structures. Although the internal disharmony and lack of program continuity characteristic of many prisons may not be dissipated solely as a result of the creation of a professionalized and stabilized central administration, such a system is a basic requirement for organizational consensus and progress. In the same way, the introduction of competent, career-oriented wardens and associate wardens into institutions would not guarantee the establishment of a "therapeutic milieu," but such a pattern could not be created without developments of that kind. Parenthetically, significant changes in this direction have taken place in a number of adult prisons throughout the United States in recent years, so that the beginnings of treatment-oriented systems can be observed.

Although detailed recipes for the creation of a positive atmosphere for rehabilitative efforts in prison are not now available, some steps can be suggested. Concerning role-conflict reduction, two things come to mind immediately: First, a detailed program of in-service training and periodic staff conferences among the various employee groups might go a long way toward reducing some of the staff communication barriers and staff hostilities found in institutions. Second, custodial staff antagonism toward therapy activities might be somewhat modified through programs in which guards are implicated in inmate counseling of either individual or group form. As stated earlier, this kind of activity creates certain problems centering around ambiguous role-definitions and evaluation of employee performance. Nonetheless, the advantages to be derived from drawing guards into therapy operations may be sufficient to outweigh the disadvantages.

What about the inmate culture and its antirehabilitation sentiments? What can be done to create protreatment sympathies in prisoners? To begin with, there is evidence which suggests that some antisocial offenders are motivated to enter into therapy. Wheeler's data cited earlier indicates that the private attitudes of many inmates are not antagonistic to therapy.[28] Along the same line, Garabedian has indicated that antisocial inmates are found in treatment programs which are inmate-sponsored, as distinct from those which are initiated by the officials.[29] Findings of this kind suggest that prison administrators might give more emphasis to provision of legitimate and meaningful opportunities and rewards to encourage a greater involvement in treatment by antisocial inmates. One step in this direction would be the alteration of conventional communication patterns to lessen the rigidity of the prisoner code and the antitreatment attitudes of convicts. A second move would be to carry out programs designed to minimize the rewards for anti-

[28] Wheeler, "Role Conflict in Correctional Communities," 234-40.
[29] Peter G. Garabedian, "Legitimate and Illegitimate Alternatives in the Prison Community," *Sociological Inquiry*, Vol. 32 (Spring 1962), 172-84.

social behavior. In other words, an attack should be made upon the patterns of inmate rackets in the institution. Modifications in parole programs which might contribute to therapy ventures in institutions can also be visualized. One major change would be in the sentence-setting and release procedures of parole boards. Instead of setting the minimum sentence at the beginning of the prisoner's term so that he then knows exactly when he will be released, the release date would be established only after enough time had elapsed to observe his institutional adjustment, treatment participation, and prison activities.

The obstacles blocking the overhaul of programs in prisons are by no means inconsequential. The sociological observer of prisons is not now in possession of knowledge and expertise which would insure dramatic and sudden results if organization reconstruction were turned over to him. All that is argued here is that the prison administrator can learn something about institutional reform from a careful reading of the literature alluded to above.

TRAINING SCHOOL ORGANIZATION

Reports on the social organization of training schools are quite scarce in comparison to those on prisons.[30] Only a few

[30] Some of this material is cited in footnote 10. See works listed there by Fisher, Polsky, Weber, and Zald. Other sources include Gordon H. Barker and W. Thomas Adams, "The Social Structure of a Correctional Institution," *Journal of Criminal Law, Criminology and Police Science*, Vol. 49 (January-February 1959), 417-22; Albert Deutsch, "A Journalist's Impressions of State Training Schools," *Focus*, Vol. 28 (March 1949), 33-40; Seymour L. Halleck and Marvin Hersko, "Homosexual Behavior in a Correctional Institution for Adolescent Girls," *American Journal of Orthopsychiatry*, Vol. 32 (October 1962), 911-17; Richard L. Jenkins, "Treatment in an Institution," *American Journal of Orthopsychiatry*, Vol. 11 (January 1941), 85-91; Ohlin, "The Reduction of Role Conflict in Institutional Staff," *Children*, Vol. 5 (March-April 1958), 65-70; Lloyd E. Ohlin and William C. Lawrence, "Social Interaction Among Clients as a Treatment Problem," *Social Work*, Vol. 4 (April 1959), 3-13; Sophia Robison, *Juvenile Delinquency* (New York: Holt, Rinehart and Winston, Inc., 1960), pp. 380-95; Arnold M. Rose and George H. Weber, "Changes in Attitudes Among Delinquent Boys Committed to Open and Closed Institutions," *Journal of Criminal Law, Criminology and Police Science*, Vol. 52 (July-August 1961), 166-77; Ruth Topping, "Treatment of the Pseudo-Social Boy," *American Journal of Orthopsychiatry*, Vol. 13 (April 1943), 353-60; Weber, "Emotional and Defensive Reactions of Cottage Parents," in Cressey, ed., *The Prison*, pp. 189-228; Mayer N. Zald, "The Correctional Institution for Juvenile Offenders: An Analysis of Organizational 'Character,'" *Social Problems*, Vol. 8 (Summer 1960), 57-68.

studies have been produced in recent years dealing with training schools, and because these have been restricted to certain specific aspects of institutional life, they do not provide any sort of complete picture. It is possible, however, to sketch a general description of the traditional form of organization in state juvenile institutions which is speculative in character, but at the same time, probably reasonably accurate. Such a description follows, after which some recent research evidence will be examined.

First, most state training schools are smaller in population size than prisons. In many states, the boys' schools handle a few hundred boys or less, and the girls' schools are even smaller. Then, too, the administrative staffs of juvenile facilities are usually smaller than in adult institutions. Training schools also normally show a physical structure quite different from that of prisons and reformatories. They are usually unwalled institutions made up of a number of dormitory buildings euphemistically called "cottages." Groups of several dozen or more juveniles, or "wards" as they are often called, inhabit these dormitories, and much of the social life of the institution goes on within these structures. Training schools include an assortment of other buildings, such as a school, trade training shops, barns and other farm buildings, and so forth. All in all, juvenile institutions more closely resemble residential academies or schools than they do prisons, although many of them are more run-down and deteriorated in appearance. Escapes or "rambles" as they are often called are frequent from training schools, partly because of the ease of escape from such places.

The superintendent of the training school traditionally has been the product of the political "spoils system," such as an ex-county sheriff or similar person to whom a political debt is owed. It goes without saying that he has often been ill-trained for the job of maintaining and managing a custodial institution. The rest of the staff tends to be divided into two general groups. The first includes work supervisors, teachers, and sometimes social case workers, who deal with the inmates in one connection or another during the day. Also included in this group are the kitchen personnel, clerks, and similar workers. The second general group of employees is made up of the cottage supervisors or cottage parents. They have the major responsibility for managing the wards at night and during those times of the day when the inmates are not involved in some formal program. The cottage workers have the greatest amount of interaction with the wards and the most difficult experiences with them. The prevention of runaways and other disturbances of the institutional routine is usually their responsibility.

Training schools in the past have usually operated a minimal treatment program. Most of the inmates have been placed in a school program or in some kind of vocational or other work experience. Occasionally, they receive some kind of individual therapy from a social case worker, but this tends to be a relatively infrequent event.

The overriding concern in juvenile institutions has revolved around the prevention of escapes and large-scale disturbances. The staff members regard runaway behavior as serious indeed, for it is serious in one important way. Even though most fugitives are quickly apprehended, and even though they normally do not create any incidents in the surrounding area, the community reacts negatively to escapes. Consequently, the juvenile institution that acquires a reputation for frequent escapes usually receives a good deal of hostile and highly vocal criticism. In turn, runaways come to be defined as extremely serious by the employees.

Juvenile facilities share certain structural shortcomings with their adult counterparts. In both places, uncooperative individuals must be restrained in some way, but a number of potentially effective control techniques are not available to the authorities. Thus, although the training school personnel can keep their charges "in line" by occasional beatings and other kinds of physical coercion, they must be circumspect in the use of force. There is a very real danger that the word will get out to the community if beatings become a regular part of the disciplinary program of the school. Then, too, cottage parents who utilize physical aggression as a main technique of control are in some considerable danger of reprisals. The worker may be physically able to dominate any individual ward, but he may not emerge the victor in a fight with a half-dozen or more inmates. This is not to say that corporal punishment is never used in juvenile institutions. Coercion which transcends the official rules is employed, but it tends to be relatively mild in form and it is used as a supplement to other control devices.[31]

The tactic commonly employed to deal with uncooperative boys parallels the arrangements in adult prisons. The institutional staff

[31] Fisher, *op. cit.*, 88.

enters into tacit bargains with certain inmate leaders in the dormitories. These older, physically mature, sophisticated juveniles operate "kangaroo courts" in which they coerce other, weaker youths into docile behavior. In addition to keeping order and preventing "rambles," these toughs often use their power to force other inmates into homosexual practices, to obtain money from them, and to victimize them in other ways.

As these remarks suggest, there is a prisoner social system in juvenile institutions. A kind of inmate code characterizes most training schools. This is a juvenile parallel of that one found in prisons, centering around the same kinds of antisocial norms as the adult counterpart, and antiadministration and antitreatment in content. It prescribes "playing it cool" as model behavior for wards, in which they are expected to do their time as pleasantly as possible but without entering into meaningful relationships with staff members.

A pattern of role-types also exists in juvenile institutions. The system tends to be a relatively simple one, based on differences in physical prowess and criminal sophistication. Two major role types emerge in training schools, "toughs" and "punks." The former are juveniles who have been in the institution for a relatively long time, who have extensive delinquency records, and who are physically superior to other inmates. The second group is made up of boys who are physically immature and who are often less sophisticated delinquents.

The preceding comments are consistent with a body of impressions about state training schools presented some years ago by Deutsch.[32] He traveled around the country looking at a large sample of these institutions, at the end of which he reported that ten "deadly sins" characterized most of them. These ten faults included regimentation, institutional monotony in the form of unvaried diets and the like, mass handling of inmates without regard to individual needs, and partisan political domination. Additionally, he listed public penury, isolation, complacency, excess of physical and mental punishment, Babelism, and enforced idleness as other deficiencies. Babelism was his term for various semantic reforms that are common in corrections, in which "the hole" is renamed the "adjustment center" but the character of the punishment program is not changed, in which the recreation program is retitled "mass treatment," or in which the name of the institution is changed from Boy's Industrial School to Brown Mountain School for Boys.

Ohlin and Lawrence have recently discussed the treatment problems which arise in places such as training schools where interaction occurs among hostile "clients" and where group norms define the model inmate as one who is "playing it cool," that is, who refrains from significant involvement with therapeutic agents.[33] Their remarks parallel the earlier ones of Topping, who noted that the treatment of "pseudosocial" delinquents (gang offenders) is complicated by the group interaction which develops among these offenders in institutions.[34] She reported that many of them exhibit a classical "crime-punishment" orientation in which they see themselves as serving time to pay their societal debt. Many of these same youngsters disavow any conception of themselves as having problems or as in need of therapy. In both of these cases, some procedures which might circumvent some of these difficulties are suggested. Among these would be the development of treatment efforts centered within cottage units, in order to utilize the inmate social organization in therapy, and employment of cottage workers who are regarded as "right" and "fair" persons by the inmates but who are also sophisticated about the manipulative techniques employed by wards attempting to "play it cool."

The social structure of a boys' training school in Colorado has been described by Barker and Adams.[35] Rigid interactional and communication barriers between inmates and staff members, along with a pervasive spirit of authoritarianism in which the offenders do not identify with the values and goals of the staff, are reported. The authors also note the existence of a status order among inmates, heavily structured around displays of physical toughness and victimization of peers. They speculate that this system may be the result, at least in part, of widespread insecurities regarding masculinity among delinquent boys.[36]

Polsky has provided a detailed description of the social structure among inmates through a study of the boys residing in a cottage

[33] Ohlin and Lawrence, *op. cit.*
[34] Topping, *op. cit.*
[35] Barker and Adams, *op. cit.*
[36] *Ibid.*, 420-42; this theme also appears in Topping, *op. cit.*, 356.

within a private correctional institution.[37] He reports a diamond-shaped status system in which a few boys have very high or low rank among their peers, with the largest group falling into a middle range. Polsky maintains that this system is independent of the particular youths who fill it in any particular period, for it persists relatively unaltered over time, even though cottage residents enter and leave the system. The departure of a leader, for example, produces competition, conflict, and jockeying among inmate aspirants for the position, followed by re-establishment of equilibrium. According to Polsky, the status types in the cottage include "toughs" and "con artists" at the apex of the order, "quiet types" in the middle range, and "bushboys" and "scapegoats" on the bottom of the system. The latter are subjected to unrelenting physical and psychological attacks by those higher in the pecking order. Probably the most significant of Polsky's observations is that the inmate system is abetted by the institutional staff. He notes that "Thus, the theme of aggression with all its authoritarian overtones is structurally configured in the cottage. Under its roof the cottage parents join the older boys in scapegoating the defenseless low-status boys—the sneaks, punks, and the sick. The latter 'deserve' the beating because of *their* provocativeness and 'unfitness.' The unwritten compact of cottage parents and toughs makes it unbearable for the 'deviants' because they are blamed for everything." [38]

Findings similar to those of Polsky come from a state training school in California. Fisher found that both the inmates and supervisors rank and victimize certain boys and, moreover, that the low-ranked boys in the eyes of the officials are also the low-status inmates in the ward hierarchy.[39] In turn, the staff workers often interpret disruptive behavior by low-status boys as evidence of psychological maladjustment rather than as flowing out of the social structure and interactional patterns among offenders. Low-ranked, victimized inmates are defined as "mess-ups," implying that they willfully engage in disapproved behavior out of psychological tensions and the like. Instead of attempting to undermine the inmate system, the authorities react to boys in terms of it, so that institutional

---

[37] Polsky, "Changing Delinquent Subcultures: A Social-Psychological Approach"; Polsky, *Cottage Six*, pp. 69-88.
[38] Polsky, *Cottage Six*, p. 133.
[39] Fisher, *op. cit.*

rewards are differentially accorded to boys with high status among their peers.

Some attention has also been given to organizational problems which develop in training schools upon introduction of rehabilitation as a major goal. One of the earliest warnings of the potential problems was sounded by Jenkins,[40] who indicated that treatment clinics are likely to become merely institutional window-dressing if they are simply grafted on to a custodial program and are unconnected to the rest of the institution. They become reduced to making diagnostic and treatment recommendations which are diverted to custodial ends or which are systematically ignored. To be effective, clinical operations must be heavily centered around cottage groups and cottage personnel. Jenkins suggested that cottage workers, who are normally persons without extensive clinical training, nevertheless represent the major group on which the success of therapy ultimately depends. Among other things, it is in the dormitories where assaults upon the antitreatment inmate system of "playing it cool" must be mounted. Otherwise, this antitherapy pattern will not be altered, and efforts of professional personnel will be nullified.

More recently, Weber has identified a number of areas in which conflict arises between professional and nonprofessional personnel in institutions where treatment is introduced.[41] One major problem which he identifies, and which is also noted by Ohlin,[42] centers around the role-difficulties that develop for cottage workers. Their authority position is often reduced or undermined with the introduction of therapy goals. They are likely to feel that their prestige has been lowered with the entry of professional personnel into the program. Redefinition of the role of the cottage worker also occurs, and he is expected to run a quiet and well-disciplined dormitory and to contribute to therapy. But because he is not given clear instructions of how he is to accomplish these ends, he experiences much the same role-dilemma that was noted earlier for prison guards. Weber and others have suggested that a number of negative consequences develop from the introduction of "rehabilitation"

---

[40] Jenkins, *op. cit.*
[41] Weber, "Conflicts Between Professional and Non-Professional Personnel in Institutional Delinquency Treatment."
[42] Ohlin, "The Reduction of Role Conflict in Institutional Staff."

into previously custodial institutions.[43] Staff cooperation is reduced and replaced by conflicts between professional and custodial personnel, defensive reactions develop among cottage workers, and other difficulties arise. In turn, inmates manipulate these conflicts to their own ends by playing competing groups against each other.

The most systematic, combined theoretical and research work produced so far on the consequences of the introduction of treatment goals into training schools is found in the work of Vinter and Janowitz, and Zald.[44] In 1959, Vinter and Janowitz presented a theoretical statement regarding the problems that are created when therapeutic functions are assigned to juvenile institutions, along with some commentary on possible solutions of these difficulties. They note that the addition of therapeutic goals produces confusion in staff-client relations as the institutional system begins to operate with a mixture of domination and persuasion as client-control techniques. They also point out, as many others have done, that bifurcation of the administrator group into treatment and custodial cliques usually accompanies the changeover to new goals. Further, they argue that the treatment-oriented facility frequently experiences considerable community hostility and resistance as the relaxation of custodial procedures in the school leads to intensified client-community contacts. Finally, they point to still another difficulty in the form of excessively high expectations for the organization by the parent agency of state government. These unrealistic expectations lead, in turn, to staff tensions and administrative instability produced by firings, resignations, and the like.[45]

Zald has reported confirmatory evidence for these propositions in a series of research studies. He studied five training schools,

[43] Weber, "Emotional and Defensive Reactions of Cottage Parents"; Zald, "Power Balance and Staff Conflict in Correctional Institutions."

[44] Robert Vinter and Morris Janowitz, "Effective Institutions for Juvenile Delinquents: A Research Statement," *Social Service Review*, Vol. 33 (June 1959), 118-30; Zald, "Power Balance and Staff Conflict in Correctional Institutions"; Zald, "The Correctional Institution for Juvenile Offenders: An Analysis of Organizational 'Character' "; Zald, "Organizational Control Structure in Five Correctional Institutions," *American Journal of Sociology*, Vol. 68 (November 1962), 335-45; Zald, "Comparative Analysis and Measurement of Organizational Goals: The Case of Correctional Institutions for Delinquents," *The Sociological Quarterly*, Vol. 4 (Summer 1963), 206-30; Robert D. Vinter, "Analysis of Treatment Organizations," *Social Work*, Vol. 8 (July 1963), 3-15.

[45] Vinter and Janowitz, *op. cit.*

two private ones and three public institutions, which differed in terms of population size, treatment goal-emphasis, form of therapy activities, and so forth. In general, he found that staff tensions and conflicts among various employee groups were highest in therapy-oriented institutions.[46]

Although it would be naive to suppose that the implementation of therapeutic interests is a task which is easily accomplished, it does appear that the problems of implementation are not insoluble. Ohlin and Weber both suggest a number of procedures by which organizational difficulties might be reduced.[47] In several cases, there is evidence that certain steps have been relatively successful. Thus Ohlin reports an experiment in a girls' training school in which closer integration of cottage and therapy activities was brought about through reorganization of the program. Social work supervisors assisted dormitory workers in the management of cottages,[48] and they also helped the cottage personnel solve problems of managing inmates. These steps, in turn, produced an attenuation of tensions and disagreements among employees.

PROBATION AND PAROLE ORGANIZATION

Parole and probation agencies can justifiably be discussed together, even though there are some important differences between them. The major dissimilarity is that parole involves more serious, criminalistic offenders than does probation; the former handles persons processed through institutions, whereas the latter does not. Penal commitment represents the harshest penalty available outside of capital punishment, so that it tends to be used with the most difficult and intractable law violators, whereas probation is a disposition commonly reserved for persons lacking in criminalistic orientation. However, even though parole and probation differ in this way, both deal with offenders in the community, and there are certain organizational features which seem to be common to both of them.

There is a paucity of empirical evidence about social-structural

---

[46] Zald, "Power Balance and Staff Conflict in Correctional Institutions."

[47] Ohlin, "Reduction of Role Conflict in Institutional Staff," 67-69; Weber, "Conflicts Between Professional and Non-Professional Personnel in Institutional Delinquency Treatment," 39-43.

[48] Ohlin, "Reduction of Role Conflict in Institutional Staff," 39-43.

characteristics of probation and parole systems. Most of the relevant literature is repetitious in the extreme, centering around "bread and butter" complaints to the effect that these services are hamstrung by case loads that are too large and wages that are too low, or around inspirational messages sermonizing upon the monetary and therapeutic virtues of probation and parole. This kind of material fills such publications as *Federal Probation*. Although these dialogues serve useful purposes, they do not illuminate the organizational features and problems of probation and parole.

In the brief discussion of probation and parole below, sketches are provided of the organizational framework of these services, that is, of the ways in which they are articulated with other aspects of local and state government. In addition, some remarks are provided regarding some of the internal organizational aspects of these programs.

The commentary on parole is mainly concerned with adult systems, in that juvenile parole programs are nonexistent or only slightly developed in many states. In particular, the notes on the general organization of parole should be read as a description of adult parole systems.

The paroling function is structured in several different ways in the various states. In some, ex officio boards made up of government officials serve as the paroling agency. In these, individuals who have major governmental responsibilities elsewhere make release decisions "on the side." The more common arrangement, particularly in the larger states, involves an agency called the "Board of Prison Terms and Paroles," "Adult Authority," or some other similar label. A group of persons are appointed by the state governor, usually for fixed terms of office, and then are given the full-time task of deciding about release of prisoners on parole. Normally no specific qualifications are required for service on the board, but members are commonly drawn from corrections, law enforcement, legal, or academic backgrounds. In some states operating under this pattern, the board discharges two major functions. It acts as a quasi-judicial board, setting release dates for prisoners, and it also administers the parole supervision organization. These boards establish policies for parole supervision and they employ and supervise parole agents as well. However, recent correctional thinking has tended to define these as somewhat incompatible functions, so that certain states such as California and Washington have removed the administrative task from the paroling agency and have placed it within the correctional department.

In theory, decisions to release or not to release an inmate are based upon such criteria as his behavioral change and favorable prognosis of success on parole. In fact, they tend not to be made in this fashion. For one thing, parole boards are often limited in the degree to which they can determine release dates by statutory minimum sentences which require that persons convicted of certain crimes spend no less than some specific period in prison. Also, minimum sentences are frequently set by the board at the beginning of the prisoner's stay in the institution, so that they are determined before sufficient time has elapsed to estimate the person's response to therapy. In addition, parole boards are often made up of members who are ill-trained to estimate the rehabilitative prospects for inmates. Perhaps the knowledge on which such decisions must be based is not at hand, so that no paroling authority however assembled could make accurate judgments of this kind. Finally, boards have to contend with factors other than the needs of prisoners. In particular, they must be sensitive to public pressures of various sorts which demand that certain offenders be kept in prison for long periods of time. For example, the decision to release a sex offender who will return to a small community from which he was convicted is frequently contingent more upon estimates of the level of community tolerance than it is upon the needs of the offender. The prisoner is paroled if the board judges that such a decision will provoke only a slight amount of "heat."

For reasons of this kind, parole decisions are normally intuitive in character. They also tend to be based on a mixture of considerations—the nature of the offense, the needs of the offender, and the reactions of the general public. In addition, they are usually not as individualized as parole theory would lead one to suppose. Instead, paroling agencies develop informal precedents, and prison terms handed out to various offenders average out to a fairly specific figure, such as three years, with little variation around that average. In turn, prisoners come to informally define three years as an equitable sentence, so that any marked departure from this standard becomes the focus of inmate grievances. Prison unrest and disturbances as inmates try to re-establish the former precedent sometimes occur as a response to shifts in parole policies.

Variations are also seen in the structure of probation services.

In some states, probation is a state operation grafted on to parole services. In this arrangement, probation is sometimes shunted aside because of the heavy work demands of parole. As a consequence, few offenders are placed upon probation. In a number of states, such as California, probation is county operated, with individual probation services in the various counties. Each of these is autonomous and is managed at the local level by county supervisors or commissioners.

One variation between probation and parole, in addition to patterns of placement within governmental systems, has to do with the involvement of probation officers in the selection of offenders to be placed under their control. Parole agents receive their "clients" from the institutions, without any option to select or reject them in terms of some set of eligibility criteria. But in both adult and juvenile probation services, the workers play a major role in the selection process. In juvenile operations, they compile information about youths undergoing court hearings. This collection of data, called the "social investigation," is a principal source of evidence on which adjudication and disposition of cases is based. Similarly, in adult probation, convicted offenders are referred to probation agents for "presentence investigations." The presentence report prepared by the officer becomes, in turn, a major consideration in the disposition of the case. This report normally includes a statement of sentence recommendations by the officer which are usually followed by the judge in his decision.

The most important bit of evidence on the internal workings of probation and parole services comes from a study by Ohlin, Piven, and Pappenfort,[49] and the material below draws heavily upon the results. Their concern was mainly upon the role-dilemmas of social workers in parole and probation settings. These seem to be much the same in both situations, except perhaps that parole "clients" are on the whole somewhat more hostile than probationers, so that they present more intense problems to the worker.

Ohlin, Piven, and Pappenfort suggest that probation and parole services have traditionally been assigned a number of not entirely compatible functions. Probationers and parolees are supposed to be supervised, assisted, and treated, but at the same time, officers are expected to collect fines, to "protect society" in various ways, and

---

[49] Ohlin, Piven, and Pappenfort, *op. cit.*

to perform other tasks having little to do with helping offenders. These agents must contend with persistent suspicion and hostility directed at them and their charges by the police and other groups in the community. Because of this antagonism, agencies often come to be as much concerned about shielding the organization from criticism as they are about protecting clients. Thus officers spend some of their time giving speeches to citizen groups, in which they argue for the merits of their services, agitate for greater financial support, and defend their agencies against charges of "softness," "coddling," and the like.

Several other specific consequences follow from the uneasy status of probation and parole in the public eye. First, the "public relations" orientations that develop frequently mean that occupational mobility in these agencies is more dependent upon "public relations" talents than it is on technical competency. Organizational "con men" ascend to supervisory positions in the operation. Second, two main kinds of workers, "punitive" and "protective" agents, have developed. The former sometimes carry guns, they regard themselves as law-enforcement officers rather than as rehabilitative agents, they are not trained in social service work, and they define their responsibilities as principally protecting society. They attempt to coerce their charges into appropriate behavior and punish non-cooperative cases by revoking their parole or probation status. The "protective" agents sometimes have had training in corrections and regard themselves as responsible for treatment, but they vacillate back and forth from protecting the public to helping clients.

Additional role-problems have cropped up in parole-probation organizations in recent years following the recruitment of large numbers of "welfare workers" into these systems. Officers trained in social work enter these fields expecting to protect clients and to treat them as they would in other welfare settings. They come prepared to apply "generic" principles in this setting. However, they soon discover that there are difficulties with treatment in corrections which their training has not covered.[50] For one, social work education is not much concerned with the special problems of dealing with captive, hostile persons. These subjects differ markedly

---

[50] For one illustration of social work literature on corrections which is not adequate to the job of preparing social workers for this kind of service, see David Dressler, *Practice and Theory of Probation and Parole* (New York: Columbia University Press, 1959).

from the conventional volunteer client who seeks help. The probation-parole social worker also finds that his training has not
equipped him to handle authority problems. He is not prepared to
function within the special structure of corrections in which he is
both a representative of the punitive social control system as well
as a helper. Third, the agent discovers that he lacks knowledge
which equips him to understand different client types or to deal
effectively with these types.

The agent trained in social work also discovers discrepancies between probation-parole settings and traditional images of the welfare agency. For one thing, the rules of client supervision, such as
those forbidding probationers or parolees from using alcohol, differentiate correctional agencies from noncorrectional ones. There
are other restraints on the kinds of decisions that workers can make,
so that the needs of the client must frequently be subordinated to
these other demands. In turn, the correctional social worker may
experience considerable identity-conflict because these agency rules
and procedures force him to act in ways which depart from the
conventional picture of his professional role.

According to Ohlin and his associates, the outcome of inadequate
educational preparation and the discrepancies encountered between
correctional settings and conventional welfare agencies is varied in
form. Some workers solve these dilemmas by getting out of correctional work or out of social work entirely. Others stay in probation-
parole, but with different "styles" of work adjustment. Those who
are in relatively autonomous systems may be able to deport themselves in a fashion close enough to their notion of the welfare
worker role to preserve a "social worker" identity. In more restrictive agencies, the agent may try to evade demands directed at him
which he regards as "nonprofessional," such as collection of fines,
and thereby retain a social worker role-conception. But this arrangement is difficult to sustain over a long period of time, and it is also
productive of a marginal and ambivalent self-identification. Finally,
some workers become reconciled to the peculiarities of restrictive
correctional settings. In turn, they redefine themselves as some special kind of social worker. They gradually lose interest in, or contact with, the general social welfare literature and social worker
organizations.

Doubtless these role-dilemmas are real ones which create adjustment difficulties for professional workers in corrections. However,

there are signs that such problems are becoming generally recognized in social work schools. In some, curriculum changes designed to provide more specific correctional training have been made, along with other modifications in social work education. Perhaps the problems identified above are relatively transitional and may become attenuated in time.

Summary

This chapter has reviewed two general kinds of obstructions to implementation of rehabilitative goals in corrections. The practical problems of inadequate finances, overly large case loads, and the like will probably continue to plague treatment efforts. The simple fact is that the financial resources of state and local governments are severely limited. There are many agencies and functions which compete for these funds, so that corrections will doubtless continue to suffer from scarce resources. They will have to make judicious use of available funds, and they will have to work out expedient solutions to their financial difficulties. For example, probation organizations will have to separate their charges into treatment groups, so that the less criminalistic offenders would get minimal assistance and the most intensive and costly efforts would then be directed at the more antisocial persons. In the same way, in other correctional settings, the authorities will have to make do with scarce finances.

The obstacles to treatment described in the latter part of this chapter will also continue to be bothersome. However, it appears that enough is known at present about some of these difficulties so that they could be remedied. At several points in this chapter, evidence was presented to indicate that many of the problems of correctional social structure can be reduced. Probably the most important single implication of the discussion is that correctional administrators should be conversant with the relevant literature on these matters. Sociologists who have studied penal organizations and other such systems have quite a bit to say to correctional administrators. They have identified a number of structural problems that develop as a result of the infusion of treatment goals into corrections. The next step would seem to be one in which the authorities begin to confront some of these situational impediments to therapy. In the same way, some dilemmas confronting treatment agents, which stem from their incomplete training, have been identified, so that it is time to begin working on new programs of correctional education.

six

TREATMENT

OF

DELINQUENTS

Introduction

Offender types and patterns of treatment are brought together in this chapter and the following one. Chapter Six advances treatment recommendations for the nine delinquent types, and in Chapter Seven, therapy tactics for the fifteen adult criminal patterns are suggested.

The reader will recall that six types of treatment were specified in Chapter Four, in which something to be done to or with law violators was outlined. One matter *not* covered in that discussion was a tactic of "no treatment." It is not necessarily true that *something* should be done to every deviant who comes into contact with control agencies. Some offenders should be segregated from persons unlike themselves, that is, they should be put into differential association with other individuals of the same type. Little else should be done to them, however, and they do not require intensive therapy. For example, certain prison inmates require assistance of various kinds from social workers, such as help in arranging a welfare check for their wives. But this kind of help is similar to general social welfare aid rendered to law-abiding citizens and is not treatment. This kind of activity is not designed to convert the inmate into a nondeviant, nor should it be, for some offenders do not need to be changed into something else.

There are juvenile and adult law violators who probably would profit from minimal interference in their activities by rehabilitative agents. Intensive therapy is something to be administered judiciously and to those violators who have some relatively obvious problem to which treatment would be directed. The term "problem" as used in this context refers to antisocial attitudes and the like, as well as to adjustment problems of some sort. In those offender types where such characteristics are missing, the recommendation will be one of "no treatment."

One indication that intensive tampering with some lawbreakers is unnecessary comes from studies of probation agency records, a number of which were mentioned in Chapter Five (pages 194-195). They indicated that most juvenile and adult probationers refrain from further illegal behavior, even though they are not given any significant dose of treatment. Quite apparently, probation agencies go about screening referrals in such a way as to sift out the more tractable persons for probation placement. They retain control over petty offenders who are not pursuing criminalistic careers, who exhibit prosocial attitudes, and who are from relatively stable social backgrounds. These individuals turn out to be "self-correctors."

The appearance of these kinds of persons who do not require therapy in correctional case loads is a function of societal reactions to acts of deviation in modern societies. An affluent society such as the United States can afford the luxury of detailed attention and concern devoted to juvenile behavior. In turn, such a social system is going to have high rates of juvenile delinquency, in part simply because it has time to spend ferreting out delinquents. In a sense, given the broad character of delinquency laws in the United States, the potential population of "juvenile delinquents" is nearly infinite in size. That is, almost every juvenile in the United States could be considered a delinquent because almost every youngster engages in at least some minor acts of law violation. Although a great many of these peccadillos are ignored and do not become the subject of official attention, some of them do become known to the police, schools, or other court referral sources. These agencies perform an initial sifting of cases, so that most of the inconsequential instances of lawbreaking are screened out and dealt with informally although some of them are reported to juvenile courts. Accordingly, the group of officially tagged delinquents comes to be made up of several components, one being career-oriented offenders needing treatment. But casual delinquents not in need of resocialization also turn up in the juvenile court, or in some instances, even in training schools.

The same general point holds for adult offenders. The police and criminal courts are given the responsibility of handling a wide spectrum of behavior patterns and offender types, many of whom are in need of therapy but others who are not. Because the latter persons are processed through criminal courts, they end up in probation case loads or, in some cases, in institutions. One illustration of the kind of offender that does not usually need therapy is the statutory rapist. Whatever the ends that are being served by incarceration of such persons, they are not therapeutic ones. The statutory rapist is not normally a pathological or atypical individual in terms of personality structure. For that matter, it could be argued with considerable merit that the statutory rapist is not a deviant in behavioral terms either. Voluntary sexual intercourse between an unmarried minor female and an unmarried adult male is not an uncommon activity in the United States.

Other cases of adult criminality can be found in which the offenders have engaged in activities that are regarded as dangerous or serious by the general public and the courts. For this reason, such persons receive prison sentences and become part of the correctional case load. Yet these same individuals exhibit remorse, contrition, and prosocial attitudes. They also show positive social backgrounds, and thus need minimal therapy.

In the pages to follow, more detailed consideration is given to types of violators who need little or no treatment. The exposition of characteristics of types in Chapter Three indicated that the group of essentially prosocial individuals includes casual gang delinquents and casual delinquents who are not gang members. It also includes "one-time loser" property offenders, professional "fringe" violators, and embezzlers. Finally, "one-time loser" personal offenders and statutory rapists are also found in this correctional group.

The commentary in these two chapters elaborates upon the earlier discussion of treatment patterns in Chapter Four. The intent of this text is to generate further attention to the basic problem of diagnostic and treatment models rather than to lay out a set of detailed therapy recipes or prescriptions.

Treatment of Delinquents

PREDATORY GANG DELINQUENT

The basic proposal for dealing with predatory gang delinquents centers around tactics involving group intervention. In brief, the task of treatment is to convert predatory offenders into members of an "antidelinquent society" by using group members as the agents of behavioral change. Predatory delinquents often get into the social control machinery through police arrest and juvenile court appearances. Many of them are found in official programs such as probation or in training schools. On the other hand, some predatory juveniles are also the focus of rehabilitative endeavors outside the framework of the legal apparatus, particularly in privately sponsored prevention programs. Predatory gang delinquents define themselves as persons without personality problems. They think of themselves as lacking in adjustment difficulties. Moreover, the research data examined in Chapter Two seem to demonstrate that these individuals are no more-or-less "pathological" than their nondelinquent peers. They are supported in these self-definitions by a peer social system which projects blame onto society rather than directing it inward upon themselves. This peer subculture is remarkably resistant to attempts to seduce individual members away from it. As a result, if individual gang members are to be changed, the group must be changed. Group therapy in which members are encouraged to develop countercriminal norms is the most likely tactic of those presently available for the achievement of these ends. Individual therapy, based on assumptions that lower-class gang offenders have personality problems about which they need "insight" is not likely to have much effect upon juveniles of this kind, judging from the results of these programs so far.[1]

Group therapy is recommended for gang delinquents who are caught up in the official system. Gang offenders on probation should

[1] For one study of treatment of this kind, apparently without effect, see LaMay Adamson and H. Warren Dunham, "Clinical Treatment of Male Delinquents: A Case Study in Effort and Results," *American Sociological Review,* Vol. 21 (June 1956), 312-20.

be put into group therapy rather than into some kind of intensive individual treatment. It would seem no great chore to assemble predatory gang members for group treatment in juvenile halls or in community facilities such as boys' clubs, recreational centers, and so forth. Of course, some minor technical problems could crop up, such as objections by community groups to the congregation of delinquents in community facilities, but it should be possible to circumvent these protests and other difficulties. Group treatment of gang delinquents on probation can be rationalized on two grounds: economy of effort and efficacy of the tactic of group work. That is, in addition to the fundamental argument for group therapy with these offenders, which is that they are most amenable to that kind of intervention, group treatment can be defended as an expedient solution to the problem of excessive case loads.

Chapter Five noted that complaints of inordinately large case loads are an omnipresent feature of probation work in the United States. Probation workers everywhere lament this situation and voice the proposition that their professional training is nullified by case loads so high that only superficial care, at best, can be given to wards. Now, it is unlikely that this situation is going to be drastically modified in the near future, and ways of dealing with these masses of juveniles will have to be found. Group therapy is one of these devices. Along the same line, there is a related possibility that has yet to be tried out on a large scale. There is a large pool of potential nonprofessional "treatment aides" or "rehabilitation helpers," as they might be termed, that might be drawn into volunteer work with delinquent groups in probation settings. In metropolitan communities, many interested laymen could be recruited and put to work under the guidance of the professional staff of the juvenile court. College students in the several social science fields that touch upon problems of deviant behavior represent a particularly promising source of volunteer therapy agents. Beyond the argument that this kind of program would help to deal with the chronic problems of insufficient staff, there is an argument of therapeutic value which could be advanced as well. A carefully executed program involving interested laymen could provide delinquent subjects with meaningful interactions with carriers of nondeviant norms. Perhaps such an operation would reduce the offender's hostility to the official agency and its personnel, at least to some degree.

Older, more sophisticated gang delinquents in institutions should also be introduced into guided group interaction. Here, too, it might be possible to involve lay persons from the community in group counseling of these wards, but probably not as easily as in the case of probation.

Ideally, group ventures with gang boys might be combined with a general program of milieu management of the Highfields form,[2] in which a variety of adjunct activities in addition to therapy would be directed at them, such as participation in work programs. Of course, this recommendation is not a very practical one in most cases. Institutions like Highfields, with very small inmate populations and favorable staff-inmate ratios, are few in number and probably will continue to be in short supply. The basic fact is that such programs are simply too costly to be widely developed. Because of their small number, they have something of the appearance of show pieces. Accordingly, institutional programs for gang delinquents will continue to be carried out in relatively conventional training schools for the most part.

If existing juvenile facilities cannot all be torn down and replaced with small, integrated living institutions, and if much of the treatment of gang offenders will continue to go on in conventional training schools, can anything be done to make these places approximate the conditions of a therapeutic milieu? Can steps be taken to contrive a situation conducive to the development of an "antidelinquency society" among gang boys in training schools? One action in this direction would be to establish a degree of physical and social segregation between the gang offenders and other boys in the juvenile facility. Gang kinds of boys could be housed together in cottages or dormitories, and many of their activities could be structured to keep these youths relatively separate from other training school residents. The intention of segregation would be twofold: to assemble similar types of boys together for purposes of therapy, and to minimize the opportunities for these offenders to engage in victimization of peers and other "system-beating" institutional adjustments. Such an organizational pattern would incorporate some features of the Korn and McCorkle model —discussed in Chapter Four (168-170)—which tries to frus-

[2] See the discussion of Highfields in Chapter Four, pp. 165-166.

trate offenders in their efforts to "play it cool" and "beat the system."

Another possibility would be to surround gang boys with cottage workers and other employees who represent the kinds of adults that gang juveniles regard as "right" persons. These workers should exhibit such characteristics as physical skill, trustworthiness, and respect for the wards. They should also be individuals who are sophisticated in the ways of delinquents, so that they could not be "conned" or manipulated by the offenders. Some of these persons might be employees who are formally designated as treatment agents or social workers, but others would be work supervisors, teachers, or cottage supervisors. These individuals would be the ones who carry out group treatment with the wards, so that although formal group activities would be carried on principally in the evenings, some informal group counseling would take place at various times of the day.

A third tactic in the institutional handling of gang boys might be to take some juvenile wards into the rehabilitation operation as treatment agents. One endeavor of this kind with adult felons in a prison was cited in Chapter Four (pages 173-174). Although this step would be fraught with difficulties if not handled with great care, the arguments for such a venture seem compelling. The employment of inmate therapists could be a viable tactic for achieving behavioral change on the part of the group. Also, participation in the role of "therapist" by the inmate would strengthen his prosocial attitudes in that such activities would serve to reinforce his view of himself as one who can "make good" (become changed into a law-abiding citizen).

A final element in an over-all program of therapy would involve the deliberate manipulation of an incentive system such that those boys showing the greatest therapeutic progress would receive the greatest share of the rewards. Two major rewards could be made the focus of attention, namely, leaves or home visits from the school, and release on parole from the institution. On the latter point, most training schools are in the enviable position of being able to release wards from custody at varied times and after varied periods of incarceration, in contrast to the adult penal institution where lengths of sentence are governed by independent paroling agencies and are not so easily adjusted to behavioral change by the inmate.

When gang boys appear in parole case loads, their involvement in group treatment should be continued in that setting. Group work with predatory gang parolees would normally take the following form: They would be returned to the community and neighborhood from which they originally came. They would be encouraged to establish conventional work attachments and would be aided in doing so by parole officers. The major treatment tactic of the parole agent would be to involve groups of such boys in therapy sessions several times per week. The postinstitutional adjustment difficulties reported by the subjects would provide grist for group discussion. In turn, such group interaction would hopefully help to insulate offenders from reinvolvement in illegal activity. The essential aim would be the creation of a mutual aid society, in which the group would provide support for each individual member in his efforts to stay out of trouble. In a fashion similar to Alcoholics Anonymous, group members would aid each other and, in rendering assistance, would also reinforce their own convictions that successful adjustment is possible for themselves. In this way, the person who helps an associate helps himself as well. Of course, all this assumes that the parole agent would have the freedom to structure a program of this kind without interference from a hostile community (or a hostile parole agency).

In some cases, an effective means of encouraging postrelease prosocial actions among parolees might be through some device such as a halfway house.[3] This might be particularly useful for working-class delinquents, who would be kept apart from the common criminalistic influences in their own neighborhoods. The halfway house is a place where offenders reside, at least temporarily, until they are ready to return completely to civilian society. The parolees work apart during the day but reside together at night and also receive treatment. Some halfway organizations have been developed in recent years, but as with treatment milieus such as Highfields, the supply of these places is not sufficient to meet the potential demand. In the immediate future, most parole programs will probably continue to be carried on outside the format of halfway organizations.

One reason why delinquency possesses considerable appeal for predatory offenders is that nondelinquent, conventional activities

[3] One recent bit of evidence on the usefulness of halfway houses is reported in Robert F. Kennedy, "Halfway Houses Pay Off," *Crime and Delinquency*, Vol. 10 (January 1964), 1-7.

are relatively inaccessible and therefore unattractive to them. The gang boy's low valuation of conventional work careers stems, at least in part, from his perception that regular, reasonable, and attractive jobs are not widely available to him. If this is so, an adjunct activity of some use in the treatment of predatory offenders would center around such things as finding jobs for them and other efforts to place them in law-abiding roles. The importance of this sort of help should not be minimized, but neither should it be confused with treatment per se.

Turning to rehabilitative efforts directed at predatory delinquents outside the framework of official agencies, two particular strategies can be suggested. Environmental change programs designed to alter the social environment of the community areas in which gang delinquency is common might be undertaken. As noted in Chapter Four, a number of environmental modifications are presently underway in certain American cities. However, activities of this kind are usually more *preventive* in aim than they are directed toward resocialization of individuals already known to be delinquent, particularly juveniles who have acquired official identities as lawbreakers through the juvenile court. A second suggestion involves group therapy in a form similar to that of existing street-worker programs in certain large American cities. In these, persons with training in social work or allied skills are employed to carry treatment to gangs in neighborhoods, or as this is sometimes described, to "reach the unreached," who do not come voluntarily seeking help at social agencies.[4] Attention is given in these programs to hiring individuals who are acquainted with the characteristics of the neighborhoods in question and who are conversant with life in the areas, so that they will be able to establish rapport with the gang offenders of the area. Workers are sought who have "savvy," who "speak the language" of lower-class society, who are mature, successful ex-working-class individuals. In all likelihood, the pro-

---

[4] See as illustrative of this approach James R. Dumpson, "An Approach to Anti-Social Street Gangs," *Federal Probation*, Vol. 13 (December 1949), 22-29; P. L. Crawford, D. I. Malamud, and J. R. Dumpson, *Working With Teen-Age Gangs* (New York: Welfare Council of New York City, 1950); Walter Bernstein, "The Cherubs are Rumbling," *New Yorker* (September 21, 1957), pp. 129-59; John M. Gandy, "Preventive Work With Street Corner Groups: Hyde Park Youth Project, Chicago," *Annals of the American Academy of Political and Social Science*, No. 322 (March 1959), 107-16; Stacy V. Jones, "The Cougars, Life With a Brooklyn Gang," *Harpers*, Vol. 209 (November 1954), 35-43.

fessional training possessed by the worker is of less significance than these other attributes. At any rate, the agents try to help the delinquent gang develop allegiance to an altered set of norms, particularly to a new set of group standards centering around substitute activities for group fighting or "bopping." Efforts are made to draw gangs into such endeavors as community services, in which boys clean up vacant lots or render other assistance of this kind. The worker also tries to get groups to sponsor dances or athletic events, and in other ways, to get them involved in status-conferring nondelinquent behavior. The fundamental premise of this activity is that whatever the nondelinquent pursuits that are encouraged, they must be ones that are meaningful to the offenders. The gang members must be enthusiastic about the activities so that they are important in their eyes as well as in those of the workers.

Detached-worker kinds of intervention are often intended to get an immediate reduction in such things as fighting and are less concerned with long-term goals of fundamental attitude changes. Also, street workers have normally been concerned with fighting gangs and not with predatory gang delinquents. Most of these detached-worker projects have been conducted in very large cities where conflict behavior is most pronounced, rather than in smaller cities where predatory activity is more common and where gangs are smaller and more amorphous in form. "Bopping" behavior is most apparent in New York City, Chicago, Detroit, Washington, D.C., and Los Angeles, and it is in communities of this size that streetworker projects have been created.[5] However, there is no readily apparent reason why detached-worker programs should be ruled out for predatory offenders. Perhaps one of the more important difficulties is that predatory groups are frequently smaller, less crystallized, and less visible in the area than are fighting gangs in large cities. The worker in these cases would have to devote some initial effort toward rounding up gang members to form therapy groups. In doing this, the treatment agent could obtain information and advice about delinquent peer groups from policemen, school employees, and other community contacts, as well as from individual boys.

[5] The data which would clearly establish this hypothesis are not at hand, but impressionistic evidence does seem to indicate that systematic violence by well-crystallized fighting gangs is most common in very large cities such as New York, Washington, Detroit, and Los Angeles.

CONFLICT GANG DELINQUENT

The recommendations for the treatment of conflict gang members are much the same as those for predatory offenders because the two types of delinquents are relatively similar. Both types of juveniles define themselves as without "problems" and both are supported in their antisocial values by a relatively well-organized peer system. The major difference between the two tends to be one of offense behavior rather than of social-psychological characteristics. On that score, there is some question concerning the extent to which gang delinquents come in two clearly separate forms as the "predatory" and "conflict" distinction implies. It may be that in a number of cases, gangs of "mixed" form, engaging in both aggression and thievery, may be found.

Because conflict gang members are in many ways similar to predatory thieves, the treatment recommendations for conflict delinquents in official organizations such as probation or training schools are much the same as those for predatory gang boys. Institutional intervention should take the form previously outlined, in which the program seeks to frustrate wards in their attempts to "play it cool," while at the same time, subjects are encouraged to develop an "antidelinquency society" through group treatment and allied activities. There is no need to repeat this commentary in detail.

For reasons centering around differences in offense behavior, conflict gang members are less likely to be netted in the official legal control system than are predatory thieves. Much of the day-to-day activity of fighting-gang boys is nondelinquent in nature, consisting of "hanging" on street corners and in gang haunts such as basements or of other aimless loitering. These boys are sometimes arrested when they get into gang fights or "rumbles," or when they engage in certain other delinquencies, but not as frequently as predatory gang boys.

At present, the most common specific program for conflict gang members is the detached-worker type, which is sometimes bound up in a larger set of actions that are directed at environmental modification, such as Mobilization for Youth or the Midcity Project discussed in Chapter Four.[6] The focus of this street-worker approach is to get offenders to discontinue street-fighting in favor of

---

[6] See footnote 4; also see Chapter Four, pp. 177-182.

nondelinquent substitutes for conflict. Attempts are made to discover alternative activities which will serve the status-needs of such boys but which will not get them into trouble with the authorities. In some cases, efforts are also made to obtain jobs for the gang members, in order to enmesh them in conventional law-abiding roles so that they will drift out of delinquency. Tactics of this sort are predicated upon the assumption that conflict gang members do not need extensive basic resocialization, that, instead, they are boys with relatively healthy personality structures but with antisocial norms which must be modified. What little evidence there is concerning the effectiveness of these strategies suggests that they do have some impact upon offenders. Many of these delinquents are ill-equipped to make a success of conventional adult criminality. In turn, they constitute raw material for the population of non-criminal citizens.

As noted above and in Chapter Four, there are some efforts directed toward conflict gang boys which are broader in scope, which are instances of environmental change. These are planned to maximize the job opportunities available to both present and potential conflict gang members or to alter their social situations in certain other ways.

There seems little question that the general tack being taken with conflict gang members is appropriate for such persons. Streetworker programs and similar ventures which are directed at utilizing gangs as the vehicle for rehabilitation seem to make good sense. The same could be said of the more complex approaches which try to alter the environment. It is highly doubtful that efforts to redirect the behavior of gang members by breaking up gangs or other strategies of that kind would be effective. The consequence of disrupting the peer associations of the offender would be to leave him without any supportive social system. In turn, he might then be driven to even more serious deviant activity such as drug use. Along the same line, conflict gang members are not likely candidates for psychotherapy. Although they may well vary among themselves in terms of general mental health, there is little evidence to indicate that their delinquent deviation can be attributed to personality pathology. If these claims are granted, the sensible direction of therapeutic intervention would be group- or community-oriented, which is not to say that detached-worker or environmental-modification approaches are panaceas for urban, conflict gang delinquency.

One comment that should be made about conflict gang members is in the form of a caveat against premature dependence upon a single causal hypothesis as the basis of treatment efforts. For example, it is perhaps too early to assume that nearly all conflict gang boys are involved in such behavior because of shared problems of perceived lack of opportunities to attain success goals. Although many lower-class delinquents may be inordinately troubled by matters of that kind, it is possible that some are not. For some boys, the deviant gang may serve as a vehicle for the expression of idiosyncratic motives. Others may be involved in a deviant peer group in response to hedonistic, "subterranean values." [7] Also, it is conceivable that life in working-class society produces a number of different but related adjustment problems, each of which contributes recruits to gang misbehavior. The worker who deals with such offenders might be wise, at this stage, to entertain the possibility that the particular motivational concerns of gang members vary somewhat from one to another. This is not a suggestion that he should adopt a broad eclectic view of delinquency. Instead, the point is that there are a number of distinct but related theories of working-class delinquency around at present,[8] each of which may contribute something to the explanation of gang behavior although none of them are perhaps complete explanations in themselves. The treatment agent would be well advised to study each of these competing theories. In turn, he may find it efficacious to try to find a job for one boy, but to help another handle status problems deriving from unpleasant school experiences. This point of view, representing a restricted position of multiple-causation, does not do violence to scientific assumptions about the explanation and prediction of deviation or other social behavior.

CASUAL GANG DELINQUENCY

The description of casual delinquents in Chapter Three indicated that they are relatively similar to predatory and conflict gang members, except that they are less involved in deviant acts and are characterized by only mildly delinquent role-conceptions. These juveniles consequently have a lower probability of getting

[7] David Matza and Gresham M. Sykes, "Juvenile Delinquency and Subterranean Values," *American Sociological Review*, Vol. 26 (October 1961), 712-19.

[8] Some of these theories are briefly discussed in Chapter Two, pp. 35-38.

swept up in the legal control operation than their more serious gang companions. Those who do get into the hands of the police and courts are frequently placed on probation, on the assumption that they are not sufficiently implicated in delinquent careers to require institutionalization. The major problem presented by casual gang offenders is to prevent their contamination by more serious delinquents. Thus group treatment should be used with these juveniles to isolate them from older, more sophisticated delinquents. This group activity, in turn, should be designed to reinforce their nondelinquent self-images and attitudes. The therapy given to offenders of this kind would be less intensive than that used for predatory or conflict gang members because casual gang boys do not need major resocialization around a new set of normative standards; rather they need reinforcement of their existing nondelinquent views.

The specific methods to be employed by treatment agents with casual gang offenders, in addition to group therapy, might be somewhat varied. The worker might be concerned about helping some of these individuals obtain jobs, whereas others might be encouraged to remain in school and to continue in that pattern. In still other specific cases, it might be useful to get groups of such juveniles into existing community facilities where they would become involved in conventional recreation programs.

CASUAL DELINQUENT, NONGANG MEMBER

Casual, nongang delinquents are often referred to as "hidden delinquents." It was noted in Chapter Three that few juveniles of this type get into the hands of the police or the courts because, essentially, much of their behavior is *both* undetected *and* minor in character. Thus even when "hidden" delinquents become visible, they still do not receive official handling.[9] Instead, the au-

[9] The argument here is that much of the behavior called "hidden delinquency" is minor and nonrepetitive in form, and much of it is handled informally for that reason. This is not to say that class biases, "power," and the like never operate. Doubtless some middle-class delinquents escape from the hands of official agencies because of intervention in their behalf by influential adults. But it is not likely that this explains most cases of undetected middle-class delinquents. It might be added that the issue of factors leading to differential handling of behavior by the police and courts is an extremely important and complex problem which has received little theoretical or research attention.

thorities make informal decisions to deal with the behavior in some nonofficial manner, on the grounds that the deviant acts are not serious enough to require formal intervention, or else they look into the social background of the casual offender and decide on that basis that he is not in need of official handling. Such juveniles commonly show conventional, stable family backgrounds, good school adjustment, satisfactory community relations, and the like.

There is merit to a program of "no treatment" for most casual, middle-class nongang delinquents. Intensive therapy is not in order for every offender. It is probably true that little or no intervention is required with casual offenders beyond some act of warning.

The probable consequence of such events as being picked up by the police in the case of violators who do not define themselves as delinquents and who are not entrapped in a network of delinquent associations is diversion from further deviant activity. It may well be that when "hidden" delinquents come to the attention of the police, that experience alone is sufficiently dramatic in its impact to deter them from further misbehavior. Colloquially, this is the phenomenon summed up in expressions of the sort: "get 'em in here and scare hell out of 'em" or "somebody should throw the fear of God into those kids." In this process, the drama of being in the hands of the police may compel them to acknowledge the deviant nature of their behavior. But instead of working out some rationalizations for deviation, the trauma of being identified as a deviant may motivate them to avoid further experiences of this kind.

The foregoing should not be read as some kind of naive, blanket endorsement of threats as a therapy tactic. Doubtless there are many offenders who would respond very differently to this limited but gruff sort of interaction with agents of the social control system. In general, the efficacy of such kinds of handling is conditional upon the degree of peer support or other kinds of social insulation enjoyed by the offender. That individual who is outside the framework of a supportive peer culture which treats deviant acts as acceptable and who is outside a system of interaction with criminalistic persons would be most likely to respond to the drama of involvement with deviant-defining organizations.

The preceding commentary should also not be taken as implying that juveniles who violate the law ought to be allowed to do so with impunity. However, it does not follow from a recommendation to do "something" about delinquent behavior that "something" necessarily means official action. Certainly it is not necessarily true that putting a person through the machinery of the juvenile court is the best or most beneficial "something" which can occur to him. Instead, other alternatives, such as turning the juvenile over to his parents, may be more beneficial than encumbering the court with the case. Why should probation officers be made responsible for petty delinquents lacking in delinquent self-conceptions? They would then be burdened with even larger case loads with even less time to devote to offenders who need help of some kind.

AUTOMOBILE THIEF—"JOYRIDER"

The portrait of joyriders sketched in an earlier chapter suggested that these are boys without seriously atypical personality structures, but who may be concerned about "toughness" and masculine identity. They are also juveniles who engage in peer-supported forms of deviation. Because they are involved in a kind of delinquency which does not lead into an adult criminal role, and because many of them seem not to be generally antisocial in orientation, these offenders represent a relatively transitional treatment problem. That is, the object of therapy is to redirect these individuals in some way during the late teen years so that they will ultimately make conventional law-abiding adjustments as young adults. Since many of them may do this independently of a particular rehabilitation experience to which they have been subjected, the aim of therapeutic intervention is to maximize the number of cases in which this occurs.

Joyriders are promising candidates for group therapy rather than for some kind of intensive individual treatment. The problems to which these boys are responding can best be tackled through a group situation in which the offender's peers can be led to attribute high status to him for acts other than stealing cars and related aggressive activity. Efforts should be made by treatment agents in settings such as probation to get such groups of boys caught up in "masculine" lines of activity which substitute for stealing cars. In some particular instances, this might involve the utilization of automobiles as a therapy tool through such programs as "hot rod clubs" and so forth.

Joyriders in institutions pose special problems to the administrators. One of these is the tendency of such juveniles to adopt "tough guy" poses in their interaction with staff members and other wards. Although fights with workers and other aggressive behavior may involve painful consequences, such actions are to a degree functional for the needs of auto thieves in that they do confer esteem upon them in the eyes of their peers. The staff must make efforts to frustrate joyriders in this kind of behavior, and in turn, to divert them toward less troublesome lines of activity such as participation in institutional recreational and athletic programs. Another problem that apparently occurs fairly frequently is runaway activity. It appears that car thieves are sometimes involved in flamboyant, "immature" actions in training schools, unlike many of their fellow inmates who are "playing it cool." Thus it may be that joyriders are more "escape-prone" than other offender types.

To summarize, joyriders seem to be boys without marked signs of personality pathology. They are relatively normal, but perhaps somewhat immature, youths who are engaged in transitory deviance in response to certain adjustment problems. In general, group relations-oriented therapy is appropriate for them. However, the worker who deals with these boys might well try out a number of innovations in specific instances. In some cases, certain mild forms of family counseling or therapy might be indicated. In others, some particular community program or organization might lure the joyrider from deviant conduct. In other words, the inventive worker might conjure up a number of specific tactics to keep joyriders from stealing cars and to get them to adopt law-abiding behavior patterns. These specific techniques could be defended as consistent with a group-relations approach to the treatment of joyriders.

DRUG USE—HEROIN

Fortunately, juveniles involved in "heavy" drugs such as heroin are not common in the delinquent population. There is good reason to assume that such deviants represent one of the most difficult kinds of juveniles with whom to work. Heavy drug use among juveniles is not an aleatory response which is dependent only upon situational opportunities to use narcotics. Instead, heavy drug users appear to be "double failures," in that they retreated from both conventional and delinquent pursuits because of personality difficulties. They appear to be juveniles who find life in lower-class settings to be even more painful, empty, dull, and un-satisfactory than more conventional run-of-the-mill offenders. In this sense, juvenile narcotic addicts represent the delinquents' "deviants." Among gang boys, repetitive use of drugs constitutes a serious form of deviation which often results in expulsion from the group.

Although drug use is not common within delinquent gangs, other than occasional experimentation with marijuana, group support for heavy drugs is frequently found with this type of offender. Many of these juveniles participate in a "cat" culture which is oriented around the pursuit of "kicks" or novel, deviant experiences.[10] In this subculture, drug use represents a major peer-supported "kick." Accordingly, resocialization of these offenders must focus upon addict groups in order to undermine these peer group influences. But treatment of a group may profitably be joined with intensive individual therapy as well. It is not unlikely that drug users could be led to internalize antidrug norms, in part, within an individual therapy arrangement. Putting the point another way, the individual's dependence upon narcotics might be partially reduced through psychotherapy which uncovers the problems that are at the root of his involvement in drug addiction. However, the question of whether to treat drug users in groups or individually is probably less important than the issue of whether or not to deal with them in some kind of more general therapeutic milieu.

On this last point, the basic stratagem for addicts should be to get them into a milieu-management program similar to that of Synanon, noted in Chapter Four. What these offenders need above all else is a lengthy period in a somewhat protective environment where they encounter a series of opportunities to try out, practice, and succeed in conventional nonaddict kinds of social roles. They also need a period of interaction with sympathetic persons who do not react toward them as though they were "fiends" and utterly depraved individuals. This kind of opportunity is central to the Synanon program, and conversely, opportunity to try out and be rewarded for success in nonnarcotics adjustments is frequently absent in other more conventional drug programs. Addicts probably are going to need some extended period of time in a protective situa-

[10] Harold Finestone, "Cats, Kicks and Color," *Social Problems*, Vol. 5 (July 1957), 3-13.

tion where they are able to stay "clean" (free from drug use) before they will be ready to re-enter the community which exacerbated their personal problems and which led to their drug use initially.

Milieu treatment for "heavy" addicts is equally relevant for adult drug users. Although there may be some uncertainty concerning the specific nature of the adjustment difficulties and personality problems of addicts, it is clear enough that these individuals have withdrawn markedly from the mainstream of normal life. They are persons who have given up on attempts to make good in the conventional worlds of either law-abiding or "normal" criminal behavior. It is unlikely that such persons withdrew into drug use because of accidental life experiences. Most of them have encountered a cumulative set of life events which have imbued them with a deep-seated sense of inadequacy. Quite probably, most of them did not renounce more conventional patterns of adjustment until they had experienced a number of failures in such endeavors.

If this account of the development of addict careers is reasonably accurate, it would be naive to suppose that the narcotic user can rather easily be redirected into nondrug patterns of activity. Thus it is not probable that if addicts are given a large dose of intensive treatment, they can then be released into the community with a high likelihood of success in nonaddiction. The drug user has been turned back into the community as a somewhat altered person, but the community has not changed in terms of the pressures it creates for the person.

This line of reasoning lies behind the judgment of many criminologists that programs of the Synanon form represent the most significant development in the treatment of drug addicts in the past fifty years in the United States. Synanon provides the addict with a protective environment which does not make unreasonable demands upon him until he is ready to completely re-enter the nonaddict world. The Synanon member must stay "clean," but he is not abruptly required to be a success in all other ways too. This situation is rather different from that of conventional drug programs, where the person is isolated for a time from the community in a narcotics hospital or institution but is then abruptly dumped back into society where he is expected to make many successful adjustments—marital, occupational, and so forth.

A specific prediction regarding the diffusion of Synanon-type programs for drug users would be hazardous. There are some obvious difficulties in creating large numbers of these kinds of organizations in the United States, difficulties of finance, community tolerance, and others. Public redefinition of addicts as "sick" rather than as "bad" is at the heart of any predictions about future directions. On this point, certain signs do indicate some swing away from punitive, repressive approaches to narcotics addicts. In the past several years, drug users have been portrayed as somewhat sympathetic and tragic figures on television programs. Articles have appeared in magazines in which contemporary law-enforcement tactics have been questioned. It may be that these signal a gradual shift toward medically oriented efforts to rehabilitate addicts. At any rate, there is little question that such programs are necessary if narcotic use is to be drastically reduced.

Several halfway houses have been established for drug addicts in the United States.[11] These operations are for parolees who have been treated for addiction. They work outside the halfway house but reside and receive therapy there. These facilities, not too different in basic outlines from Synanon, are consistent with the broader proposals outlined here.

OVERLY AGGRESSIVE DELINQUENT

The outlines of appropriate therapy for overly aggressive delinquents are well established in existing programs such as private, psychiatric residential-treatment facilities.[12] In these, unsocialized aggressive persons are subjected to a multifaceted program. First, they are restrained from flamboyant and dangerous displays of aggression during their initial period of treatment. In the beginning, appeals to behave reasonably are not likely to keep them from assaulting other patients or staff members. Instead, they have to be forcibly controlled. At the same time, great effort is made to demonstrate to these persons that they are not being punished for being

[11] Gilbert Geis, "Narcotic Treatment in California," paper presented before the conference, "Perspectives on Narcotic Addiction," sponsored by the Massachusetts Health Research Institute and the U.S. Public Health Service, Chatham, Mass., September 1963.

[12] See, for example, Fritz Redl and David Wineman, Controls from Within (New York: The Free Press of Glencoe, Inc., 1952); Bruno Bettelheim, Truants from Life (New York: The Free Press of Glencoe, Inc., 1955).

"bad," that instead, they are being restrained to prevent them from injuring themselves or someone else.

After a while, residential therapy programs try to create an awareness on the part of the offender that contrary to his usual beliefs, not all people are out to "get him." Treatment workers try to give him the sense that although they cannot and will not tolerate his more violent activities, they accept him and have affection for him. In turn, the expectation is that such experiences will awaken his latent dependency needs, so that he will ultimately take some initiative in establishing and sustaining an intimate, trusting relationship with one or more therapists.

Assuming that such a breakthrough is achieved and that the asocial person does develop some relationship with a therapist, it usually does not occur until the patient has repeatedly "tested" the worker through verbal and physical abuse and attacks to find out if he really can be trusted. Eventually these outbursts diminish and the individual begins to enjoy a quasi-parent-child relationship with one person. Hopefully, the gains made there will be extended to other interpersonal relationships with other persons. When the therapist and patient have established a bond of warmth and trust, the aggressive patient is then directed through an individual therapy experience in which he comes to develop an awareness of the factors behind his aggressive behavior. Once he begins to see that his hostility was warranted to some degree when directed at specific individuals who have victimized and abused him in the past, presumably he will also begin to understand that aggression is not justified when directed at other persons.

The aim of this entire set of actions is to reduce the extent of psychological crippling manifested by the offender, or conversely, to socialize him beyond the stage he represented at the start of treatment. This result is difficult to obtain, even under the best of circumstances. Appropriate residential treatment programs are costly and lengthy and they require personnel of extraordinary patience and sympathy for others. But on the other hand, the general strategy appears to be well grounded. Alternatives such as group therapy are not in order, for such deviants lack the *sine qua non* of candidates for group treatment. At the start of therapy, they have a very low ability to engage in meaningful group experiences. There may be some sense to involving offenders of this kind in group treatment at some advanced point in their rehabilitative ex-

perience, but not until they have been subjected to a lengthy prior
program of the kind outlined above.

FEMALE DELINQUENT

The description of female delinquents in Chapter Three
centered around one pattern among delinquent girls which is extremely common, namely, sexual promiscuity. Girls who appear in
the juvenile court and who are representatives of this category are
charged variously as "ungovernable," "wayward," or "sexually promiscuous," but in most cases they have been reported to the court
because of repetitive and visible violations of social expectations
regarding chastity and kindred matters. Not all female delinquents
are involved in sexual misbehavior; other activities, such as shoplifting, also get some girls into trouble. In turn, the treatment proposals for delinquent females will vary with the different characteristics of such girls. The following therapy recommendations for
girl offenders are oriented toward sexually deviant females, who
represent the largest single class of delinquent girls.

The behavior of girl delinquents is commonly a response to
perceived inadequacies in affectional relationships within the family
group. In turn, the girls seek out affectional associations with boys
as a substitute for normal parent-child relationships. Partly because sexual favors represent a kind of currency with which to obtain affectional contacts, and for other reasons as well, many of
these relationships ultimately become sexual in character. The girls
acquire a reputation among boys as "easy lays," and this reputation
eventually comes to be a matter of more general public knowledge.
Quite possibly, this process involves a kind of vicious circle in which
the girl's attempts to deal with perceived difficulties of adjustment
create more problems for her, so that her concerns and anxieties
become multiplied.

Although there is intragroup variation among delinquent girls,
it appears that many of them are relatively well socialized but are
concerned about their affectional relations with others. Although
they are often "tough" in pose, with a chip-on-the-shoulder attitude
and verbalizing sentiments well larded with profanity, diagnoses
of "psychopathy," "sociopathy," or other personality abnormalities
are not in order. The "tough" characteristics and manners of the
girls form a protective outer shell which they have developed in re-

action to a series of experiences of abuse and distorted primary group associations encountered in the past. Beneath this surface hostility, many of these girls show reasonably stable personality structures.

Contemporary policies for delinquent girls frequently involve commitment to training schools at a relatively early age, following an initial probation placement in which they made an inadequate adjustment. In the training school, the girls engage in intensive peer interaction, usually with other inmates in a particular cottage. In some institutions, they also receive some amount of individual, client-centered therapy. The common outcome of this set of experiences appears to be that most of these females ultimately get married and refrain from further deviant behavior. Apparently, most of these offenders do not "graduate" into adult criminality, although this is scarcely to be credited to the therapeutic effects of conventional institutions. This "rehabilitation" is more the product of normal maturation processes, the paucity of opportunities for careers in crime, and factors of that kind. These girls have few opportunities available to them in the world of adult criminality. On the other hand, they have personality structures sufficiently healthy to provide the basis for relatively satisfactory marital relationships and other adult adjustments. Thus, when they get out of institutions, they rather quickly become involved with a particular male in a satisfactory affectional relationship, which in turn removes the principal motivating force behind their delinquent activity.

Some suggestion of the importance of emotional-affectional needs of delinquent girls is provided by the widespread pseudohomosexual attachments which they establish in training schools.[13] At first glance, these relationships could lead to the conclusion that institutions are breeding grounds for lesbianism, but on closer examination, it looks as though most of these "crushes" or "girl stuff" relationships are essentially nonsexual in character. They are liaisons between two girls which are patterned after conventional boy-girl relationships. They do not usually involve overt manifestations of more extreme lesbian activities, and they are transitory adjustments which are not normally continued outside of the institution.

[13] Seymour L. Halleck and Marvin Hersko, "Homosexual Behavior in a Correctional Institution for Adolescent Girls," *American Journal of Orthopsychiatry*, Vol. 32 (October 1962), 911-17.

If the core notions regarding affectional problems in the genesis of girl delinquency are correct, the implications for treatment would include the following: On probation or in training schools, such offenders should be put into group therapy or into individual, client-centered counseling, designed to help them adopt realistic perspectives on their past experiences. They need to become aware of the sources of their hostility toward others—sources located close to the parental situation. In turn, unsatisfactory parent-child relationships are something they must learn to live with. Under some circumstances in probation case loads, the worker might attempt to conduct a program of joint therapy with the girl and members of her family, although it would be the fortunate probation officer who has time for much of that sort of activity. But even with family therapy, it would be unrealistic to create an expectation in delinquent girls that their former parental relationships are going to miraculously change as they go through therapy. Conversely, they must be directed to the realization that affectional relations and support can be obtained in marital situations so that the solution of their dissatisfaction lies there or in some other nonparental pattern of interpersonal associations. In the same way, on parole, such offenders need to be assisted in managing the tensions and anxieties that flow from inadequate parent-child relationships. For some of them, a realistic program might involve girls' residence apartments and places of that sort, out of contact with their family members.

The role of the therapist in client-centered treatment of girl delinquents would be one of quasi-parent or good friend. Doubtless such a relationship between a worker and the female offender will be difficult to establish, for it would develop in many cases only after an initial period of "testing" by the girl. Nonetheless, the basic ingredients from which such a relationship can be built are apparent in many delinquent females. The worker, who would usually be an older woman, is in a position to serve as a kind of mother-substitute figure, particularly because many of the real mothers of girl delinquents have inadequately operated in that role.

"BEHAVIOR PROBLEM" DELINQUENT

A variety of "behavior problem" forms of delinquency are lumped within this residual category. It includes juveniles who set fires and engage in certain deviant sexual acts or in other activities which are usually seen as symptoms of some fairly deep-seated personality maladjustment. These offenders normally show some evidence of seriously disturbed family relationships. Most of them also exhibit distorted peer group associations. For reasons of this sort, they are not good prospects for either group therapy or some kind of client-centered individual treatment. Instead, they need depth psychotherapy, administered by a clinical psychologist or psychiatrist, aimed at discovery of the sources of deviant motivational patterns, sources commonly located in family-interaction patterns. Ideally, the entire family group should be the subject of therapy, but this frequently is difficult to arrange.

Detailed discussion of therapy tactics for disturbed delinquents is not in order here, as this text is concerned with treatment tactics to be used with common kinds of delinquent and criminal behavioral roles. It is also designed as an articulation of tactics and procedures which could be carried on by professional correctional workers with modest training, including cottage personnel, group supervisors, correctional officers, and the like, as well as social workers and kindred workers. Extreme cases of behavior problem delinquency are not common in the offender population, and such individuals are not usually made the responsibility of regular correctional agents. Instead, they are diverted to special treatment agencies for disturbed children and to psychiatrists. As far as treatment recommendations to be made by correctional workers are concerned, the obvious recommendation would be to put the behavior problem offender into an intensive depth psychotherapy experience. The worker, however, would not be expected to carry out such a recommendation.

Summary

No detailed summary of this chapter is required. Treatment suggestions have been made for delinquent types, and similar comments must be made about criminal patterns, to which the next chapter turns.

seven

TREATMENT
OF
CRIMINALS

Introduction

This chapter, a continuation of the discussion in Chapter Six, concerns treatment recommendations for adult offenders. Fifteen types of adult criminals were specified in Chapter Three, but all fifteen will not be discussed at the same length or detail in this chapter. Although some of these types, such as "white-collar criminals," represent important analytical categories of behavior to be explained, they are not common in the population of candidates for therapy. Also, several of the adult types are counterparts of juvenile patterns analyzed in the previous chapter, so that they will be only briefly touched upon here.

Treatment of Criminals

PROFESSIONAL THIEF

This is one of those offender role types which is rare in treatment populations. Professional thieves are a disappearing aristocracy in crime—an elite group which has always been a criminal minority. Then, too, professional thieves have a low likelihood of arrest because of the sophisticated character of their criminal behavior. As a consequence, those professional thieves who are still around in any quantity, such as those who ply the trade of "pigeon-drop" grifting, are rarely found in prisons or in other correctional settings.

Although skilled professional thieves are rare in prison, there is an offender type fairly common in institutions which bears some resemblance to professional thieves—the group of prisoners Schrag has identified as "pseudosocial" inmates.[1] These are persons who exhibit manipulative behavior patterns and who shift their loyalty attachments in prison back and forth from prisoners to administrators, depending upon the exigencies of particular situations. Such individuals are often in prison for embezzlement, forgery, and other rather sophisticated crimes. They normally do not have extensive delinquency records. Schrag suggests that such offenders are skilled role-players who have acquired manipulative role-playing techniques from certain early parent-child relationships. These are the kinds of deviants that Jenkins has described as "budding grifters."[2] Although pseudosocial inmates are not strictly comparable in terms of criminal behavior to the extremely skilled professional thieves that have been described in the literature,[3] they do resemble them in social-psychological characteristics. Thus they might be labeled "quasi-professional thieves."

What should be done with these persons? The available evidence suggests that "budding grifter" kinds of offenders are not characterized by markedly crippled personality structures, deep-seated problems, or similar characteristics. They are individuals with developed role-playing skills but with somewhat attenuated loyalty ties to others. In a word, they are ingratiating, glib "lone wolves." For reasons of this sort, they are not candidates for intensive individual

[1] Clarence C. Schrag, "Some Foundations for a Theory of Correction," in Donald R. Cressey, ed., *The Prison* (New York: Holt, Rinehart and Winston, Inc., 1961), pp. 309-57; Schrag, "A Preliminary Criminal Typology," *Pacific Sociological Review*, Vol. 4 (Spring 1961), 11-16.

[2] Richard L. Jenkins, *Breaking Patterns of Defeat* (Philadelphia: J. B. Lippincott Co., 1954), pp. 148-58.

[3] Edwin H. Sutherland, *The Professional Thief* (Chicago: University of Chicago Press, 1937); David W. Maurer, *The Big Con* (New York: Bobbs-Merrill Co., 1940); Maurer, *Whiz Mob* (Gainesville, Fla.: American Dialect Society, 1955).

treatment. Moreover, not only are they not in need of such therapy, they would probably try to manipulate the psychotherapist in order to obtain special favors.

The treatment of these offenders should center on systematic frustration of their "con politician" behavior. At least some of the elements of the Korn and McCorkle treatment model (discussed on pages 168-170) might be applied to these persons. The therapist must be aware of efforts by the inmate to manipulate him. The con politician must be given opportunities to try out his manipulative modes of adjustment, but he must fail. Of course, this is much easier said than done, particularly in conventional institutional settings in which pseudosocial prisoners have traditionally been employed in various positions of power and responsibility, such as classification office clerks, orderlies, and so forth. These prisoners, more intelligent and versatile than the average inmates, customarily have been utilized by staff members in positions of importance to alleviate the problems of insufficient personnel. If con politicians are to be moved out of these informal positions in the institution, the authorities must be able to replace them with civilian clerks and other noninmate employees.

The argument for frustrating the pseudosocial offender is quite simply that such negative experiences might play some part in directing him into law-abiding activities upon release from prison. As it now stands, the institutional experience of such persons tends to be relatively short and one in which they enjoy a number of illicit privileges that mediate the harshness of "doing time." Manipulative behavior "pays off," and the inmate does "easy time." However, it should be made clear that by itself, a more rigorous prison experience would be of no major consequence to the offender. The argument here is not a "classical" one to the effect that if the punishment is made severe enough, it will automatically deter the person from further violations of law. Accordingly, a part of the program for the con politician would be placement in group therapy with other "politicians" or perhaps in a mixed group of "right guys" and pseudosocial inmates. Hopefully, some learning of prosocial norms would take place in that setting as a result of group pressure on the individual regarding his manipulative techniques and rationalizations.

Although almost nothing is known about the effects, positive or negative, of various sentence lengths upon offenders, there is some reason to suppose that the postprison adjustment of pseudosocial inmates might vary directly with length of sentence. In other words, the longer the sentence served (up to some point), the greater the likelihood of success on parole. The reasoning behind this hypothesis is that pseudosocial prisoners might be motivated to avoid further criminality, in part, from awareness of the unpleasant consequences of such behavior. Again, this hypothesis is contingent upon the assumption that some direct therapy is given the inmate as well.

Recommendations that prisoners be given long sentences are not in favor at present, largely on nonempirical grounds. That is, it is widely argued that existing prison terms are, on the average, much longer than required for therapeutic purposes, although little direct evidence can be marshaled to demonstrate that this argument is true. The author is in sympathy with the hypothesis that many prison terms are too long and probably detrimental to rehabilitative ends. But it is perhaps true that for certain kinds of offenders, pseudosocial inmates included, relatively long prison sentences have positive rather than negative effects. At any rate, this line of argument is worth pursuing further, for at this point, such a possibility cannot be discarded as certainly false. There is some evidence on parole violation rates which indicates that success rates do vary with sentence length and not always in an inverse fashion. Garrity's findings show that for some parolees, low violation rates on parole are associated with relatively lengthy prison terms and, conversely, that higher violation rates are seen for similar inmates who have served shorter sentences.[4]

Another suggestion, which might seem facetious but is not designed to be, is that treatment of con politicians might profitably point the offender toward law-abiding occupations where his role-playing skills would be utilized. Stated differently, pseudosocial criminals should be encouraged to seek out civilian jobs which call

---

[4] Donald L. Garrity, "The Prison as a Rehabilitation Agency," in Cressey, *The Prison*, pp. 358-80. It should be noted that Garrity's data does *not* show that the postrelease adjustments of politicians improve with longer sentences. Instead, his findings show just the opposite. However, these results do not necessarily invalidate the argument of this book. The politicians studied by Garrity were able to engage in manipulative behavior in prison; thus he argued that the longer the sentence served, the more practice in manipulative activity, and the lower the likelihood of success on parole. The hypothesis advanced here is conditional upon frustration of the politician in his "conning" endeavors, which could result in a different outcome.

for talents they have been using in crime. One occupation of this sort which immediately comes to mind is automobile salesman. No doubt car salesmen have varied personalities, but it does not seem that they are a random sample of the general population. Instead, it seems that they are a law-abiding version of behavior patterns and personality types which has parallels in the world of pseudo-social crime and criminals. It may be that the most optimistic post-release prognosis for con politicians would apply to those prisoners who obtain jobs selling cars or in allied occupations.

PROFESSIONAL "HEAVY" CRIMINAL

This is another of those categories for which treatment recommendations are not too meaningful. Criminals who fit the model of highly skilled, career-oriented, professional "heavies" are not common in the population of offenders. Then, too, as in the case of professional thieves, the criminal skills of true professional heavies are such as to insure a low risk of apprehension and prison commitment. As a result, the number of these persons found in institutions is extremely small. Most prison inmates or offenders in treatment populations outside the walls range in crime skills and professional commitment to crime from gross amateurs to offenders with modest criminal talents and semiprofessional orientations to criminality.

It is fortunate that professional heavies can be passed over lightly in discussions of therapy on the grounds that they are too few in number to be worth much attention. The treatment problem in these cases can be compared to what would be involved in attempting to convince physicians that they should take up garbage collecting! To put the matter another way, the therapy agent is presented with formidable obstacles in the case of professionals because such persons are often highly successful criminals in financial and other terms. Noncriminal equivalents into which to divert these offenders are not abundant. The job of directing such persons into law-abiding pursuits is quite different from what is involved in turning run-of-the-mill offenders toward noncriminal paths. In the latter case, a reasonably compelling argument can be advanced to the effect that law-abiding behavior is potentially more satisfying and rewarding for them than criminality. But how is such a case to be made to the professional criminal who has an illegal income greatly exceeding the salary of the warden or the director of corrections?

Quite independent of therapy efforts, there does seem to be a common career line represented by professionals in which they ultimately "reform" themselves; that is, they retire from criminality. Apparently, many professional criminals eventually reach a certain age at which they decide that the hazards of crime have become sufficiently severe as to suggest that other lines of work be taken up. One example of this pattern is represented by Everett DeBaun, a former heavy who is now a successful free-lance author and television writer. Parenthetically, DeBaun's discussion of armed robbery suggests that it is possible to repress heavy crimes of certain kinds by law enforcement and legislative tactics which increase the risks of detection and apprehension.[5] He indicates that shifts in the form of armed robbery have occurred in the United States as a response to such developments as federal statutes regarding bank robbery. In these cases, the risks of certain crimes have been perceived by professional heavies as too great in relation to the financial returns so that they have turned to other "low risk" kinds of robbery. The marked trend away from "bank heists" as a form of professional robbery is one case illustration. Bank stick-ups in the United States in the past several decades have been almost exclusively the work of amateurs, rather than professional, robbers.

SEMIPROFESSIONAL PROPERTY OFFENDER

Unlike the two previous types, semiprofessional property criminals make up a major part of the offender population. They are the adult counterparts of predatory gang offenders—they are gang delinquents "grown up." Although the frequently voiced assertion that "the delinquents of today are the criminals of tomorrow" is a gross oversimplification, it does describe this case. There is a wealth of evidence which demonstrates that many predatory gang offenders graduate into adult criminality of a semiprofessional kind. Many of them persist in this activity for a number of years in adulthood, so that the career line of semiprofessional violators often involves repeated commitment to penal institutions

---

[5] Everett DeBaun, "The Heist: Theory and Practice of Armed Robbery," *Harpers* (February 1950), 69-77.

Individual client-centered or depth therapy is not in order for these persons because they do not usually verbalize "problems" nor do they exhibit causally important emotional problems which can be readily identified and to which their deviance can be attributed. This is not to say that they never express hostility, bitterness, or feelings of being abused by a hostile social environment. Certainly they do, but these expressions are not indicators of emotional maladjustment or personality pathology, nor are they causally significant. These feelings are often the *result* of involvement in deviance, rather than the cause of it. Semiprofessionals occasionally do show idiosyncratic personality problems which would respond to psychotherapy, but the existence of adjustment difficulties does not mean that the etiology of their criminality can be traced to those problems. Because amelioration of personality problems that are not causally related to the individual's criminality may be required to get that person out of deviant conduct, no suggestion is made that incidental features of specific persons should be totally ignored.

Semiprofessional property criminals are supported in their view that "society" is the villain, rather than themselves, that they have been "done in" by an unjust and capricious cultural system, and other notions of this kind, by an inmate system of antiadministration, antisocial values. This is a major reason for regarding them as unamenable to psychotherapy. Finally, many semiprofessional criminals are poor candidates for individual therapy because they are strikingly dissimilar to the middle-class professional therapists with whom they would be in interaction. The conditions for rapport between client and worker are not apparent in these cases. Nonetheless, such offenders now do engage in individual therapy, but this is normally an attempt to manipulate and "con" the worker into according them special privileges or to "use" him in some other way, such as receiving a favorable recommendation directed to the parole board.

Inasmuch as semiprofessional offenders represent adult versions of gang delinquents, the treatment recommendations for the two types are relatively alike. The basic stratagem would be to place these offenders in intensive group therapy experiences in the various correctional settings in which they are found.

For reasons that are easy to find, probation systems in the United States and elsewhere tend to systematically exclude semiprofessionals from their case loads. One reason for this is simply that such individuals are difficult treatment cases who cannot be given sufficient attention under the present work conditions of probation. Thus they are shunted off to prisons and reformatories, and case loads are filled principally with "square John" offenders. The net result is that the main service rendered by probation agencies is to prevent criminalistic contamination of offenders through interaction with each other in institutions. Little or no direct therapeutic intervention is carried on in probation agencies. Also, probation departments are chary of dealing with semiprofessionals because of concern about the "heat" that might be generated as a result. That is, the probation agency that began to acquire a large load of antisocial offenders would become subject to public criticism to the effect that criminals are being "coddled." Finally, judges tend not to be sympathetic to the notion that "hardened" criminals should be placed on probation, so that probation officer recommendations in this direction would often be overruled by judicial decisions.

Under existing conditions, suggestions to the effect that semiprofessionals be placed on probation in large numbers would be unrealistic. Among other things, a program of that kind would demand a public conditioned to expect and accept higher violation rates than now customary for probation groups. It would be naive indeed to suppose that probation organizations could sustain their present low violation rates if they were to begin handling a large number of antisocial law violators. Also, in order to treat these persons within probation settings, case loads would have to be reduced in some way. This might be accomplished by putting square John types into very large case loads so that a few officers could work with small, special case loads of semiprofessional offenders. However accomplished, probation settings would have to be modified in order to manage the job of therapy with these violators.

Quite probably, no dramatic modifications will occur in the near future in the probation area. Thus recommendations that semiprofessionals be placed on probation will continue to be somewhat unrealistic. Still, from another perspective, such a suggestion makes sense. There is no apparent reason to assume that such individuals could not be effectively treated outside of penal institutions. Quite the reverse, under certain conditions, therapy might well be more effective outside of prisons than within. It is obvious enough that prisons do not represent the ideal milieu in which to resocialize individuals. If anything, quite the opposite is true. Prisons are a human invention which manage the functions of punishment, social sanitation, and the like reasonably well, but they hardly serve as the optimal device for the achievement of rehabilitative goals.

The treatment of semiprofessionals on probation should center around group therapy. The focus of attention would be the same as that for gang delinquents, namely, the development of collective norms among offenders of a prosocial kind to replace antisocial attitudes and definitions. Group therapy would direct attention and criticism at such sentiments as "only slobs work" and "everyone has a racket—everyone is on the 'take.'"

The treatment of semiprofessionals in prisons should take the same group form as outlined previously for gang delinquents. Group therapy would strive to create a primary group relationship among offenders in which a new set of shared standards would eventually be generated. The therapist in this kind of treatment would be a parliamentarian, and to some extent, an "expert" on human behavior who would on occasion serve as a "resource person" providing information which group members would utilize in their discussions. His role would not be one of creating "insight" on the part of individual members regarding their particular problems. The aim of group treatment is to produce *group insight,* that is, to generate group-shared interpretations of prior conduct as undesirable and group-shared new definitions of situations. Shared sentiments are the product of group creation rather than the handiwork of the therapist.

One issue regarding therapy of various forms in prisons centers around the question, should treatment be voluntary or compulsory? One argument for voluntary participation in rehabilitation programs is that the treatment agent in this case knows that he is dealing with motivated persons who are amenable to change. The other side of the thesis is that persons who are reluctant or hostile participants cannot be resocialized. However, these assertions are not convincing. For one thing, it might be held that positive involvement in therapy can be generated *after* a person becomes engaged in group experiences as a result of pressure placed upon him by members of a meaningful reference group. Also, those entrants into therapy who appear to be enthusiastic seekers of help may be "con artists" trying to manipulate workers in order to get special privi-

leges. Another counterargument to the notion of voluntary participation is that those individuals least in need of assistance would
be the ones getting it. Antisocial offenders would not usually volunteer for treatment. It is true that rehabilitative programs in
prisons in the past have often been filled with square Johns. In
these cases, the services of the institution have been directed at the
wrong subjects as square Johns are not the ones who are most in
need of change. It may well be that it is possible to run a quiet,
well-ordered correctional plant when antisocial and prosocial persons are handled in these ways, but no one should suppose that
such an arrangement produces much rehabilitation.

Prisoner involvement in treatment must be and should be compulsory. Unless participation is mandatory, many of those persons
most in need of treatment will not get it. Moreover, there is reason
to believe that many antisocial inmates are not as hostile as they
seem·to be at first glance. Many of them are privately more interested in having therapy than some of their public utterances would
imply. Wheeler's findings cited in Chapter Five imply more enthusiasm for treatment by individual inmates than is initially apparent in prisons.[6] Prisoners are involved in "pluralistic ignorance"
in which each sees other offenders as more antagonistic than they
actually are. Because they overperceive the degree of inmate aver-
sion to treatment, they are in turn reluctant to voice protherapy
attitudes publicly. Now, if prisoners are loath to express protreatment motivation, and if they are apprehensive about getting involved in programs for fear of loss of status in the inmate system,
mandatory assignment gives them an "out." They can engage in
treatment without being held accountable by their peers for violation of the inmate code. This argument for compulsory treatment
is a persuasive one.

Another stratagem for group treatment and other kinds of therapy might be alterations in the customary routine in prisons. In
most existing systems, inmates are subjected to a continuous diet of

---

[6] Stanton Wheeler, "Role Conflict in Correctional Communities," in Cressey,
The Prison, pp. 229-59. Also see J. E. Baker, "Social Education in a Penitentiary," *Federal Probation*, Vol. 27 (December 1963), 32-36. Baker presents evidence from a group discussion program in the U.S. Penitentiary, Terre Haute,
Indiana, which indicates that inmates eagerly engaged in the program when
ordered to do so because they were able to argue that they "had to go along
with the program."

therapy throughout their institutional stay. Perhaps much of this is something of a waste of time. For many prisoners, the business of "making out" in the social system of "the walls" demands their full attention, even when many of these same persons might be concerned about behavioral change. Treatment programs during the midpoint of the inmate's term may not be able to compete effectively with the demands of the prison community. It might be advisable to concentrate group treatment of semiprofessionals (and other types of inmates, also) immediately prior to their release from prison, or at least, to carry on the most intensive group therapy at that point. The evidence from several studies suggests that prisoners go through a "prisonization" pattern in which they are attentive to "outside the walls" concerns at the beginning and end of their institutional stay, but they are not so oriented during the intervening period.[7]

The parole experiences of semiprofessional offenders should be centered around group treatment as a continuation of institutional therapy. Parole officers should be involved in work with groups of parolees as the principal tactic of help. At the same time, the parole agent is in a strategic position to render assistance to parolees in a number of situations where adjustment difficulties are common, but particularly in employment. Parole agents perform a major task by helping the parolee to deal reasonably and effectively with the job problem. As a result, one measure of the effective parole officer is the degree to which the agent has managed to build up a pool of "contacts" where jobs for ex-inmates can be found.

There are some harbingers that halfway houses may become more common for adult parolees in the United States in coming years. Such a development would be encouraging. The commentary about halfway houses for semiprofessionals is similar to that which has previously been made for gang delinquents. A halfway house would provide a convenient location where group treatment could be made a systematic part of the parolee's supervision experience.

---

[7] Stanton Wheeler, *Social Organization in a Correctional Community*, unpublished doctoral dissertation (Seattle: University of Washington, 1958); Daniel Glaser and John R. Stratton, "Measuring Inmate Change in Prison," in Cressey, *The Prison*, pp. 381-92; Peter G. Garabedian, "Social Roles and Processes of Socialization in the Prison Community," *Social Problems*, Vol. 11 (Fall 1963), 139-52.

Placement in a halfway house would also serve to remove the offender, temporarily at least, from some of the criminogenic influences in the community which contribute to recidivism.

There is one negative note worth sounding regarding halfway houses. The entire system of parole is often a matter of considerable offender hostility. Many prison inmates take a retributive posture regarding their crimes, claiming that they should receive a certain amount of punishment in the form of imprisonment. When they have served their time, they see their "debt" as paid. Accordingly, the regulations of parole and parole supervision are defined as gratuitous and unwarranted double punishment. In short, many prisoners would prefer to serve "flat time" in which their obligation to the state would cease at the end of their prison terms.

Given these sentiments about parole, it is likely that assignment to a halfway house would be regarded by many parolees as extended incarceration rather than as an aid to their adjustment. However, the reactions of offenders to halfway houses are probably not uniform. Some individuals without well-developed social ties might welcome such a parole situation, whereas others would resent assignment to such a place. Accordingly, halfway house placements should be selective and voluntary, not compulsory. Only those individuals with relatively positive attitudes toward them would be sent there.

The treatment of semiprofessional criminals could probably be improved in some sort of milieu management operation, as contrasted with treatment in conventional prisons. Ideally, there would be much to be said for institutions holding less than one hundred offenders of this type, in which educational-vocational programs could be integrated with intensive group therapy provided by skilled, trained workers. Such an organizational system would reduce the degree of artificiality that is found in group treatment within prisons, where the social life of the inmate outside of therapy groups is markedly at variance with the social climate within the counseling group. But there is not much reason to suppose that institutions of this kind are going to become very numerous. The capital outlay for them would be prohibitive, so that the likelihood that any campaign to "break down the walls" will succeed seems slight indeed. Large prisons are a fixture on the landscape and it is in them that the treatment of many criminals, including semiprofessionals, will continue to take place.

PROPERTY OFFENDER—"ONE-TIME LOSER"

It was suggested in Chapter Three that persons who fall into this category are, in a social-psychological sense, noncriminals who have engaged in criminality because of situational pressures and factors. Legally, these individuals are criminals, but they do not exhibit role-conceptions centered around definitions of themselves as deviants. They stoutly maintain that they are different from "real criminals." They verbalize prosocial sentiments in which they agree that they should be punished in some way for their illegal behavior and in which they demonstrate neutral or positive feelings toward law enforcement and correctional persons. Finally, as the term implies, the criminal careers of "one-time losers" are brief ones. Their offenses usually take the form of unsophisticated, naive, and petty property crimes.

What kind of treatment problem do these persons present? There is no therapy task here comparable to that represented by semiprofessional offenders. One-time losers are not in need of change, they do not need to be resocialized, for they are already noncriminals in social-psychological terms. Accordingly, the main task to be performed with one-time losers centers around their isolation from differential associations with antisocial criminals, and conversely, around reinforcement of their prosocial ties.

One-time losers are presently found in abundance in probation case loads. This is all to the good, for probation placement restricts the contacts that they can have with criminalistic persons. In some probation offices, attempts are made to provide these persons with case work assistance, but this is usually quite sporadic and superficial in character. Yet because such offenders usually refrain from further criminality, the success rates of probation organizations seem quite impressive. These high success records can be attributed to the fact that many probation clients, particularly one-time losers, are square Johns in criminal orientation. They are "self-correctors" who keep themselves out of further difficulties quite independently of any intensive therapy.

There is little reason to advocate wholesale revisions of the probation handling of one-time losers. Perhaps intensive therapy would make these individuals even more "healthy" in mental health terms, but this is largely irrelevant to treatment. Thus the major recommendation for probation dealings with these persons is that they should be given aid of various kinds by probation officers which would assist them in remaining law-abiding. The agent can render help in finding jobs and in providing other services to these probationers, but he should not make any special effort to engage them in more than minimal supervision or in programs of relatively superficial assistance.

One-time losers do occasionally make their way into prison settings. The number of them in different institutions varies with such factors as the differential availability of probation services in various locales, the size of the community in which the offender resides, and other contingencies. In institutions, these inmates come to be labeled "square Johns." They also get caught up in differential association with other prosocial persons and in differential avoidance of "right guy" prisoners. The program for one-time losers very often includes fairly intensive involvement in vocational or educational programs or in treatment activities. But on logical grounds, there is not much justification for placing them in therapy. Instead, the major approach should be maximizing their isolation from the criminalistic elements of the prison community. These are the kinds of prisoners who should be confined in a minimum security section of the institution or in a satellite facility outside the walls of the prison. Such offenders might also be included in group counseling, particularly near the end of their institutional stay. But these activities would be designed to help them make the transition from the prison community to the free one, rather than to rehabilitate them. Group therapy would take the form of prerelease preparation which would aim to give the offenders realistic notions of the parole difficulties they will encounter as a consequence of their new "ex-convict" public identity and to provide them with the ability to handle these problems of adjustment. Group rather than individual counseling is recommended partly for reasons of expedience, in that more persons can be handled with the same expenditure of time and effort in groups than in individual counseling.

The parole tactics to be used with one-time losers should center mainly upon the agent rendering reasonably intense assistance to the parolee at the start of his parole experience, with release from intensive supervision taking place rather quickly thereafter. Once the one-time loser is re-employed and resettled in his marital situation, he would need little supervision and assistance.

AUTOMOBILE THIEF—"JOYRIDER"

This criminal pattern needs little discussion, for Chapter Six devoted some detailed commentary to juvenile joyriders. Adult car thieves are not much different from juvenile ones except that they are usually older males. What this silly-sounding assertion means is that to some extent, the matter of being labeled a criminal as opposed to a juvenile car thief is a chance phenomenon. Car thieves who are dealt with as delinquents in one area frequently are handled as adult offenders in other jurisdictions because of variations in juvenile court utilization of concurrent jurisdiction provisions. Juvenile courts can transfer subjects to criminal courts at their discretion, but individual courts vary in their practices regarding remand of individuals to adult courts.

The major outlines of treatment for adult joyriders are the same as for youthful car thieves. These center around group activities designed to provide the subjects with status-conferring equivalents to car theft. Such offenders need programs which are "masculine" in definition, in which they can resolve their masculinity needs in noncriminal ways.

Perhaps the principal cautionary recommendation for joyriders in prisons is that they should be isolated from intensive contacts with "right guy" prisoners. Automobile thieves must be directed toward the realization that their criminal activities are immature forms of behavior, but this is a lesson which they should teach each other in group therapy. Pains should be taken to prevent any kind of contamination of joyriders by "right guys," in which the former come to emulate the "tough guy" attitudes and behavior of the latter group. Isolation of this kind could be created and sustained by several different arrangements, such as housing car thieves in institutional areas with other prosocial inmates.

NAIVE CHECK FORGER

Naive check forgers appear to be persons with histories of adjustment difficulties of various kinds who stumble upon check writing as a solution to their problems. They often represent a marked departure from other kinds of property criminals in that they frequently exhibit prosocial attitudes and also enter into individual treatment with some enthusiasm. Also, many of them are from more comfortable economic backgrounds than other property offenders. As a result, naive check forgers are often placed upon probation, for they appear to be more tractable than many of the hostile and antagonistic individuals who are processed through the courts. But the behavior of check forgers on probation is frequently disappointing. Their violation rates are relatively high, and after several probation placements, many of them are sent to prisons.

These individuals need some form of client-centered counseling or group therapy designed to build up a fund of acceptable solutions to "problems." Common attitudes of the form, "you can't kill anyone with a fountain pen" and "what I did was not serious because banks have lots of money—therefore nobody was hurt by my activities," must be replaced with internalized definitions of check forgery as unacceptable problem-solving behavior. Perhaps many check forgers would also profit from a form of "shock therapy" administered early in their deviant careers. It appears that many of them drift into repetitive check forgery, in part, out of a perception that they can engage in this problem-solving technique with impunity. As indicated above, a common career line for these offenders shows a number of informal actions taken against them, as well as several probation placements. It is not until the check writer has engaged in repetitive episodes of this activity that he is brought up short by the stringent penalty of being sent to prison.

What kind of "shock therapy" would be in order? One rather obvious shock experience would be to put check forgers in jail for a short period, perhaps for a week or two, immediately after their conviction in court. At the end of this period, they would then be placed on probation where they would be provided with intensive therapy by a treatment agent. Also, in the initial probation period, the probation officer might find it necessary to utilize warnings and threats of certain kinds in order to obtain compliance with his directives. By "threats" is meant such things as explicit indications by the officer that certain behavior on the part of the probationer will result in revocation of probation.

No claim is intended that by themselves jail terms and threats are effective tools in rehabilitation. Instead, the thesis is that tactics of this kind may be of some utility *when accompanied by direct therapeutic activities*. Views of this kind, holding that jail sentences and warnings may have positive value, are not very fashionable ones in the correctional literature. About the only time this theme gets expressed is in the mass media where naive and blanket suggestions are advanced to "get tough" with offenders. This book is not a plea for repressive and punitive tactics as the major corrective diet for law violators. Yet it may be that under certain well-defined circumstances, the judicious application of coercive measures might deter further deviant conduct. There is no firm evidence to support such notions, but it is equally true that there is no data which show that such tactics are harmful. Arguments of this kind are not to be settled by fiat, so that some empirical evidence is called for on this point. Thus the hypothesis that jail terms might be useful for naive forgers represents a specific notion worthy of research.

The kind of therapy to be administered to check forgers on probation could be client-centered individual therapy, group treatment, or a combination of both forms. Check forgers are, on the one hand, candidates for individual therapy because of their pro-treatment attitudes. Also, they are relatively similar to probation officers in terms of social backgrounds, so that the conditions for client-worker rapport are apparent in these cases. At the same time, group treatment of collections of check forgers would make considerable sense, particularly because of the homogeneity of characteristics of both the worker and the group members. Finally, a combination of group treatment and client-centered therapy could possess advantages over either individual or group treatment taken alone. In this instance, group sessions could provide individual check forgers with detailed observations and information about the adjustment problems faced by other offenders, and in turn, with some guidance regarding appropriate techniques for handling these difficulties. Thus the two forms would complement each other.

The same general kinds of treatment intervention would be suggested for those naive forgers who turn up in penal institutions. They could be provided with some degree of individual, client-centered therapy or with group therapy. They should also be isolated from "right guy" inmates. However, the prevention of criminal contamination in this case is relatively easily accomplished, for check forgers tend to engage in self-segregation from the prisoners they define as the "real criminals" in prison. Thus segregation of them is not a major administrative problem for prison officials.

The treatment procedures to be employed with naive check forgers on parole are similar to strategies for working with these persons in other settings. However, in the case of parole supervision, check forgers would probably require rather intensive supervision and assistance at the initial stage of the parole period, with declining attention from that point onward. The parole agent's major task with these offenders centers around helping them find jobs and motivating them to stay out of difficulties with their employers, or other postrelease matters of this general kind.

One commonly voiced hypothesis by correctional workers is that check forgers are "dependent" personalities and, as a consequence, difficult individuals to treat. In the view of correctional agents, check forgers are not difficult persons to induct into therapy, quite the contrary. The problem with them is that it is hard to disengage them from therapy. Stated differently, workers sometimes lament that they cannot get naive forgers to "stand on their own two feet." Note first that this matter of possible "dependency" is presently just a "hunch" unsupported by any firm evidence. It may be that check forgers do not, in fact, exhibit this kind of personality pattern. But if it is assumed for a moment that this perception of treatment workers is frequently accurate, the agent must be concerned with the reduction of client dependence upon him. For what it is worth in this regard, some of the findings of Rogers and his associates relative to client-centered therapy suggest that dependency upon the therapist can be reduced in the course of treatment sessions, so that it is possible to develop assertive and independent behavior on the part of the client.[8]

WHITE-COLLAR CRIMINAL

A paragraph or two is all that is required to deal with treatment for white-collar criminals. Such offenders are rare in correctional case loads, for most cases of white-collar crime are handled outside the system of criminal proceedings. Moreover, because white-collar offenders are not characterized by antisocial attitudes or criminal self-images, they do not need resocialization.

Although white-collar criminals are unimportant within the conventional population of therapy candidates, they present some very thorny theoretical and policy questions for criminologists and citizens alike.

[8] Carl R. Rogers, " 'Client-Centered' Therapy," *Scientific American*, Vol. 187 (November 1952), 66-74.

One question which is both theoretically and pragmatically significant centers about the contribution, if any, that white-collar crime makes to conventional lawbreaking. It is not unlikely that the existence of white-collar criminality, along with differential handling of the individuals involved in it, provides run-of-the-mill offenders with powerful rationalizations for their own conduct. The latter can argue that "everyone is crooked" and that they are the "little fish" who are the victims of a corrupt and hypocritical society. In the same way, some rather obvious problems for treatment of conventional offenders may arise from their perception of widespread illegality among individuals of comfortable economic standing. Although definitive evidence on this matter is lacking, it is possible to gather up an abundance of statements by articulate criminals and delinquents in which these individuals allude to the facts of white-collar crime as one basis for their grievances against "society."

A different point regarding white-collar criminals is that prosocial individuals who define themselves as upright, honest persons violate the law in ways which are serious indeed in terms of financial cost to the general public. Specific white-collar offenders are involved in organizational networks and associations in which norms have developed that exempt the actors from culpability as "criminals." Normally there is little question that the actors are fully aware that their actions are illegal. Nonetheless, these persons think of themselves as very different from "real criminals."

What should be done about white-collar crime and white-collar criminals? This is not a question to be answered solely, if at all, by the criminologist. It is an issue of public policy in the same way that the question of what should be done with drug addicts, cigarette smokers, or sex offenders is to be adjudicated publicly. Of course, the criminologist may have an important part to play in identifying the results to be expected from one policy or another. If it is assumed for the moment that some consensus eventually develops that white-collar crime should be treated as "crime" and vigorously repressed, the criminologist could then lay out certain recommendations.

Certainly the first action that would be taken to reduce white-collar criminality should be one of vigorous and consistent law enforcement. The regulatory agencies charged with enforcement of business and financial regulatory statutes would go about ferreting out violations of law with the same diligence as is now found in narcotics bureau operations. In turn, detected law violators would be dealt with in the criminal courts. Those convicted of criminal offenses would be handed sentences involving large fines and prison terms. The rationale for this approach to white-collar criminality is obvious enough, namely, that it would make it difficult for deviant persons and organizations to "have their cake and eat it too." That is, offenders would find it difficult to assert that they are noncriminal and virtuous when confronted with the clear evidence that other persons who have engaged in similar actions have been defined and dealt with as "criminals."

A parallel action designed to reduce the extent of business criminality would center about endeavors to generate a code of ethics among business and financial organizations which stresses scrupulous fidelity to the law. The question of precisely how such an ethical code might be generated is not so easy to answer, although a diligent law enforcement approach to white-collar crime might lead to greater concern within business organizations for ethical and legal conduct.

The basic point in all this is that if white-collar crime is to be reduced, the steps needed to attain that end have more to do with alterations in patterns of social organization than they have to do with tampering with individual persons.

PROFESSIONAL "FRINGE" VIOLATOR

Hard facts concerning criminal behavior of the professional "fringe" variety are hard to come by because few of the participating individuals are subjected to official actions. Thus only a few doctors who commit abortions are arrested for such activities and sentenced to prison. Instead, because it is the lay, unskilled abortionist who runs the considerable risk of apprehension, conviction, and prison commitment, professional fringe violators do not represent a numerically significant group in corrections.

Those few professional fringe violators in correctional case loads are normally prosocial, noncriminal individuals in orientation. They are not in need of intensive resocialization. The major problem to be dealt with in their case centers around postrelease adjustment in situations where the individual is barred from reinvolvement in his preprison professional occupation. In this instance, the parole agent may help the person find some occupational activity which will make use of his professional skills. As an example, a doctor-abortionist may be prevented from practicing medicine, at least temporarily, so that some job as a laboratory technician or similar activity must be found for him. The parole agent in this case can make representations to prospective employers on behalf of the parolee. Of course, this is not treatment in any important sense, but it may nonetheless be an important form of parole assistance.

EMBEZZLER

Embezzling is still another kind of deviant behavior which frequently is handled outside the framework of correctional agencies and processes. Also, it is another form of criminal behavior in which the actors are essentially prosocial in attitudes and are lacking in criminal self-images. Thus those embezzlers who do fall into the hands of correctional workers do not need intensive treatment.

There are two main considerations with respect to the handling of embezzlers in correctional settings. In prisons, these persons should be isolated from intensive contacts with criminalistic inmates, but this is not usually a difficult matter to arrange. For one thing, embezzlers normally define themselves as different from the "real criminals" in the institution, so that they segregate themselves and associate differentially with other square Johns. Also, some of them are recruited into administrative activities in the prison, such as clerical positions, and are often housed separately from other inmates. Such prisoners make up one part of the group of "politicians."

The second and major concern in the case of embezzlers has to do with postrelease adjustment problems. Once an individual has acquired an official record for financial defalcations, employment in situations where additional embezzlement could occur is unlikely. As a consequence, the paroled embezzler faces the problem of finding a job. Although this is not basically a treatment problem, it is nonetheless an important adjustment difficulty. The parole agent can be of important assistance in helping the paroled embezzler to find employment. Insofar as the parole worker succeeds in this respect, the prospects of acceptable parole adjustment by the offender are rather good. Accordingly, the embezzler represents a case where parole supervision and assistance would decline markedly after an initial period of release from prison.

PERSONAL OFFENDER—"ONE-TIME LOSER"

This is another type in which the recommendation of "no treatment" is the main therapy strategy. The majority of these offenders are persons who have committed homicides or serious assaults. They usually have been involved in some form of "victim-precipitated" violence that developed from situations of long-term stress between the interactional partners. The common pattern of spouse-homicide or assault which has culminated from an extended history of marital tension and violence is one of the major forms of behavior included in this type. Most of the offenders have had only minor records of prior delinquency or criminality. They are usually persons without criminal attitudes or self-images who assume the square John role in prison settings.

Although personal offender, one-time losers do not fit the picture of the hostile, defiant, antisocial criminal, such individuals are on the receiving end of intense societal reactions. They are normally sentenced to correctional institutions for long terms. The murderers in this group are normally given "life" sentences (or are executed in some instances). The "life" sentences are somewhat misleading, however, for many murderers are paroled from prisons after serving sentences of a half dozen years or so.

The prison program for one-time loser personal offenders should center around their segregation from antisocial inmates. This is normally an easy matter to arrange, for such square Johns tend to self-segregate themselves from the "right guy" prisoners. As far as program recommendations are concerned, these persons are candidates for any number of specific institutional activities, such as religious or educational programs and so forth. The main concern should be in finding activities that are compatible with the interests of the offender in order to keep him busy in prison. No intensive therapy is called for in this case.

Although these offenders do not need treatment in institutions or on parole, they do frequently require some help from parole officers upon release. Because of the long period of confinement that most of them have experienced, they are likely to encounter a variety of adjustment difficulties when they return to civilian society. The parole officer can render a variety of services which help to minimize the shock of postrelease adjustment.

"PSYCHOPATHIC" ASSAULTIST

Deviants of this type are recognized more on the basis of asocial attitudes and self-images than of specific offense activities. They show a diversity of criminal behavior patterns—some of them have been involved in assaultive activities, and others have engaged in property offenses—but they all exhibit indices of an asocial personality structure. These offenders are adult versions of "overly aggressive" delinquents. However, the degree of personality maladjustment of some "psychopathic" assaultists is less than that of the more extreme unsocialized juvenile offenders.

"Psychopathic" assaultists in prison come to be recognized in the inmate argot by such terms as "gorillas," "toughs," "outlaws," or "hard guys." [9] They are very difficult persons to deal with in any setting, but particularly in penal facilities. They are feared by other inmates and are avoided by them as much as possible. The authorities attempt to control such persons by isolating them in the most secure area of the institution. They also try to cope with them by handing out the most severe punishments to them such as isolation in the "hole" or segregation unit. Still another tactic for controlling them has been to ship them off to the most secure prison in the correctional system, or on occasion, to a unit for the "criminally insane" persons in a state mental hospital. In any event, variations in tactics aside, not much, if any, treatment has been attempted with these persons.

The reasons why "psychopathic" assaultists have received little therapy are not hard to find. Many institutions are without rehabilitative programs into which such persons could be placed. In addition, it is by no means clear as to what should be done with these individuals even when therapy programs are available.

On the whole, the kind of program that is required by "psychopathic" assaultists parallels that for "overly aggressive" delinquents. Some kind of combined tactic is needed to control the

[9] Schrag, op. cit.; Gresham M. Sykes, The Society of Captives (Princeton, N.J.: Princeton University Press, 1958), pp. 84-108.

asocial actions of the offender at the same time that attempts are made to resocialize him. Attempts must be made to carry the socialization of the person beyond the point at which his earlier experiences have taken him. Having said this, it should be immediately made clear that these individuals represent one of the least hopeful groups of candidates for treatment in corrections. Although they need the kind of program outlined for juvenile, asocial delinquents, they are not going to receive much treatment. This kind of activity is simply not compatible with the programs of most conventional correctional institutions. Moreover, this is not the sort of responsibility that can easily be shifted to a state mental hospital because these offenders are extreme custodial and escape problems.

Perhaps the most reasonable solution to the problem of psychopathic assaultists who are a minority in any single correctional facility would be to develop a regional or federal institution for them. In a very general sense, what is needed is a kind of "Alcatraz" to serve as a collection place for these individuals from different state prisons. This facility would have to have extremely detailed security systems and a comprehensive and detailed therapy program.

VIOLENT SEX OFFENDER

Violent sex assaultists are, at the same time, serious therapy problems and outside the scope of treatment. That is, they are psychiatrically abnormal persons who need a great amount of attention if they are to be "cured." On the other hand, they commit extremely violent and bizarre offenses, often culminating in the death of the victim, so that they are given long prison sentences. In the case of sex assaults leading to homicide, the offenders are frequently dealt with as capital cases and executed. Those who are not executed are given "life" sentences, but unlike the personal offender, "one-time loser," life in this case frequently means life imprisonment in fact. Parole boards are noticeably reluctant to release such individuals on parole because under present circumstances it is almost impossible to be certain that they have been rehabilitated. Therapy is not often provided for them because of the slight development of treatment programs. In addition, even if therapy is provided, this behavior pattern is sufficiently obscure in terms of causal background that it is extremely difficult to be certain that therapy has accomplished a "cure."

In view of the paucity of good evidence or theory regarding causal processes in violent sex behavior, no attempt will be made here to specify treatment strategy for such offenders other than the very general recommendation that they be given psychotherapy. One appealing device for avoiding an explicit confrontation with the problem of sex assaultists would be to shift the responsibility for explaining or treating them to psychiatrists. But that ploy will not be used, for it would be grossly misleading to suggest that psychiatric theory is equal to the task of explanation or therapy. Instead, one can search the psychiatric literature in vain for significant theory, research findings, or treatment strategies for these deviants.

Violent sex offenders were seen in Chapter Three as developing within atypical family settings, such as those having seductive interaction patterns among family members. Also, they were identified as extremely hostile toward females, and their behavior was interpreted as embodying more aggressive than sexual motivation. It should be made clear, however, that these are very sketchy statements that are not supported by any systematic body of research data.

Another reason for not shifting responsibility for this behavior pattern to psychiatrists is the good possibility that such behavior is as legitimate an interest for social psychologists as for psychiatrists. Although social psychology has tended to be asexual in orientation, there is no clear warrant for excluding normal and deviant sexual development from social-psychological study. Quite the contrary, sexual socialization is as legitimate a subject for social psychology as the more usual topics that are now addressed. Then, too, the interactional framework of social psychology has much to recommend it as applied to sexual adjustment patterns. Whatever else that might be said about various forms of sexual behavior, these are learned responses: they develop out of socialization experiences and differential interaction patterns. Hence the behavioral perspective which has proven to be of value in the study of other forms of deviant behavior could perhaps illuminate matters of sexual deviation as well. But if so, this is virgin territory for social-psychological exploration.

NONVIOLENT SEX OFFENDER—"RAPO"

These offenders are individuals who have committed exhibitionist acts or who have engaged in nonviolent sex acts with immature victims. They are termed "rapos" in the argot of prisons and are accorded extremely low status among inmates. They are looked upon as markedly peculiar, depraved, and repulsive persons, both by inmates and by the general public. These persons are aware of their low standing in the eyes of others, but they frequently resort to various rationalizations or denials of guilt to avoid accepting definitions of themselves as "bad" persons. Nonviolent sex criminals are usually much older than other prison inmates and they often show a record of little or no prior criminality.

The available theory and research data on this pattern of deviant sex behavior is not abundant, but it is more impressive than the literature on violent sex assaultists. The most marked impression that emerges about persons involved in nonviolent sex behavior is that they share certain characteristics such as timidity, communication difficulties with adult peers, and feelings of sexual inadequacy. In brief, they are caught up in concerns about whether they are "men" or "mice." Many of them are married to aggressive, domineering spouses, so that their personality problems are bound up in a particular interaction context which may exacerbate their adjustment difficulties.

As stated in Chapter Three, the term "nonviolent" is sometimes misleading because some offenders in this category do harm their victims. But violence is not a central ingredient of the behavior in that it tends to stem from fears of the offender that the victim will report him to someone. Violence is not a fundamental interest or motive of the offender as it is of the sex assaultist.

Those "rapo" criminals who kill their victims are, of course, usually given life terms or are executed. Even in the more common case where the sexual actions do not culminate in violence, long prison sentences are the norm, particularly for child molesters who provoke a societal reaction of abhorrence and violent antagonism. Exhibitionists, on the other hand, are sometimes dealt with less harshly and are placed on probation or in psychiatric therapy. Exhibitionists are often viewed as "funny" or "crazy," but child molesters are regarded as depraved monsters.

Offenders in this category are candidates for psychiatric treatment of a fairly intensive kind. Although it is doubtful that they require long-term analysis designed to probe deeply into their psyches, they do need to be handled by skilled and perceptive therapists. Thus what is suggested here is therapy along client-centered lines, but carried on by trained therapists, preferably clinicians or psychiatrists.

Nonviolent sex criminals must be helped toward an awareness of the basis of their activities, that is, certain insecurities. In turn, they must be led to a firmer definition of themselves as "men" rather than as "mice." Also, such persons need to be directed toward more assertive and outgoing behavior, particularly with respect to such immediate interactional partners as fellow workers and spouses. Some reports are at hand to suggest that this kind of therapy does produce behavioral change in a favorable direction.[10]

The optimal device for implementing this kind of program would be one combining out-patient psychotherapy with a long-term probation placement. In it, the offenders would first receive an intensive dose of psychotherapy. Following this intensive therapy, they might be drawn into group therapy sessions on probation in which they would engage in mutual reinforcement of new self-images and adjustment patterns. Group treatment would not be in order at the beginning point in therapy because such persons might be traumatized by being forced too early to face up to negative societal reactions which might emerge as a common theme in group interaction. The initial individual therapy would be designed to prepare these offenders for group interaction by helping them conceptualize themselves as needing help.

This optimal program is predicated upon an assumption that psychiatric services are available within probation organizations. Now of course this is not usually the case—such services as a part of probation operations are quite rare.

A similar approach would be recommended for those nonviolent sex offenders who are sentenced to prison. They should first be given intensive therapy by psychiatrists or clinicians, or failing this, by the most experienced and skilled therapist in the institution. At the point that the offender has developed some ablity to admit and "live with" the facts of his deviant conduct, that is, has managed to accept the behavior without feelings of extremely low esteem, he might then be placed in group treatment with other "rapos." It would be inadvisable to assign such prisoners to therapy activities with "right guy" inmates in view of the hostile attitudes held by

[10] J. H. Conn, "The Psychiatric Treatment of Certain Chronic Offenders," *Journal of Criminal Law and Criminology,* Vol. 32 (March-April 1942), 631-35.

the latter toward "rapos." At least, such a course of action would be ill advised until the nonviolent sex offender has made marked progress in therapy. Until that point has been reached, interaction with persons who will direct verbal hostility toward him would destroy therapy and would devastate an already fragile ego.

Nonviolent sex offenders in parole case loads should be continued in group treatment as a part of their therapy program. Doubtless the parole period is the most difficult time for many of these persons, in that members of the community are likely to be antagonistic toward him, quite apart from any change in behavior that might have taken place on his part. For this reason, one tactic of nontreatment would be to work out parole programs for "rapos" in which they would be encouraged to re-establish civilian ties in a new community.

NONVIOLENT SEX OFFENDER—STATUTORY RAPE

This is another of those criminal behavior patterns for which the recommendation of "no treatment" is in order. Statutory rapists have been convicted of normal heterosexual acts with voluntary sex partners under the legal age of consent. The crime partner in these cases normally shows up in juvenile courts charged with "immorality," "ungovernability," or similar activity. The most obvious thing that can be said about statutory rapists is that they are persons who were engaging in a very common form of behavior but who were unfortunate enough to get caught.

Because statutory rapists are normally lacking in antisocial attitudes or criminal self-images, they are ideal candidates for probation and for minimal supervision on probation. However, some of these persons are on occasion sentenced to reformatories or prisons. In these cases, no formal treatment is called for, but attempts should be made to restrict the contacts of these persons with "right guy" elements in the institution. Statutory rapists are good prospects for assignment to minimum security facilities, prison farms, and other parts of the facility where they will have few associations with antisocial offenders. It is probably also true that the shorter the prison sentence the offender serves, the better. Penal commitment is of no positive value in rehabilitation of the offender, and such individuals are in prison for punishment. But the less punishment, measured in terms of time served, the higher the likelihood that the institutional experience will have only a slight negative effect. Conversely, the longer such individuals are kept in prison, the greater the chance that some of them will develop feelings of bitterness and antagonism toward "society" and its social control agents. In turn, these changes could increase the probability of statutory rapists interacting with "right guys" as a reference group through which they may acquire crime skills and an orientation toward criminality as postrelease behavior.

NARCOTIC ADDICT—HEROIN

The treatment remarks in the preceding discussion of programs for juvenile narcotic users apply with equal force to adult narcotics addicts. The essentially punitive and law-enforcement orientation of existing drug programs needs to be modified toward rehabilitative efforts directed at heavy drug users. More important, the specific form which therapy activities should take seems clearly to be in the direction of long-term milieu management patterned in a general way after Synanon. Although causal factors and processes in drug use are not fully understood, one thing is clear enough: Most drug addicts are not able, for one reason or another, to remain free from drug use following conventional treatment when they are returned to the community and to contact with drug users and the criminal underworld. Instead, they need consistent support from a subculture of former drug users to help them withstand the pressures to relapse into narcotic use. Until this general form of program is rather widely adopted, narcotic addicts are likely to continue in the pattern of drug use, apprehension and confinement, relapse into drug addiction, repeated confinement and relapse, over and over until it is finally terminated in some cases by death from an overdose of narcotics or untimely death from some other cause.[11]

Summary

This concludes the commentary on strategies of treatment for juveniles and adult offenders. At this point, the major

[11] For one graphic example of this process, see Helen M. Hughes, ed., *The Fantastic Lodge: The Autobiography of a Girl Drug Addict* (Boston: Houghton Mifflin Co., 1961).

business of this book is also finished, but there are some observations in the form of an epilogue regarding needed theory and research which would form a fitting conclusion to this argument in this text. This summary comment is the topic of the final chapter.

eight

RECENT TRENDS
AND
FUTURE
NEEDS

Introduction

In science, the usual view is that what is known at any point in time is only a fraction of the ultimately knowable, so that science does not deal in final truths. Such a posture of modesty is particularly appropriate in the basic and applied behavioral sciences because of the relatively recent origins of these fields. The amount now understood about human behavior seems clearly to be only a segment of the knowledge eventually to be discovered. This book has presented as a venture in applied social science a brief inventory of much of the theory and research on two matters: (1) the etiology of criminalistic behavior patterns and (2) treatment tactics to be employed with lawbreakers. As an appropriate conclusion, this chapter reviews some recent work on causal and treatment theory and investigation. It also provides some comments and suggestions for future efforts on these matters. In short, this chapter enumerates some answers to the question "Where do we go from here?"

Causal Theory and Research

In Chapters Two and Three much of the etiological product of criminological attention that has accumulated so far was identified. Among other things, it was noted that analysis has lately moved toward typologies and the search for separate causes for different patterns of criminalistic behavior. This trend has been uneven, however, in that some types of lawbreakers have been much studied and others have been relatively ignored. Hence, the summary characterizations of offender role-careers in Chapter Three are based on differential amounts of evidence. Some of these descriptions are buttressed by a large and comprehensive body of supporting research data, whereas others are based on fragmentary and less numerous empirical sources. In general, more theorizing and research has been directed at juvenile offenders than at adults in the past several decades. Also, criminological inquiry has been particularly concentrated upon lower-class, gang, "subcultural" delinquency.

It was noted in Chapter Two that Albert K. Cohen's essay on working-class, gang misbehavior, which appeared in 1955, stimulated much subsequent speculation by Cloward and Ohlin, Bloch and Niederhoffer, Miller, Sykes and Matza, Yablonsky, and others as well (see pages 35-38). Indeed, for a time this surfeit of theory cried out for supporting facts, but the ferment stirred up by Cohen has begun to produce a large amount of research, some of which has already been mentioned in Chapter Two. For the most part, this activity has turned up findings consistent with the portraits of gang offenders in Chapter Three, although as is often the case, these empirical reports indicate that actual persons are more varied and complex than their sociological images.

The recent investigations by Chilton centering around working-class patterns of delinquency include an ecological examination of urban area social correlates of delinquency rates in Baltimore, Detroit, and Indianapolis.[1] In general, he discovered that high rates of juvenile misconduct are consistently related to transience, poor housing, and low-income conditions in neighborhoods. A somewhat

[1] Roland J. Chilton, "Continuity in Delinquency Area Research: A Comparison of Studies for Baltimore, Detroit, and Indianapolis," *American Sociological Review,* Vol. 29 (February 1964), 71-83.

parallel study by Reiss and Rhodes throws more light upon the relationships between deviant conduct and socioeconomic class position.[2] Their results dealing with a large number of juvenile males in the Nashville, Tennessee, metropolitan area show that there is no simple or uniform linkage between social class position and delinquency. Although those boys most frequently found in the population of officially designated delinquents are from the lower class, delinquency life-chances or risks are not uniform for all working-class males. Juvenile misbehavior is most common in homogeneous lower-class neighborhoods and less usual in neighborhoods of mixed social status. Thus Reiss and Rhodes argue that the behavior of working-class boys is conditioned by the social class structure and the cultural traditions of the community areas in which they live. Youths whose parents are working-class individuals have a high risk of delinquent involvement if they live in areas populated by similar kinds of persons, but they are not likely to become offenders if they live in neighborhoods of mixed or predominantly middle-class socioeconomic character.

A fair amount of information has begun to appear on another question regarding lower-class delinquents, namely, "What do delinquents do?" Historically, criminologists have not paid much attention to the detailed description of the behavioral forms taken by criminalistic deviance. Yet it hardly needs to be pointed out that satisfactory explanation of behavior is unlikely in the absence of good information about the phenomena to be explained. One report on the action patterns exhibited by gang members has been made by Robin.[3] In an investigation carried on in Philadelphia, he examined the official and unofficial police records of over 700 male Negro members of 27 delinquent gangs in that city. Most of these youths came to the attention of the police before they were 15 years of age. They exhibited progressive movement toward illegal acts of increasing seriousness, in many cases culminating in involvement in adult criminal careers. Robin also maintains that although most of these subjects engaged in a versatile collection of

[2] Albert J. Reiss, Jr., and Albert Lewis Rhodes, "The Distribution of Juvenile Delinquency in the Social Class Structure," *American Sociological Review*, Vol. 26 (October 1961), 720-32.

[3] Gerald D. Robin, "Gang Member Delinquency: Its Extent, Sequence and Typology," *Journal of Criminal Law, Criminology and Police Science*, Vol. 55 (March 1964), 59-69.

delinquent acts, about two-thirds of them had committed at least one offense involving physical violence. He interprets this finding as support for the claims of Cloward and Ohlin concerning the existence of a "conflict" subculture in delinquency.[4]

A second bit of information on gang behavior is found in a paper by Reiss dealing with "the social integration of queers and peers."[5] This material concerns a group of lower-class delinquent males in Nashville whose activities include participation in a complex structure of relationships with adult homosexuals. The boys submit to adult fellators in exchange for pay, an interaction pattern which they conceptualize as a business transaction.

Still another statement regarding behavior patterns of gang delinquents is found in a report by Short, Tennyson, and Howard, regarding the delinquent and nondelinquent conduct of about 600 members of Chicago gangs.[6] Their findings indicate that most of the offenders are involved in a wide range of deviant and non-deviant acts rather than in narrowly focused patterns, suggested by Cloward and Ohlin, which center around stealing, violence, or drug use. The former investigators aver that an undifferentiated "parent delinquent subculture" exists from which more specialized delinquent groups emerge. In other words, they indicate that the generic form of gang behavior is one in which behavioral versatility is the rule and that from this "parent" form, cliques and subgroups branch off into more specialized careers in deviant conduct.

Inquiry has begun on still another facet of gang delinquency, namely, the test of various causal generalizations that have been put forth. For example, Spergel has uncovered supporting evidence for some of the claims of Cloward and Ohlin in two separate studies in New York and Chicago.[7] In New York he discovered community

---

[4] *Ibid.*, 64-65.

[5] Albert J. Reiss, Jr., "The Social Integration of Queers and Peers," *Social Problems*, Vol. 9 (Fall 1961), 102-20.

[6] James F. Short, Jr., Ray A. Tennyson, and Kenneth I. Howard, "Behavior Dimensions of Gang Delinquency," *American Sociological Review*, Vol. 28 (June 1963), 411-28.

[7] Irving Spergel, "Male Young Adult Criminality, Deviant Values, and Differential Opportunities in Two Lower Class Negro Neighborhoods," *Social Problems*, Vol. 10 (Winter 1963), 237-50; Spergel, "An Exploratory Research in Delinquent Subcultures," *Social Service Review*, Vol. 35 (March 1961), 33-47; Spergel, *Racketville, Slumtown, Haulburg* (Chicago: University of Chicago Press, 1964). See also Delbert S. Elliott, "Delinquency and Perceived Opportunity," *Sociological Inquiry*, Vol. 32 (Spring 1962), 216-27.

areas in which delinquent subcultures of the "criminalistic" or "conflict" form predominate. These areas exhibited neighborhood characteristics of the kinds suggested in the Cloward and Ohlin argument.[8] In addition, consistent with the orienting theoretical perspective, the delinquents in all the areas studied showed a greater discrepancy between their aspirations and their expectations regarding their economic and occupational futures than did the nonoffenders.[9] The offenders view their life-chances in relatively dismal terms because they anticipate that they will achieve far less in life than they would prefer. Spergel's findings from Chicago, dealing with young adult criminals, parallel those for New York, in that he discovered that two community areas which show differing patterns of criminality also have variant forms of neighborhood social organization.[10]

A final concentration of recent work on gang misbehavior has centered about the study of value patterns of gang members. In one of these investigations, dealing with lower-class gang boys, nongang lower-class youths, and middle-class, nongang males in Chicago, the three groups were shown to differ only slightly in their evaluation of behavior governed by middle-class prescriptive norms.[11] All three groups placed positive emphasis upon such matters as going to college, saving money, and similar orientations. On the other hand, the working-class gang boys demonstrated the greatest degree of tolerance or approval for activities proscribed or forbidden by middle-class norms, such as use of narcotics or sexual activity. Parallel observations from a number of areas in Pennsylvania have been reported by Rothstein, who indicates that delinquent and nondelinquent boys at several social class levels generally agreed upon the items or criteria making for high social status.[12] That is, all of them evaluated college education, popularity with girls, and like matters in similar terms.

[8] Spergel, "An Exploratory Research in Delinquent Subcultures," 37-39.
[9] *Ibid.*, 41.
[10] Spergel, "Male Young Adult Criminality, Deviant Values, and Differential Opportunities in Two Lower Class Negro Neighborhoods."
[11] Robert A. Gordon, James F. Short, Jr., Desmond S. Cartwright, and Fred L. Strodtbeck, "Values and Gang Delinquency: A Study of Street Corner Groups," *American Journal of Sociology*, Vol. 69 (September 1963), 109-28.
[12] Edward Rothstein, "Attributes Related to High Social Status: A Comparison of the Perceptions of Delinquent and Non-Delinquent Boys," *Social Problems*, Vol. 10 (Summer 1962), 75-83.

Doubtless even more data regarding gang delinquency would be useful, such as comparative evidence from a wide range of different community types, from varied regions, or even from different nations. In the same way, additional research on the causal backgrounds of gang members, of the impact of agency intervention on the careers of offenders, or of kindred matters can be visualized. Yet at the same time, it can fairly be said that the descriptions of lower-class gang delinquents in Chapter Three are reasonably accurate ones, drawn from a sizeable store of supporting evidence.

The same claim could be made about some of the other role-career descriptions in Chapter Three. The picture of overly aggressive delinquents, represented by offenders who engage in individualistic acts of aggression against human and nonhuman targets, is based upon a large body of empirical findings which indicate the nature of this deviant career.[13] This material is also emphatic in underscoring the importance of parental rejection as a major condition serving to generate such behavior. There is no serious quarrel to be had with the broad claims that overly aggressive behavior is an important category of deviant conduct, that aggression varies from the relatively mild deviation described by Bandura and Walters[14] to the severely atypical conduct examined by Jenkins, Redl and Wineman, and others,[15] or that aggression varies concomitantly with the severity of rejection experienced by the individual.

However, not all delinquent role-careers are equally well understood. For example, the several studies on young car thieves are in agreement on one point, namely, that many of them concentrate their deviant actions upon joyriding and that they are commonly from comfortable economic backgrounds.[16] In the words of Wattenberg and Balistrieri, this is frequently a "favored-group" delin-

---

[13] Richard L. Jenkins and Lester E. Hewitt, "Types of Personality Structure Encountered in Child Guidance Clinics," *American Journal of Orthopsychiatry,* Vol. 14 (January 1944), 84-94; Fritz Redl and David Wineman, *The Aggressive Child* (New York: The Free Press of Glencoe, Inc., 1960); Albert Bandura and Richard H. Walters, *Adolescent Aggression* (New York: The Ronald Press Company, 1959); Leonard Berkowitz, *Aggression* (New York: McGraw-Hill Book Company, Inc., 1962).

[14] Bandura and Walters, *op. cit.,* passim.

[15] Jenkins and Hewitt, *op. cit.;* Redl and Wineman, *op. cit.*

[16] Erwin Schepses, "The Young Car Thief," *Journal of Criminal Law, Criminology and Police Science,* Vol. 50 (March-April 1960), 569; Schepses, "Boys Who Steal Cars," *Federal Probation,* Vol. 25 (March 1961), 56-62; Leonard D. Savitz, "Automobile Theft," *Journal of Criminal Law, Criminology and Police*

quency. In terms of the typological description of joyriders in Chapter Three, the significance of these studies is that they verify the existence of this pattern. They also suggest that car thieves are not usually from particularly disordered or tension-ridden homes, but instead, they are often the product of relatively stable middle-class family backgrounds.

Existing studies of car thieves do not so clearly support some of the other allegations contained in Chapter Three. They reveal little about the behavioral activities of automobile thieves and they are relatively mute on the issue of etiological variables in joyriding. For example, they contain very little information relating to the hypothesis of "masculine-protest" which holds that middle-class boys are commonly troubled by personal concerns about masculinity during adolescence and that some of them turn to car theft as a technique by which they can assert themselves and resolve identity problems.

These studies of car thieves are generally instructive, for their deficiencies are common to a number of investigations of other types of offender behavior. The principal reason why explorations of car theft (and analyses of other types as well) are not as revealing as they might be is that they have been restricted to the assessment of official data collected by some agency such as a police department or juvenile court. The record-keeping systems of most official organizations attend to only a limited number of facts about offenders, such as age, sex, official charge for which the person has been apprehended, and so forth. Not uncommonly, even these sparse items are unreliably or unsystematically recorded. But most important, these fact-gathering procedures are usually insensitive to the accumulation of data on theoretically significant dimensions with which the investigator is concerned. Thus few facts are recorded on such critical matters as the structure of the social behavior which has resulted in the offender being labeled a deviant. For example, statements about victims and their relationship to the offender are usually absent from official records. In short, an investigator can only draw out of official reports those facts which have been put there by agency officials, and in many cases, he will be lucky indeed if some of these happen to be related to the concepts and categories in which he is interested.

Science, Vol. 50 (July-August 1959), 132-43; William Wattenberg and James Balistrieri, "Automobile Theft: A 'Favored Group' Delinquency," *American Journal of Sociology*, Vol. 57 (May 1952), 575-79.

Given these deficiencies of official sources of information on offenders, investigators will have to pay more attention in the future to collection of original data. Correctional and social control agencies cannot be charged with the major responsibility of gathering theoretically significant basic data for the criminologist. Accordingly, studies of car thieves are necessary in which some detailed evidence would be acquired about automobile theft through interviewing or questionnaire techniques. These would be concerned with spelling out the details of joyrider behavior, the presence or absence of masculinity concerns by car thieves and by a comparison group of nondelinquent, middle-class males, and so forth. It is quite probable that researchers will also be required to contrive instruments for the measurement of some of the hypothesized dimensions or variables in certain forms of deviant behavior, so that "masculinity" scales, "dependency" measures, and the like will have to be developed.

The remarks to this point hold for forms of adult criminality as well as for the study of juvenile offenders. Some of the role-career descriptions of adult criminals in Chapter Three are drawn from a relatively abundant body of supporting empirical evidence, much of which was alluded to in Chapter Two (see pages 28-33). On the whole, the available data support the claims in Chapter Three that a number of different property offender careers and varied roles in crimes against persons do exist, but some of these are not completely understood. For example, although there is little doubt that many naive check forgers are found in correctional case loads, there are various gaps in existing knowledge about them. It is not clear as yet, for instance, precisely how common certain self-image notions are among these individuals. Research is needed which involves the collection of original data dealing with some of the social-psychological notions about check writers and the hypotheses about their marital and occupational backgrounds presented in Chapter Three. In particular, the frequently voiced contention of correctional workers mentioned in Chapter Seven that naive forgers are "dependent" individuals is a worthy hypothesis for study. Lemert's recent study of dependency among alcoholics provides a relevant model of the kind of work that is needed.[17] In that analysis, measures of dependency on the part of alcoholic persons were

[17] Edwin M. Lemert, "Dependency in Married Alcoholics," *Quarterly Journal of Studies on Alcohol,* Vol. 23 (December 1962), 590-609.

obtained from observations on domination of the person by his spouse, on economic dependence of the alcoholic on others, and on dependence imputed to the person by his wife. Evidence of dependency existing prior to the onset of drinking problems was uncovered in about two-fifths of the cases.

There are also other forms of adult criminality which call for additional study, for example, nonviolent sex offenders ("rapos") and the behavior patterns and causal backgrounds of violent sex offenders.

To summarize this discussion of etiological theory and research, this book has argued that a role-oriented approach to offender types is needed in which deviant patterns are described in terms of offense activity and social-psychological characteristics. Certain broad causal dimensions were also noted. Earlier chapters have presented a skeleton statement regarding identifying attributes of offender types and the causal processes which generate them. Many of these descriptions are supported by reasonably detailed evidence, although some are not. Thus more exploration of types is required through research studies of the kind sketched above.

Treatment Research

Until very recently, virtually no studies have been undertaken regarding the effects of various programs upon offenders. Opinions pro and con particular strategies of therapy have been visceral ones, rather than cerebral and empirical in form. That is to say, estimates about the efficacy of treatment procedures have been based on hunches and hope, rather than on research evidence. But in the past decade, some extremely significant changes in this situation have occurred in which research studies have begun to scrutinize tactics of treatment. Some investigations of the effects of therapeutic or preventive experiments have been alluded to earlier. These were the Provo Experiment (pages 8-9), Mobilization for Youth (pages 8-9, 180-182), the Highfields Project[18] (pages 59-60,

[18] In addition to the McCorkle, Elias, and Bixby report on Highfields, see H. Ashley Weeks, *Youthful Offenders at Highfields* (Ann Arbor: University of Michigan Press, 1958); for a brief excerpt from this work, see Weeks, "The Highfields Project and its Success," in Norman Johnston, Leonard Savitz, and Marvin Wolfgang, eds., *The Sociology of Punishment and Correction* (New York: John Wiley and Sons, Inc., 1962), pp. 203-12.

165-166), and the Midcity Project (pages 177-179). In several states, including California, program research has come of age; corrections is now beginning to move from simple record-keeping or "head counts" to operations research in which some crucial evidence is being systematically assembled on the impact of various tactics and programs upon offenders. In California, the state delinquency agency and the state adult correctional organization have both developed permanent research units. These research offices have turned out a sizeable body of valuable empirical evidence concerning the effects of various programs upon offenders in those systems. One of these studies, noted earlier, which is in progress is the Intensive Treatment Program at Chino (pages 173-174).[19]

The PICO Project (Pilot Intensive Counseling Organization) in California is one of the well-known instances of program evaluation.[20] In that investigation experiment, treatment and control groups of inmates at Deuel Vocational Institution were subjected to study. The subjects were California Youth Authority wards between 17 and 23 years of age. The experimental (treatment) subjects were given intensive, individual, interview therapy similar to what has been called individual depth psychotherapy in this book. They were administered individual therapy several times per week, and they received some group treatment as well. The controls were subjected to the conventional program of the institution, which meant that they received much less attention. The individuals in the project were also sorted out into "amenable" and "nonamenable" groups at the outset of involvement in the study. Those cases rated as amenable to treatment were judged to be characterized by a level of anxiety which would make them likely to respond to therapy, whereas the nonamenables were assessed as lacking this prerequisite for therapy. The treatment and control groups both contained a mixture of amenable and nonamenable subjects.

The therapists in this project were persons trained in clinical psychology or psychiatric social work. They conducted therapy on their assigned experimental group wards for a period which aver-

[19] A summary of recent California Youth Authority research studies can be found in *The Status of Current Research in the California Youth Authority* (Sacramento: Department of the Youth Authority, 1963).

[20] Stuart Adams, "The PICO Project," in Johnston, Savitz, and Wolfgang, *op. cit.*, pp. 213-24.

aged about nine months per subject. Each therapist worked with a case load of about twenty-five wards.

The effectiveness of this program was measured in a variety of ways, but a principal criterion of failure was "return to custody" or parole violation. The results, in brief, were these: In general, the treated amenables showed the best postrelease performance, followed by the control group amenable patients and the control group nonamenables. Surprisingly, the treated nonamenable inmates made the poorest postrelease adjustment. They apparently got worse rather than better as a result of therapy. The investigators concluded that the treated amenables learned adjustment skills from the program, and the treated nonamenable persons may have received the wrong kind of therapy.

Another California program, reported by Guttman, concerns the effects of short-term psychiatric treatment on boys in two training schools.[21] Treatment (experimental) and control groups of boys were established at Fred C. Nelles School and at the Preston School of Industry. In both places, the treatment wards were processed through a Psychiatric Treatment Unit staffed by psychologists, psychiatric social workers, and a psychiatrist. In each case, the boys were given individual, interview therapy. The wards at the two schools were not identical, as the Preston inmates were generally older than the Nelles boys. Other differences concerning personality characteristics of wards were reported by workers at the schools.

The evidence from this investigation indicates that the Nelles parolees who had been subjected to intensive treatment had lower violation rates than did the control group boys from the same school, whereas at Preston the controls had a lower recidivism rate than the treated boys. Guttman suggests that the discrepant results from the two institutions may be explained on the basis of differences in the organizational "climate" of the two facilities. At Nelles School, the Psychiatric Treatment Unit was new, and a kind of therapeutic milieu with high staff morale and other positive features existed. At Preston, the Psychiatric Treatment Unit was the focus of considerable hostility of staff members. Boys in the special treatment program received invidious handling from staff members and

[21] Evelyn S. Guttman, *Effects of Short-Term Psychiatric Treatment on Boys in Two California Youth Authority Institutions,* Research Report No. 36 (Sacramento, Cal.: Department of the Youth Authority, 1963).

other inmates. Thus it is possible that certain features of the general training school structure worked against the psychiatric intervention at Preston.

Still other examples of program research now underway in California are found in the Fricot Ranch School Study[22] and the Community Treatment Project.[23] The former is a treatment-control group investigation of the effects of intensive treatment at Fricot Ranch, a California Youth Authority facility. The treatment boys live in a twenty-boy experimental living group, whereas the control subjects are in regular fifty-boy living arrangements and receive regular institutional care. So far, the findings on success rates, measured in terms of postrelease adjustment, suggest that the treated boys are performing better on parole than the control subjects.

The Community Treatment Project is also an experimental control group investigation going on in Stockton and Sacramento. One group of California Youth Authority wards who would normally be assigned to institutional care are instead being placed directly on parole from reception centers, whereas other comparable youngsters are sent on to institutions as a control group. The wards in question are also subdivided into types on the basis of I-levels (Interpersonal Maturity Levels). The intention of this study is to determine whether or not intensive community intervention can be substituted for institutionalization, and further, to investigate differentials in program impact upon different kinds of wards. The treatment wards are also given many kinds of treatment, including individual counseling, individual and group psychotherapy, guided group interaction, group psychotherapy, family treatment, and certain other kinds of therapy. Not all boys get all of these forms of help, but rather, the worker uses varied strategies with different cases.

No doubt as this trend toward research evaluation of programs continues, it will ultimately be possible to make statements about the effects of certain tactics of therapy which will represent more than faith or guesswork. That is, in the past, persons have argued

[22] California Youth Authority, *The Fricot Ranch School Study: An Analysis of a Training School Experience*, Progress Report No. 4 (Sacramento, Cal.: Department of the Youth Authority, 1963).

[23] California Youth Authority, *Community Treatment Project: An Evaluation of Community Treatment for Delinquents*, Research Report No. 3 (Sacramento, Cal.: Department of the Youth Authority, 1963).

for this program or that one, mainly on emotional grounds rather than in terms of any conclusive evidence that the program accomplishes any significant alteration of behavior. But as more evidence develops from studies of specific treatment experiments, it will be possible to declare that "program X has been shown to achieve a success rate of n per cent with offenders of some kind." In turn, "program X" could be compared with "program Y" in terms of success rates, so that an objective decision could then be made that one of these tactics should be adopted over the other.

These studies cited above, along with others not discussed here, augur well for the future. But there are some formidable problems encountered in research activity of this kind which ought not to be slurred over. One of these has to do with the interpretive difficulties that arise when the impact of some program upon an undifferentiated sample of offenders is studied. To illustrate this point, several existing studies of program impact can be offered. One ambitious investigation into treatment effects was carried on several years ago in California, under the label of the IT Project (Intensive Treatment).[24] Groups of inmates from San Quentin and Chino were placed in experimental and control groups, in accordance with conventional experimental design. The treatment (experimental) group was then subjected to a program of intensive individual and group psychotherapy, while the controls received the regular institutional program. The hypothesis underlying this research was that offenders suffer from emotional problems and that their illegal behavior is produced by psychological difficulties. From this it follows that they need intensive psychotherapy designed to uncover these problems and lead to their solution.

At the end of the experiment, parole violation rates for the intensively treated and control subjects were compared. For all practical purposes, these were found to be the same. What conclusion can be reached about these results? Is it the case that intensive treatment is of no value whatsoever? Probably not, for there are persons who would benefit from intensive psychotherapy. In all likelihood, this study failed to point to any specific conclusion or therapeutic progress by some offenders because of methodological and conceptual deficiencies that were built into it. The major defect of the

[24] California Department of Corrections, *Second Annual Report, Intensive Treatment Program* (Sacramento, Cal.: Department of Corrections, 1958).

IT Project was simply that the hypothesis—that all or most of-fenders are emotionally troubled and in need of intensive psycho-therapy—was too broad. Instead of singling out a segment of the inmate group as candidates for intensive therapy, this treatment was administered to a cross-section of all inmates. Some of the treated prisoners may have been positively effected, but if so, this was not observed because they were lumped together with a num-ber of other persons for whom the therapy was not relevant and upon whom intensive treatment achieved no result. Accordingly, intensive treatment should be used in some judicious manner with relevant offender clients.

Another example of correctional research which failed to take variations among offenders into account was the SIPU (Special In-tensive Parole Unit) Project in California.[25] This project was an attempt to test the hypothesis that parole violation rates could be markedly reduced if parolees were placed in small case loads where they would receive intensive parole supervision. In this study as in the IT Project, experimental and control groups were utilized. At the end of the experiment, the violation rates of the intensively supervised parolees were about the same as those for the parolees in regular case loads. Here again, there may have been some posi-tive effect of intensive supervision upon some parolees, but if so, this did not show up in the results. Perhaps the kind of parole program needed by individuals varies from one group to another, so that some persons need intensive help whereas others would benefit from minimal supervision. In the same way, some parolees might respond to group treatment on parole, whereas others would be more responsive to individual therapy. Certainly such possibilities were suggested in Chapters Six and Seven. Thus research on the ef-fectiveness of parole programs might profitably be more narrowly focused than was the SIPU Project.

In the light of the above, policy research must proceed toward investigations of the impact of specific programs upon particular types of violators rather than upon offenders en masse. Several of

[25] Walter T. Stone, "Administrative Aspects of the Special Intensive Parole Program," 126-31; Bernard Forman, "Report on the Special Intensive Parole Unit-Research Investigation by the Division of Adult Paroles, Adult Authority, State of California," in *Proceedings of the American Correctional Association, 1956*, pp. 132-39; Ernest Reimer and Martin Warren, "SIPU: Relationship Between Violation Rate and Initially Small Caseload," *N.P.P.A. Journal* (July 1957), 222-29.

the studies in California which were cited earlier have attempted to do this through examination of program effect upon amenables and nonamenables or upon offenders of different interpersonal maturity levels.

There are some problems which develop when research concentrates upon the analysis of program effect upon types of violators. For one, it is sometimes difficult to build up a supply of eligible candidates to assign to experimental and control groups when a study is restricted to some specific offender patterns. However, the more important difficulty is a theoretical one. What types of violators should be studied? How should offenders be classified? What kinds of treatment should they be given? It is not enough that some kind of classificatory procedure be employed. Rather, the types that are singled out for investigation should be significant ones so that by administering particular forms of therapy to them, rehabilitation will be maximized. Quite probably there are many ways of sorting offenders into types which would not produce such results. Suppose that a group of violators were classified into two types, "property criminals" and "personal criminals," with the first receiving group therapy and the second, individual counseling (with matching control groups who receive no intensive therapy). Little difference might be observed in terms of successful treatment between the experimental and control groups because the forms of strategy were not utilized with the proper cases. Yet it is possible that group treatment would be highly effective *when* administered to the right persons. But which are the right persons? At this point, the problem that gave rise to this text emerges, namely, the need for diagnostic and treatment theory as a guide to research.

In California, typologies centering around the notions of treatment amenability and interpersonal maturity levels are regarded as significant. It is not yet clear, however, whether these are the most useful classificatory schemes or whether some other might be more productive. At any rate, no single taxonomic device which is objective in form and which can be reliably applied to offenders has been adopted for research purposes everywhere, nor is such a typology now in sight. Policy research is so new a development that matters of this sort have not yet received much attention. But it is probably clear enough that such a device is needed if research results on treatment strategies are to have a cumulative effect, so that a study in one state regarding one form of therapy and another in a second state would contribute to a growing stockpile of systematic knowledge.

Parenthetically, there are other obstacles to program investigations, particularly concerning treatment in institutions. When the success of the activity is measured in terms of postrelease adjustment, such as by parole violation rates, variables which were not included in the experiment may influence the experimental outcome. To put the point another way, there is the problem concerning research on institutional treatment that any effects which therapy may have could be drastically altered, distorted, or nullified by conditions existing in the community during the offender's parole experience.

Investigations of treatment impact upon offenders are not easy to accomplish. Some of the obstacles to program inquiry have been mentioned, although anyone of a pessimistic persuasion could easily find still other difficulties to enumerate. But for all this, it should be remembered that very few matters worth investigating are easy to study, and granting all the impediments to policy research, this kind of activity must be pressed forward. If society is to tamper with certain persons in the name of therapy, that tampering ought to be based on knowledge, not guesswork.

The purpose of this text is not to lay out an inventory of hypotheses for test regarding various forms of treatment with offenders. Nonetheless, the earlier chapters do contain a number of potential hypotheses for study. These include such questions as the optimum group size for effective group therapy, the effects of different membership patterns of therapy groups upon treatment success, the influence of varied leadership structures upon group programs, and so forth. Inquiry could also profitably be directed at such things as attitudes of different offenders toward programs of different kinds, such as halfway houses, probation, and the like. In the same way, careful examination of the possible efficacy of jail sentences and kindred experiences is much needed.

One optimistic aspect of the question of policy research is that there is an abundance of opportunities for such work. Funds have become available in relatively generous amounts for experiments, demonstration projects, and similar efforts. Also, there are a large number of "natural experiments" in process which provide the locus for significant research work. For example, there is in San Francisco a Catholic-operated residential training school for girls with an inmate population of under 100 which has traveled some distance toward the creation of a therapeutic milieu. The institution appears to have developed a degree of staff harmony and goal consensus which is unusual for this kind of organization. Consequently, much might be learned from a study of the workings of this school. This place is only one example of a large number of ongoing organizations that could reveal much about effective therapy if they were scrutinized through careful research.

Summary

This brief chapter has considered some of the research implications of the theme of the book.

INDEX